American Bards

WALT WHITMAN

AND OTHER

UNLIKELY CANDIDATES

FOR NATIONAL POET

Edward Whitley

American Bards

THE UNIVERSITY OF NORTH CAROLINA PRESS

CHAPEL HILL

Designed by Kimberly Bryant and set in Merlo by Tseng Information Systems, Inc. Manufactured in the United States of America. The paper in this book meets the guidelines for permanence and durability of the Committee on Production Guidelines for Book Longevity of the Council on Library Resources. The University of North Carolina Press has been a member of the Green Press Initiative since 2003.

Library of Congress Cataloging-in-Publication Data
Whitley, Edward Keyes.
American bards : Walt Whitman and other unlikely candidates for national poet / by Edward Whitley.
p. cm.
Includes bibliographical references and index.
ISBN 978-0-8078-3421-3 (cloth : alk. paper)
1. Whitman, Walt, 1819–1892—Appreciation—United States. 2. National characteristics, American, in literature. 3. Poets, American—19th century. 4. Whitfield, James Monroe, 1822–1871. 5. Snow, Eliza R. (Eliza Roxey), 1804–1887. 6. Ridge, John Rollin, 1827–1867. 7. Whitman, Walt, 1819–1892—Influence. I. Title.
PS3233.W44 2010
811′.309—dc22
[B]

2010010142

Portions of Chapter 3 appeared in modified form in "'The First White Aboriginal': Walt Whitman and John Rollin Ridge," *ESQ* 52, no. 1–2 (2006): 105–39, reprinted here with the permission of the Board of Regents of Washington State University. Portions of Chapter 4 appeared in modified form in "Whitman's Occasional Nationalism: 'A Broadway Pageant' and the Space of Public Poetry," *Nineteenth-Century Literature* 60, no. 4 (Fall 2006): 451–80. Reproduced with permission of University of California Press—Journals in the format other book via Copyright Clearance Center.

14 13 12 11 10   5 4 3 2 1

For my parents and my teachers

CONTENTS

PREFACE

*The American bards shall be marked for generosity and affection and
for encouraging competitors. . . . They shall be kosmos . . . without monopoly or
secrecy . . . glad to pass any thing to any one . . . hungry for equals night and day.*

— *Walt Whitman, Preface to* Leaves of Grass *(1855)*

American Bards tells the story of three antebellum poets whose names are seldom, if ever, mentioned in the same breath as that of Walt Whitman, despite the fact that their respective projects for American poetry ran parallel to Whitman's own. At one time or another, each of these poets adopted a posture similar to that of Whitman's now-famous persona of the social outsider who audaciously claims to be the nation's representative bard. A large part of Whitman's enduring appeal is due to his ability to stand at the center of American culture while retaining the outlaw swagger of a figure on the fringes of society. He was not, however, the only antebellum poet to do so.

Laboring in mutual obscurity from one another and unaware of Whitman's own unlikely bid to be the nation's representative bard, the three poets I write about in this book—James M. Whitfield (an African American separatist and abolitionist), Eliza R. Snow (a Mormon pioneer and women's leader), and John Rollin Ridge (a Cherokee journalist and sometime advocate for Native rights)—similarly claimed to speak for a nation that deemed them unfit national representatives. Today, that the quintessential American bard would emerge from the working-class neighborhoods of antebellum New York can feel inevitable. But it is just as (un)likely that the national poet would be affiliated with an African American separatist movement, a utopian religious group in the deserts of the American West, or an exile community of Cherokees living in gold-rush California. These three poets positioned themselves with respect to the nation much as Whitman did: by recasting their liabilities as assets and claiming to be uniquely suited to address the nation because of, and not in spite of, their status as national outsiders.

In addition to sharing with Whitman the persona of the national out-sider who defiantly steps forward as the national bard, these three poets also echoed some of the central aspects of Whitman's project for American poetry. Two years before Whitman first proposed that *Leaves of Grass* be read as a textual embodiment of the nation, James M. Whitfield published *America and Other Poems* (1853), a book that also sought to render the nation as verse. Similarly, at the same time that Whitman presented himself as the poet of a new American religion, Eliza R. Snow had already been christened "Zion's Poetess" by the members of the faith that Leo Tolstoy (among others) is said to have called "the American religion."[1] Finally, just as Whitman's poetry was being characterized in the press as "resembl[ing] nothing so much as the war-cry of the Red Indians" and the poet himself was cast as a semisavage mouth-piece for the indigenous energy of the continent, John Rollin Ridge was pub-lishing poems under his Cherokee name, Yellow Bird, that attempted to bring Native culture more fully into the American mainstream.[2]

When I first began working on this book, Whitfield, Snow, and Ridge were of interest to me as counterpoints to Whitman, and for a time I focused on charting the points of connection between Whitman's career and the careers of these lesser-known poets. As I continued my research, however, I started to see a pattern emerging in these poets that I had not previously noticed in Whitman. I began this book intending to use Whitman as a lens through which to view a group of poets who might not otherwise get much attention in the study of nineteenth-century poetry, but I soon found that the lens I was holding up worked both ways, and that a common thread run-ning throughout Whitfield, Snow, and Ridge was forcing me to reconsider what it meant to call Whitman an American bard.

I found that, at crucial moments in their careers, these would-be national bards were not primarily interested in creating poetry about the American experience, but rather, they were caught up in a complex set of loyalties—either real or imagined—to communities both smaller and larger than the nation itself, communities, that is, better defined as local and global than as explicitly national. I saw that the efforts of these three poets to step out of the margins and into the center of national life were complicated by a sense that the nation was something of an afterthought to more essential commit-ments to communities alternately local and global in scale. As I continued my research, I found moments in Whitman's antebellum career that simi-larly bear the traces of a poet whose desire to represent the nation was complicated by his conflicting allegiances to a local subculture of working-class New Yorkers, the global community, and the United States itself. These moments jumped out at me as essential to understanding Whitman's life and work before the Civil War, even though the prior scholarship on Whitman's antebellum period did not explicitly flag them as such.

In addition to seeing a pattern where national loyalty ceded ground to local and global allegiances, I also noticed that these poets tended to gravitate toward a particular mode of poetic expression to articulate their complex relationships with the nation. Whitfield, Snow, and Ridge often turned to public commemorative verse—poetry written to observe some moment of cultural or political importance—as a way to interact with an audience of readers who may or may not have been willing to acknowledge their claims as American bards. Commemorative poetry is an interesting species of verse, differing in crucial ways from the received notion that lyric poems are necessarily dramatic monologues that require the poet to turn his or her back on an imagined audience while contemplating the depths of consciousness in solitude. Commemorative poetry, in contrast, opens up a dialogue with the audience and creates a space for debate over what it means to be the representative voice of a community. As I turned my attention to Whitman's antebellum attempts to commemorate public events, I found that his efforts to address the nation—the same nation that he so enthusiastically believed would accept him as its representative bard—were marked by conflicts similar to those expressed by Whitfield, Snow, and Ridge.

Throughout this process of comparing and contrasting the most well-known American poet with three much more obscure figures, the legacy of multiculturalism has always been at the back of my mind. The multicultural critique of the canon of American literature that took place during the 1980s and 1990s has, in many ways, made this project possible, even if my primary goal is neither to challenge Whitman's place in the canon nor to chastise the scholars who put him there. In the final chapter I offer some thoughts on what it means to do multicultural scholarship in the early twenty-first century, but for now let me say that I am just as hopeful that Whitfield, Snow, and Ridge will make their way into anthologies and course syllabi as I am that Whitman will emerge from *American Bards* more rather than less relevant to the study of American poetry. I take Whitman at his word that there is no "monopoly" in poetry and offer this book as testament to that encouraging thought.

ACKNOWLEDGMENTS

I am grateful for the opportunity to dedicate this book, in part, to the many teachers in whose classrooms I have been privileged to sit over the years. Of all these teachers, however, to none do I owe more thanks than Robert S. Levine and Martha Nell Smith of the University of Maryland. Their support was essential to both the genesis and the completion of this project. I will forever be indebted to them not only for teaching me how to be a scholar, but for believing that I could actually become one.

I also owe a debt of gratitude to other members of the University of Maryland community. Special thanks are due to Carla Peterson, Ralph Bauer, Kandice Chuh, R. Gordon Kelly, Neil Fraistat, Bill Sherman, John Auchard, Sue Lanser, Manju Suri, Tim Helwig, Ingrid Satelmajer, Maria Ramos, Koritha Mitchell, Andrew Rennick, and Myles Weber. I am grateful for the positive climate for research in the Washington, D.C., area in general and offer my thanks to the librarians at the Library of Congress and Howard University's Moorland-Spingarn Research Center, as well as at the University of Maryland's own McKeldin Library. I would be remiss if I did not also thank Jack Jones, Tom Creamer, and my former colleagues at the McNeil Technologies Language Research Center for their friendship and support during my time in Maryland.

Since I moved to Pennsylvania in 2004, my colleagues at Lehigh University have consistently provided me with encouragement and support. I hesitate to single out specific members of the English Department at Lehigh because of what the department as a whole has done on my behalf, but I would like to recognize Barry Kroll, Ed Gallagher, Seth Moglen, and Dawn Keetley for the mentorship that has seen me through the process of writing and publishing this book. Lehigh has graciously provided me with generous research support—including summer funding and time off from teaching—that has made completion of this book possible, and it has also given me supportive colleagues across the university, especially among librarians such as Julia Maserjian and Robert Weidman. The undergraduate and graduate students that I have had the privilege to work with at Lehigh have given me numerous opportunities to test the ideas I have written in this book. Among all of these intelligent and hardworking students I am particularly grateful to Kurt Hoberg for being the best research assistant I could possibly hope for, and to Jameson Garcia for being a valued friend.

Outside Lehigh, I am grateful for the community of Whitman scholars who have welcomed me into their ranks: Ed Folsom, Ken Price, Betsy Erkkila, David Haven Blake, Michael Robertson, Donald Kummings, Tyler Hoffman, Ted Genoways, Matt Cohen, and Ivy Wilson, among others. David Blake deserves an additional helping of gratitude for reading the entire manuscript for the University of North Carolina Press and for providing so many useful insights and corrections. I also thank other scholars of American literature and culture who have provided me with advice and counsel along the way: John Ernest, Michael Borgstrom, Marianne Noble, James Holstun, Terryl Givens, Jill Mulvay Derr, Karen Lynn Davidson, Lisa Steinman, Timothy Sweet, James W. Parins, Andrew Jewell, Amanda Gailey, Ed Cutler, Gloria Cronin, and Suzanne Lundquist. I also give my heartfelt thanks to Ed Folsom and Ken Price (again), along with everyone who has helped them to make *The Walt Whitman Archive* an indispensable resource for scholarship on Whitman's life and work.

At the University of North Carolina Press I have been privileged to work with Sian Hunter, Beth Lassiter, and Stephanie Wenzel, whose professionalism is matched only by their personal investment with the authors whose works they publish.

I am glad to be able to dedicate this book to my parents, Tom and Colleen Whitley, who have spent most of the last four decades teaching me and encouraging me at every opportunity. The strongest motivation I have to write another book is the knowledge that I now owe a dedication to the members of my immediate family—Marguerite, Milo, Clara, and Violet—who have been patient and loving (and patient again) throughout the time I have spent writing this one.

ABBREVIATIONS

America   James M. Whitfield, *America and Other Poems* (Buffalo, N.Y.: James S. Leavitt, 1853)

LG   Walt Whitman, *Leaves of Grass* (Philadelphia: David McKay, 1891–92)

LG55   Walt Whitman, *Leaves of Grass* (Brooklyn, N.Y.: n.p, 1855)

LG56   Walt Whitman, *Leaves of Grass* (New York: Fowler and Wells, 1856)

LG60   Walt Whitman, *Leaves of Grass* (Boston: Thayer and Eldridge, 1860)

NUPM   Walt Whitman, *Notebooks and Unpublished Prose Manuscripts*, 6 vols., ed. Edward F. Grier (New York: New York University Press, 1984)

PW   Walt Whitman, *Prose Works, 1892*, 2 vols., ed. Floyd Stovall (New York: New York University Press, 1963–64)

Ridge   John R[ollin] Ridge, *Poems* (San Francisco: H. Payot & Co., 1868)

Snow   Eliza R Snow, *Poems: Religious, Historical, and Political*, vol. 1 (Liverpool: F. D. Richards, 1856)

WWC   Horace Traubel, *With Walt Whitman in Camden*, vol. 1 (Boston: Small, Maynard, 1906); vols. 2–3 (New York: Rowman and Littlefield, 1961); vol. 4 (Philadelphia: University of Pennsylvania Press, 1953); vols. 5–7 (Carbondale: Southern Illinois University Press, 1964–92); vols. 8–9 (Oregon House, C.A.: W. L. Bentley, 1996)

INTRODUCTION

Walt Whitman occupies at the present moment a unique position
on the globe, and one which, even in past time, can have been occupied
by only an infinitesimally small number of men. He is the one man who
entertains and professes respecting himself the grave conviction that
he is the actual and prospective founder of a new poetic literature, and
a great one — a literature proportional to the material vastness and
the unmeasured destinies of America: he believes that the Columbus of
the continent or the Washington of the States was not more truly than
himself in the future a founder and upbuilder of this America.
— *William Michael Rossetti, preface to* Poems by Walt Whitman *(1868)*

When William Michael Rossetti credited Walt Whitman with being
"the one man" in America to have created a school of distinctively
national poetry, he nurtured the persona that Whitman himself
had already cultivated as the "solitary singer" of the United States.[1]
As Whitman wrote nearly a decade earlier, "I alone advance among
the people en-masse, coarse and strong / I am he standing first there,
solitary chanting the true America."[2] Generations of readers and critics since Rossetti have similarly ceded this point to Whitman, calling
him the most representative of American bards and the definitive national poet of the United States. This impulse to identify a single individual — or at most, as Rossetti allows, "an infinitesimally small number
of men" — as the articulate voice of a nation corresponds with a belief
harbored by many nineteenth-century Americans that U.S. national
identity was sufficiently well defined and delimited to be expressed by
one single poet. As Liah Greenfeld has argued, when the identity of a
nation "is seen in unitary terms, it tends to assume the character of a
collective individual possessed of a single will, and someone is bound
to be its interpreter."[3]

Accordingly, the idea of a national tradition in literature—with its assumption that literary texts bear witness to a nation's primal essence—necessitates the existence of a poet who can render intelligible that essence in both his poetry and his own representative identity. When Whitman hailed himself as "an American bard at last!" in an anonymous self-review of the first edition of *Leaves of Grass* in 1855, he made clear his intention to be the poet whose name and poetry would become synonymous with what he and other Americans took to be the nation's collective identity.[4] In the same review where he claimed to have filled the theretofore vacant slot of poetic interpreter of the nation's essential character, however, Whitman also marked himself as an unlikely candidate for the job, writing that he came "rough and unbidden" onto the scene.[5] Although he would adopt the pose of the grandfatherly "Good Gray Poet" following the Civil War, throughout the antebellum period Whitman said that he was "one of the roughs," and in so doing he aligned himself with the gangs of "toughs" and "rowdies" whose lawlessness earned them a negative reputation in New York City's bestiary of urban types: "A more despicable, dangerous, and detestable character than the New-York rough does not exist," noted one nineteenth-century commentator. "He is an epitome of all the meannesses [*sic*] and vices of humanity."[6]

Throughout his antebellum career, Whitman's self-identification as "one of the roughs" took advantage of a symbolic economy that put working-class men at the rhetorical heart of Jacksonian democracy while at the same time considering them "rough and unbidden" participants in civil society. Betsy Erkkila has described how Whitman's antebellum self-identification as "one of the roughs" allowed him to be both a representative American poet and an unwanted social outsider; she writes that the posture of "the rough" presents "the author as a democratic presence, a common man who speaks as and for rather than apart from the people," but as "'one of the roughs', he also identifies with an unruly segment of the American populace."[7] The aura that Whitman has generated as a national outsider who leverages his position on the margins of society into a bid for the office of national bard is central to his enduring mystique as the quintessential American poet. This aura has been perpetuated by 150 years of literary criticism that has found ways to harmonize Whitman's social position on the periphery of national culture as a "dangerous" figure tainted by the "vices of humanity" with a successful, albeit unlikely, claim to the title of U.S. national poet.

The prevailing critical narrative goes something like the following: By defining American democracy as the homosocial bonds between men in a republic of artisan laborers, Whitman took those things that jeopardized his bid for public acceptance—his homosexuality and his working-class roots— and turned them into his rationale to be America's representative national bard.[8] According to this narrative, the sexual "deviancy" and lower-class "incivility" that would otherwise be liabilities for Whitman become instead tremendous assets in his efforts to speak to and for the nation. Literary critics may have challenged the notion that Whitman is an unproblematic embodiment of national identity by reminding readers of his affiliation with fringe elements of national society, but they have often done so in a way that has retained what Rossetti called Whitman's "unique position on the globe" as a "founder of a new poetic literature." In an effort to counteract this tendency toward Whitmanian exceptionalism, *American Bards* tells the story of three antebellum poets who, like Whitman, presumed to address the United States as representative Americans despite their membership in communities deemed, to one degree or another, to be decidedly un-American.

Just as Whitman did, the three poets who are the focus of this study— African American separatist James M. Whitfield, Mormon pioneer Eliza R. Snow, and Cherokee journalist John Rollin Ridge—took those aspects of their identities that potentially disqualified them from national citizenship and recast them as their qualifications to speak to and for the nation as American bards. While never as bold or as insistent as Whitman was in his claim to be the representative voice of the nation (there were no proclamations comparable to "an American bard at last!" from either Whitfield, Snow, or Ridge), these three poets nevertheless shared with Whitman an awareness of the symbolic value that came with speaking for the nation from the fringes of national culture. From the outset of his career, Whitman said that he welcomed "competitors" and "equals" who would join him in writing American poetry. "The American bards shall be marked for generosity and affection and for encouraging competitors," he wrote in the 1855 preface to *Leaves of Grass*. "Without monopoly or secrecy . . . glad to pass any thing to any one . . . hungry for equals night and day" (*LG55* vii). More often than not, however, both Whitman himself and subsequent generations of critics have depicted these fellow bards as "poets to come" rather than as contemporaries from the nineteenth century, thereby preserving the assumption that Whitman's only peers are his twentieth-century heirs (*LG* 18).[9] In contrast, *American Bards* recovers a moment of antebellum literary history when three poets who knew nothing about Whitman—and who were virtually unknown to the nation at large—adopted similar personae as national outsiders who leverage their liabilities into assets while assuming the role of national bard.

Admittedly, Whitfield, Snow, and Ridge are not the only nineteenth-century poets who could correct the critical myopia that has cast Whitman as the "solitary singer" of American poetry. Each poet does, however, serve as a provocative case study, as an instance that, as Lauren Berlant writes, "points to something bigger . . . an offering of an account of the event and of the world."[10] Rather than comprise an exhaustive list of such poets, Whitfield, Snow, and Ridge are, instead, like the opening salvo of a poetic catalog that, while starting small, promises to grow increasingly larger once further names are added and it expands into a sprawling testament to a complex and richly imagined world. Given that the populations from which these poets emerged were particularly troubling to antebellum constructions of national identity, they are remarkably well suited to reexamining the persona of the national outsider as national bard. The fact that these poets also shared some of the primary features of Whitman's project for American poetry—his hope to create a book of poems that would embody the nation in all its contradictions (Whitfield), his desire to be the poet of a new American religion (Snow), and his eagerness to cull the indigenous energy of the American continent (Ridge)—makes them even more appropriate candidates to initiate an ongoing project of rethinking Whitman's place in nineteenth-century U.S. poetry.[11]

As did Whitman when he claimed that "the United States are essentially the greatest poem," James M. Whitfield similarly attempted to render the nation as verse in his one published volume of poetry, *America and Other Poems* (*LG55* iii).[12] The first chapter of *American Bards* details Whitfield's efforts to structure *America and Other Poems* in a way that would reflect the contradictory nature of black life in the United States, torn as the nation was between its dependence on chattel slavery and its promise of democratic equality. Whitman himself acknowledged that slavery was one of the defining contradictions of American culture, writing in an early manuscript that a representative national bard would have to be both "the poet of slaves and of the masters of slaves" (*NUPM* 1:67). Whitfield, for his part, was less sanguine about the possibility that the United States could find a peaceful resolution between black slaves and their white masters, whether in poetry or in reality. As such, in the early 1850s he joined a separatist movement that encouraged African Americans to leave the United States entirely and establish an independent black republic in Central or South America.

As incongruous as it may now appear for an avowed separatist to write a book of poems titled *America*, it is precisely this sense of being excluded from the nation that allowed Whitfield to claim the title of American bard. The separatist group to which Whitfield belonged challenged the racist belief that people of African descent were rootless nomads who could be shuttled back and forth across the Atlantic either as American slaves or as repatriated citizens of a U.S.-backed colony in Liberia. Whitfield and his fellow separatists turned this belief on its head. They insisted that the transatlantic mobility ascribed to African Americans as a rationale for both their enslavement from as well as their repatriation to Africa was the very same mobility that allowed the first Africans brought to the New World to lay the foundations for a future American nation. In arguing that the mobility and adaptability of people of African descent were essential to the existence of the United States, they made the case that African Americans could create a new "America" wherever they went, either in Central or South America or, as Whitfield extended the argument with *America and Other Poems*, in poetry.[13]

The second chapter of *American Bards* begins with a consideration of Whitman's claim that *Leaves of Grass* was an American sacred text, a new bible for a new nation. He wrote in 1860 of his plan to "inaugurate a religion" and prophesied in 1858 that *Leaves of Grass* would be the "Bible of the New Religion" (*LG* 22).[14] While Whitman would have to wait a number of years for the disciples who would receive him as the poet-priest of a new national religion, by the middle of the nineteenth century Eliza R. Snow was already the undisputed poet-priestess of an American-born faith. As the recognized poet laureate of the Church of Jesus Christ of Latter-day Saints, Snow penned numerous hymns, occasional verses, and theological poems that established for her a position of authority that extended beyond her status as a poet: The Mormons considered Snow to be a "priestess" and a "prophetess" as well as a poetess, a singular achievement in a patriarchal religion that granted limited authority to women.[15] Whitman was confident that, given enough time, his new religion would be embraced by the entire nation. The Mormons, however, were well aware of the struggle they faced to win over the American people.

Most Americans felt either casual disdain or outright hostility toward the Mormons, sentiments that reached their fullest expression in the mid-1840s when the Saints were expelled from their prosperous settlements in Ohio, Illinois, and Missouri and forced to move to the valley of the Great Salt Lake. Political and territorial conflicts notwithstanding, a number of core ideological differences made it difficult for the Mormons to live alongside their American neighbors, differences that made this particular American religion seem, to many, to be entirely un-American. The Mormons engaged in communal living, they believed in the absolute ecclesiastical and political authority of prophets, and most conspicuously, they entered into polygamous marriages. All of these practices were seen as a step backward on the scale of historical progress that, according to most Americans, had culminated in the U.S. embrace of the free-market economy, political democracy, and domestic monogamy. In her poetry, however, Eliza R. Snow depicts the recovery of such ancient practices as polygamy and theocracy not as a historical aberration but as an essential precondition for an American millennium, arguing that the Mormons had made a compact with sacred history that would unite the deep past of the ancient world with the millennial future of the New World. The very thing that Snow's countrymen saw in her as un-American—the fact that she and the Mormons appeared to be moving backward while the rest of the nation was moving forward—was what she believed would qualify her to address the nation as its representative bard.

The third chapter of *American Bards* compares Whitman's desire to bring Native American themes into his poetry with John Rollin Ridge's own efforts to create a space for Indians in American society. In a literary culture that often drew upon images of Native peoples and customs, Whitman distinguished himself not merely by making frequent mention of Native Americans (which he did) but by presenting his poetry itself as having become a species of indigenous expression. D. H. Lawrence's characterization of Whitman as "the first white aboriginal" of American literature and as the poet who channeled the "true rhythm of the American continent" aptly summarizes Whitman's hope that the indigenous vitality of the New World would so thoroughly permeate his consciousness as to replace his European ancestry with something more essentially American.[16] As the son of a Cherokee father and a white mother, however, John Rollin Ridge experienced being a "white aboriginal" rather differently than did Whitman. For Whitman, the figure of the white aboriginal was a way to pay homage to the nation's Native American legacy without having to account for the actual Native bodies that continued (albeit in diminishing numbers) to inhabit the continent. For Ridge, the figure of the white aboriginal was a way to imagine a nation that embraced racial and cultural amalgamation rather than the extermination of Native peoples and the wholesale appropriation of Native culture. Ridge faced a number of considerable challenges, however, in his effort to cast a mixed-race Cherokee in the role of representative American bard.

Ridge, along with thousands of other Native Americans, was expected to vanish into oblivion as white Americans moved the national frontier increasingly westward. The literature of the period, from *Hiawatha* to *Hobomok* to *The Last of the Mohicans*, was replete with images of Native peoples who silently resigned themselves to disappearing into the West. In many ways, Ridge had lived the life of the vanishing Indian. After leaving the Cherokee homelands in Georgia as part of the Indian Removal policies that culminated with the Trail of Tears, Ridge resettled in the Midwest and then continued westward to California. According to the imagery of the period, the westernmost edge of the frontier was the place where Indians were supposed to vanish from existence, thereby leaving the continent free for settlement by whites. Instead, Ridge's poetry characterized the melting-pot environment of gold-rush California as a place that welcomed an Anglo-Cherokee poet as a representative of the cultural hybridization that was defining the Pacific frontier. Situated in California, Ridge attempted to reimagine the entire nation as an amalgamation of the peoples and cultures that he believed his multiracial heritage as a "white aboriginal" had uniquely positioned him to represent.

THE FIRST CONTRIBUTION OF *American Bards* is to take a group of poets who are not Walt Whitman and place them in the Whitmanian role of the national outsider-*cum*-national bard for long enough to rethink Whitman's relationship to antebellum literary culture. Though such a venture is long overdue, it is not without its risks.[17] Ed Folsom, among others, has cautioned against uncritically using Whitman as a frame of reference for studying American poetry, warning that "any poet so powerful threatens to turn his nation's poets into an indistinguishable mass of epigones."[18] Similarly,

Timothy Morris has shown how attempts to introduce new poets into the study of American poetry often produces "images of literary artists that will correspond to the Whitman template."[19] Whitman himself posed a rhetorical question about his relationship to other U.S. poets that can sound vaguely threatening in this light: "Must not the true American poet indeed absorb all others, and present a new and far more ample and vigorous type?"[20] Given Whitman's overwhelming presence in American literary studies, however, it would be evasive (if not disingenuous) to consider a group of poets assuming to speak for the nation from the margins of national culture without directly acknowledging both Whitman and the critical tradition that has grown up around him.

Taking these warnings into consideration, the first three chapters of *American Bards* do more than merely present Whitfield, Snow, and Ridge as a trio of antebellum pseudo-Whitmans. Instead, these chapters draw from the works of Whitfield, Snow, and Ridge to identify a model for rethinking Whitman's legacy as the nation's outsider bard. Just as something akin to what Morris calls "the Whitman template" forms the basis throughout *American Bards* for reading the poetry of Whitfield, Snow, and Ridge, there is a pattern by which these poets approach the office of national bard that, in turn, provides an alternative template for rereading Whitman. This template has two components, both of which center on questions of form: (1) the social and geopolitical form of the nation and (2) the form of address that a poet takes toward his or her audience. The first component, which treats the nation's physical and ideological shape, deals with how these poets identify pressure points on the national form, spaces where allegiance to the nation is challenged by a complex set of loyalties to localized communities within the nation as well as to populations that reach beyond national boundaries. The second component takes up the persistent notion that every nineteenth-century poem be read as a lyric utterance: an indirect address to an absent (or nonexistent) audience that serves to express the emotive state of an individual in solitude. In contrast, the form of poetic address that Whitfield, Snow, and Ridge employ at pivotal moments of their careers could be termed a bardic utterance: a direct address on a public occasion to a community of readers who seek from the poet (often in vain) a confirmation of the common cultural values that define them.

The issue of national form recalls William Michael Rossetti's contention that Whitman had created "a literature proportional to the material vast-ness and the unmeasured destinies of America," a statement that would have resonated with antebellum literary nationalists who believed in a one-to-one correlation between the nation and its representative poetic voice.[21] This equation of the national bard with both the geopolitical boundaries ("material vastness") and ideological mission ("unmeasured destinies") of the nation is based in a *one race, one place* theory of nationalism, a theory that views the nation in Joseph Stalin's now-famous formulation as "a historically constituted, stable community of people, formed on the basis of a common language, territory, economic life, and psychological make-up manifested in a common culture."[22] Whitman, who wrote that "a bard is to be commen-surate with a people" because "his spirit responds to his country's spirit," endorsed the idea that the identity of the nation could be reflected in the identity of a single bard with what could be called a *one race, one place, one poet* theory of American poetry (*LG55* iv).

Rather than bind themselves exclusively to the nation, however, Whit-field, Snow, and Ridge depict national identity as merely one aspect of a tri-partite cultural formation wherein the nation surrenders its primary claim on allegiance to subcultures within the United States as well as to people and places beyond national boundaries. In shifting their focus away from the exclusivity of national identity and moving it toward intranational and supranational allegiances of various kinds, these poets foreground an alter-native to the literary nationalism that has long been considered the defining feature of the antebellum period, an alternative that tempers the primacy of the nation with influences both local and global in scope. For Whitfield, being African American meant belonging to a community that was circum-scribed by, but not equivalent with, the larger nation. As such, he joined with the leaders of the separatist movement to which he belonged in classifying African Americans as a "nation within a nation."[23] Employing language simi-lar to that used by Whitfield and other black separatists, one nineteenth-century observer said that the Mormons constituted "a kingdom within a kingdom," an apt description of how the Latter-day Saints thought of them-selves as a self-contained unit within the nation as a whole.[24] As a member of the Cherokee Nation—which the United States officially classified as a "domestic dependent nation"—Ridge had also experienced what it meant to belong to a group that was both a part of and apart from the nation. This experience continued for Ridge the more he thought of his adopted home of California, with its distinct regional identity, as culturally separate from its host nation.

At the same time that they united themselves with circumscribed communities within the nation, all three of these poets felt connected in some way to people and places beyond national borders. Whitfield and other black separatists believed that people of African descent were an inherently cosmopolitan population that had a claim on the entire globe. In arguing, as Henry Bibb did, that "the world is the Colored man's home," these separatists contended not only that African Americans inhabited a social sphere that was smaller than the nation as a whole, but also that they had access to spaces across the world.[25] Similarly, just as their western settlement allowed the Mormons to think of themselves as a coherent national subgroup, it was also a space that they conceived of as a millennial gathering place for people from across the world (Snow herself wrote that the "City of the Saints" is "the place destined for the gathering of people from every nation, kindred, tongue, and people").[26] By the same token, Ridge thought of California as the central node in an international network of nations that was poised to usher in a global cultural amalgamation that would begin with the interracial children of whites and Native Americans (such as himself) and then extend to people of all races. Ridge called the immigrants to California "strange compounds" of people from across the world, and he believed that this global convergence heralded "a universal amalgamation of the races" that would result in "the present identity of nations and tribes" becoming "entirely lost in the commingling and absorption of specific elements."[27]

As opposed to the model Rossetti used to describe Whitman as the poetic "founder and upbuilder" of a national literary tradition, then, Whitfield, Snow, and Ridge conducted their projects for American poetry from spaces where national loyalty ceded ground to subnational and transnational associations. To borrow Djelal Kadir's formulation, "America," for these poets, "is both smaller and larger than it thinks itself."[28] By triangulating the nation between smaller-than-national and larger-than-national frames, these poets identify dynamic spaces that do not uniformly bind their work to an exclusively nationalistic tradition. Rather, by articulating a relationship with the United States in ways that require the nation to acknowledge both local and global forces, these poets present an image of the antebellum era that differs significantly from the overblown cultural nationalism that has long been considered the dominant feature of the period. These poets imagined spaces of possibility—pressure points on the national form—where the tensions surrounding the nationalist project of the antebellum era were put into high relief by a complex framework of local and global alliances.

This repositioning of the nation between cultures either circumscribed by or external to the United States demands a reconsideration of the overly familiar notion that Whitman is simultaneously both an insider and an outsider to American culture. The spatial metaphors of being "inside" or "outside" the nation—and the correlative metaphors of being on the "margins" or at the "center" of national culture—have heavily influenced the critical vocabularies of Whitman studies and American literary studies alike. While the metaphors of being outside or marginal to the nation promise an escape from the constraints of national identity, the idea of an "outside" or a "margin" necessarily reinforces the sense of the nation as possessing a clear and distinct "inside" or "center" that continues to serve as a stable frame of reference, thus compromising attempts to separate oneself from the nation at all. Perhaps more significantly, these metaphors also encourage a critical model that has a tendency either to fetishize the subversive potential of outsider figures on the margins of the nation, or to place undue emphasis on the restrictive powers of a centralized and dominant national culture. Conversely, placing notions of national identity between the coordinates of the subnational and the transnational allows for a more dynamic interplay between nationalist sentiments and other potentially denationalizing forces, an interplay that is essential when dealing with complex figures like Whitman.

An undue reliance on the metaphors of margin/center and outside/inside to explain Whitman's uneven relationship to U.S. nationalism has, accordingly, resulted in schizophrenic depictions of Whitman as either an ardent nationalist or a rebellious dissident. Shira Wolosky's observation in the *Cambridge History of American Literature* that Whitman has come to be read as both "transgressive and yet also centrally defining within American culture" as his work is "persistently split into contradictory and opposing stances" aptly summarizes the last century or so of Whitman criticism.[29] This tendency to see Whitman as both a defiant outsider and the quintessential insider has persisted, in part, because the drama of American literature itself is often cast with social and literary outsiders in the starring roles. When F. O. Matthiessen, in his seminal 1941 study *American Renaissance: Art and Ex-*

pression in the Age of Emerson and Whitman, for example, placed Whitman among his pantheon of nonconformist writers who championed American ideals from the fringes of national society, he set in motion a critical apparatus for understanding the place of literary outsiders in U.S. culture that continues to inform discussions of American literature.[30] In the years since *American Renaissance* defined the field of antebellum literary studies, scholars have made the figure of the literary outsider a consistent point of reference for asking a larger set of questions about the possibility of dissenting from the dominant national ideology. One of the most influential responses to Matthiessen came in the 1970s and 1980s when Sacvan Bercovitch argued that the nineteenth-century figure of the writer on the margins of society—which he identified with the Puritan tradition of the jeremiad that critiques the culture while reinscribing its most basic assumptions—was merely an agent of national ideology who, in his words, was "radical in a representative way that *reaffirmed* [American] culture rather than undermining it."[31] In the 1990s, Donald Pease challenged Bercovitch's insistence that "every oppositional movement is susceptible to co-optation" and argued instead that national ideology can be genuinely subverted by writers from outside mainstream American culture.[32]

Bercovitch and Pease are representatives of the two major schools of thought that have dictated how scholars of American literature deal with the figure of the national outsider. For Pease, American culture is porous: It is full of gaps and holes that outsiders exploit in their efforts to expose the constructed nature of national identity. For Bercovitch, American culture is pervasive: it is both malleable enough to accommodate new forms of dissent from cultural outsiders and aggressive enough to silence them at virtually every turn. Accordingly, scholarly studies in the Bercovitch vein operate in an elegiac mode that laments the overwhelming power of a cultural ideology that makes dissenting outsiders conform to national consensus and renders all but hopeless any attempt to completely escape the limiting purview of the nation. Studies such as those encouraged by Pease, conversely, contend that literary outsiders can legitimately subvert the dominant national ideology and bring about both cultural and political change.

More recently, scholars who are eager to continue Pease's "post-nationalist" approach to American literature have expressed interest in recovering what Edward Soja calls "the powerful mediating role of the national state," but without necessarily returning either to Bercovitch's sense of U.S. nationalism as a virtually inescapable prison house of ideology or to the celebratory mode of literary scholarship from Matthiessen's era.[33] For example, when the contributors to John Carlos Rowe's *Post-Nationalist American Studies* argue for a less nation-centered approach to U.S. cultural studies while still acknowledging that the nation "cannot easily be wished away by the application of the *post-* prefix," they gesture toward a theoretical model that performs a balancing act between the schools of thought advocated by Bercovitch and Pease.[34] Such a model draws on Bercovitch's insistence that the ideology of American nationalism can, in his words, "enforce compliance" upon would-be dissidents, but it avoids granting this ideology the power to suppress virtually all forms of opposition.[35] This model also embraces Pease's faith in what he calls "the possibility of countering [nationalist] hegemony," but it does so without downplaying the continuing influence of the nation on postnationalist movements.[36]

This theoretical model has taken a number of different forms in recent years—including the hemispheric, transatlantic, and diasporic approaches that have recently complemented the multicultural critique of U.S. literature—all of which share, to some degree, a focus on explicating those moments when the nation finds itself in tension with potentially denationalizing forces. These moments of tension are not identified as either a subversion of the nationalist paradigm or the triumph of national ideology; rather, the tension itself is suspended as the primary site of critical exegesis, thus enabling nuanced treatments of national identity in figures with particularly problematic relationships to the nation. "The key" for such scholarly approaches, Kenneth Cmiel nicely summarizes, "is not to destroy the nation but to put it in its proper perspective."[37] The template that *American Bards* finds in Whitfield, Snow, and Ridge for situating the nation in a space of tension between subnational and transnational frames is one such effort to put the nation in the "proper perspective" of a field of local and global influences, particularly as that tension provides a model for rethinking the antebellum Whitman.

Moments of tension between Whitman's cosmopolitanism, his nationalism, and his allegiance to local cultures appear throughout his body of work. For example, on one occasion Whitman speaks of "a sense in which I want to be cosmopolitan: then again a sense in which I make much of patriotism—of our native stock, the American stock," and on another he fantasizes about rejecting "the timid models of the rest, the majority" for an eroticized comradeship with a fellow working-class New Yorker who "ever at parting kisses me lightly on the lips with robust love," a kiss that he calls the "salute of American comrades" in a self-consciously ironic gesture for someone expressing contempt for "the majority" of the nation (*wwc* 3:132; *lg*60 364). While such comments appear sporadically throughout Whitman's prose and poetry—and have provided material for numerous insightful analyses by Whitman scholars—there was a pivotal (though heretofore underappreciated) moment at the peak of Whitman's antebellum career when he articulated in a single poem how his erstwhile nationalism came into conflict with his cosmopolitanism, on one hand, and his loyalty toward working-class Americans, on the other.[38] This moment, which is the focus of Chapter 4 of *American Bards*, surrounds the composition of "A Broadway Pageant," a poem Whitman published in the *New York Times* on 27 June 1860 to commemorate a parade held for the Meiji Japanese ambassadors who had come to Manhattan as part of a diplomatic mission to ratify a trade agreement with the United States.

More so than any other poem he wrote before the Civil War, "A Broadway Pageant" succinctly illustrates what Whitman meant when he identified himself as "an American, one of the roughs, a kosmos" in every antebellum version of "Song of Myself": As "an American" he celebrates U.S. diplomatic and economic power; as "one of the roughs" he emphasizes his allegiance to the working-class New Yorkers who filled the parade route; and as a cosmopolitan "kosmos" he expresses his devotion to the idea of global community represented by the Japanese embassy (*lg*55 29). "A Broadway Pageant" not only places the central aspects of Whitman's antebellum persona in a state of dynamic tension, but it does so at a moment that allowed Whitman to fulfill the obligation of the bard to publicly commemorate an event of national significance. In 1855 Whitman introduced himself to the world as "an American bard at last!" but not until five years later with "A Broadway Pageant" did he take upon himself the bardic mantle to write a commemorative poem for a high-profile national event. Despite having no legitimate claim to the title of American bard in the summer of 1860, Whitman nevertheless took a number of modest gains in publicity from the preceding months as evidence that his ascension to the office of national poet was imminent. Confident that his fellow countrymen and -women were on the cusp of acknowledging him as their bard, Whitman felt that writing a poem to commemorate an event such as the visit of foreign ambassadors was precisely the sort of thing that he should do.[39]

Because the office of poet laureate would not officially be recognized in the United States until well into the twentieth century, Whitman's belief that a national bard should commemorate important events would have been borrowed from a model set in England, where state-sanctioned poets laureate had been writing commemorative verses since the seventeenth century.[40] The idea that a poet could act as the voice of the state also drew upon a domestic precedent that had been set in the early republic's culture of public celebration, a culture that required the person tasked with commemorating an important event to be worthy to speak not only *to* the nation but *for* the nation as well. Recalling Whitman's dictum from the 1855 *Leaves of Grass* that "an individual is as superb as a nation when he has the qualities which make a superb nation" (*LG55* xi), David Waldstreicher has noted that antebellum Americans "were seeing grave implications in *who* spoke in public on festive occasions as well as in *what* was said."[41] Poetry written to commemorate occasions of national importance let the citizens of the new republic project a sense of collective identity onto what Kristen Silva Gruesz has called the "national author whose writing would best represent 'our' essential values and character." But given that the United States had not formally instituted the office of poet laureate, anyone presuming to represent the nation as its bard faced an uphill battle: "In what ways do self-ordained poets," Gruesz asks, only somewhat rhetorically, "claim to stand in for their readers, offering their lyric voice as exemplary?"[42] Whitman's attempt to speak for the nation in "A Broadway Pageant" did not, strictly speaking, take the form of a "lyric voice" at all but was instead—and this distinction is crucial—the bardic voice of commemorative poetry.

Nineteenth-century commemorative poems function differently than do their lyric counterparts, and it is this difference in function that constitutes the second half of the template that *American Bards* provides for rethinking Whitman's posture as a national outsider who would be the national bard. Most of what is traditionally considered lyric poetry, as Mutlu Blasing has recently written, "is still understood to be the self-expression of a prior, private, constitutive subject."[43] Because lyric poetry "privileges the mind in its solitary and private moments," as Helen Vendler writes, the author of a lyric poem "does not have to make any special effort to place [her- or] himself in solidarity with 'the collective.'"[44] Rather than adopt the posture of solitary isolation that Vendler and others have long attributed to the lyric—a posture that recalls John Stuart Mill's definition of poetry as "feeling confessing itself to itself, in moments of solitude" or Northrop Frye's description of poetry as "preeminently the utterance that is overheard"—commemorative poetry is instead characterized by direct address to an audience whose presence looms large in the poet's mind.[45] Jonathan Kamholtz has said that commemorative poetry requires "an agreement between speaker, subject, and audience about how to identify [the] virtues" that have united a group of people in celebration of an event such as a national holiday, the inauguration of a president, or the anniversary of a battle.[46] Regardless of whether or not a poet ever reaches the "agreement" with his or her audience that Kamholtz describes, commemorative poetry opens up a space for what Jonathan Culler calls a "rhetorical transaction" between poets and audiences as they deliberate over the meaning of the event that has brought them together. "Whether listeners at a ceremony or readers of poems," Culler continues, the audience in such a situation is "expected to make observations about what [is] praiseworthy, worthy of belief."[47] Audiences that feel entitled to contribute to how a poet approaches his or her subject often expect a high return on their investment: They expect the poet to commemorate the event in a way that best reflects their values and identity, and they hope to see those values and that identity exemplified in the person of the poet. This self-contained space of reciprocating identity formation between poet, poem, and audience, however, is not guaranteed to remain stable.

Commemorative poetry takes place in a moment of cultural (mis)recognition, a moment when audiences experience either a sense of solace as they see an imaginary reflection of their own best selves embodied in a poet, or a sense of discord as they are forced to admit that the poet who is addressing them does not represent them. A similar type of author-audience interaction has long been recognized as a fundamental aspect of nineteenth-century public speaking—think of the commentary on Frederick Douglass's "What to the Slave Is the Fourth of July?" for example—but because of what Virginia Jackson calls the "lyricization of poetry" (the tendency to read all poems, regardless of genre, as if they were lyrics), commemorative poetry has not received a comparable amount of critical analysis. As critics and scholars continue to treat all nineteenth-century poetry as the lyric expression of poets in solitude, writes Jackson, "fewer actual poetic genres address readers in specific ways."[48] This tendency to read every poem from the period as a lyric utterance renders invisible the ways in which commemorative poetry functions as a species of bardic utterance. If a lyric utterance is the expression of an interior consciousness, a bardic utterance, in contrast, aspires to be the expression of a cultural consciousness. This is not to say that only poets with a legitimate claim to represent the collective will of an audience are entitled to write commemorative poetry and to speak in the voice of the bard. The opposite, in fact, is equally true. The (mis)recognition effect of commemorative verse can be appropriated and exploited by poets who, knowing full well that they have been deemed unfit representatives of their audiences' values and norms, nevertheless issue forth in bardic utterance as a way to challenge or redefine the nature of collective identity.[49]

This is precisely what James M. Whitfield, Eliza R. Snow, and John Rollin Ridge did at key moments of their careers. None of these poets ever wrote commemorative poetry under the presumption that his or her ascendance to the office of national bard was imminent. They all appreciated, however, the symbolic value of commemorative verse and took advantage of the moment of cultural (mis)recognition that the settings for such poems provided. Ridge, for example, was enlisted on several occasions to write and deliver commemorative poems in his adopted home state of California. In 1860 Ridge was commissioned to write a poem by an agricultural society who believed that their efforts to cultivate the Pacific Coast were the fullest expression of the civilizing mission of Manifest Destiny, and that as an Anglo-Cherokee poet whose "civilized" half had conquered his "savage," Ridge was the perfect candidate to address them. Ridge, however, had other ideas. Not only did the broad themes of the poem he wrote for this occasion refute the assumption that European immigrants to the New World were solely responsible for having settled the American continent, but at key moments in the poem Ridge also broke the fourth wall and addressed his audience directly, as when he commanded them to "Smile not!" with sneers of superiority at his depiction of hunter-gatherers in a supposedly "primitive" state (*Ridge* 116). Ridge knew that commemorative poetry gave him the opportunity to quarrel directly with his audience over the meaning of American history and how that history is projected onto a representative bard.

Snow, too, was frequently called upon to write commemorative verse.

Rare was the New Year's Day or Fourth of July in the middle decades of the century when Snow's services as "Zion's Poetess" were not required by her fellow Latter-day Saints. In "Ode for the Fourth of July," a poem that was published in a number of different contexts over the years, Snow self-consciously toys with the conventions of commemorative poetry by refusing to present her readers with a poem that appeals to the values of the nation's Revolutionary heritage. Instead, she begins the poem by asking her readers if they should even acknowledge the holiday at all: "Shall we commemorate the day / Whose genial influence has pass'd o'er?" she asks a group of Latter-day Saints who had been expelled from their prosperous settlements in the Midwest. "Shall we our hearts' best tribute pay / Where heart and feelings are no more?" (*Snow* 257). Other than in its title, the poem never mentions either the Fourth of July or the Revolutionary history celebrated on that day. Instead, the poem functions as a meta-commentary on bardic utterance by inviting its audience to consider the meaning of a national holiday for a people at odds with their nation. In a similar vein, Whitfield strategically arranged the commemorative poems he included in his 1853 collection, *America and Other Poems*, to question what it means for different audiences with different values and assumptions to coexist within the same nation. By pairing an elegy for a white statesman (John Quincy Adams) with an encomium for an African revolutionary (Cinque, the leader of the revolt on the *Amistad*), or an ode for the Fourth of July with a poem on the anniversary of the end of the British slave trade, Whitfield reminded his readers that there were different audiences within the same nation, and that these audiences had different criteria for what did and did not merit commemoration. Knowing that commemorative poems are grounded in a consensus of community values, Whitfield highlighted the fact that deciding *what* deserved commemoration was tantamount to deciding *who* was part of the nation.

A growing number of scholars have recently turned their attention to the social function of nineteenth-century poetry, noting, as does Shira Wolosky, that poetry played a "vibrant and active role within ongoing discussions defining America and its cultural directions."[50] While prose narrative has been the primary site of analysis for nineteenth-century U.S. cultural studies, these scholars have begun to carve out a space for poetry under the rubric of "historical poetics," a term that Wolosky and Yopie Prins, among others, have used to classify this effort to study how the "poetic forms of the era," as Augusta Rohrbach writes, "represented cultural practices and consciousness."[51] Antebellum commemorative poetry constitutes one such formal practice, even though these poems have been largely underexamined and incompletely theorized. In order to better appreciate how this mode of poetic discourse functions within its cultural environment, scholars will need to turn their attention to the writers from the period who sought to bring poetry into the public sphere. Wolosky notes that "Walt Whitman of course figures as the outstanding example of such a vision of poetry as participating in American public and cultural life," but she is wise to add the caveat that Whitman "is only the greatest exemplar of a fundamental impulse in nineteenth-century poetic enterprise."[52]

At the heart of *American Bards* is a similar effort to identify the relationship between poetic form and the cultural tensions of the period, particularly as those tensions played out in the works of poets who redefine Whitman's exemplary status as the representative poet of the United States. *American Bards* explores points of both convergence and divergence between Whitman and these relatively unknown poets, identifying shared affinities and unexpected parallels as well as points of disagreement and contrast. As a metaphor for how Whitman's work crossed paths with those of these poets, each of the first three chapters begins by recounting a moment when Whitman came close to but never actually met Whitfield, Snow, or Ridge. There are no records to suggest that Whitman knew anything about any of these poets — or, conversely, that they knew anything about him — but the fact that he nearly missed meeting with them on three separate occasions further illustrates how their lives and careers ran along parallel lines.

The chapter on John Rollin Ridge begins in the spring of 1866, when Ridge traveled from California to Washington, D.C., to attend a meeting at the Bureau of Indian Affairs in the very office where, less than a year earlier, Whitman had been employed as a clerk. The chapter on Eliza R. Snow begins in September 1879 with Whitman on a trip to the Pacific Coast that would have taken him through the Utah Territory had he not fallen ill and been forced to return home to New Jersey without traveling farther west than Denver. Many journalists, literati, and other curious observers of the period routinely stopped in Salt Lake City to meet with representatives of the Latter-day Saints, and Snow was often called upon in such settings to serve as the public face of the church. The chapter on James M. Whitfield, which immediately follows this introduction, begins in 1848 at a political rally in Whitfield's hometown of Buffalo, New York. Both Whitman and Whitfield attended this rally, unaware of each other's presence and even, at this early date, unaware that they were both about to start down the path toward becoming American bards.

chapter one

THE POET OF SLAVES

I am the poet of slaves and of the masters of slaves.

— Walt Whitman,

unpublished poem fragment, 1854

In early August 1848, the first national convention of the newly formed Free-Soil Party took place in Buffalo, New York. Those in attendance were a mix of former Democrats, Whigs, and Liberty Party members who, for various reasons, opposed the extension of slavery into territories acquired by the United States during the Mexican War. Walt Whitman attended the convention as one of the official delegates from Brooklyn. Like many other Democrats who split with their party when it failed to support the Wilmot Proviso's ban on slavery in the new territories, Whitman joined the Free-Soil Party not because he opposed slavery per se but because he was worried that white laborers would be economically disadvantaged—"degraded," as he put it—by the presence of slave labor in the West.[1] Despite this disregard for African American civil rights held by many Free-Soilers, the platform of the party was broad enough to attract African American abolitionists who saw in the Free-Soil movement an opportunity to extend the national debate on slavery. Frederick Douglass, one of the featured speakers at the convention, said in retrospect, "Anti-slavery thus far had only been sheet lightning; the Buffalo convention sought to make it a thunderbolt."[2]

James M. Whitfield was living in Buffalo at the time of the Free-Soil convention. The son of free northern blacks, Whitfield had moved to Buffalo from his hometown in rural New Hampshire and was working as a barber, contributing to the local African American political community, and beginning to contemplate a career as a poet.[3] While

James M. Whitfield

the scant historical documents regarding Whitfield's life do not definitively place him at the Free-Soil convention, it is all but certain that he was
aware of it and more than likely that he felt an investment in its outcome.
(The abolitionist newspaper the *North Star*, which heavily promoted the
convention, lists Whitfield as one of its subscribers for the year and mentions Whitfield's involvement in other abolitionist activities in upstate New
York.)[4] As an active participant in local antislavery efforts in Buffalo, Whitfield would have seized the opportunity to interact with the black abolitionists who came to the convention, including Douglass and his *North Star*
coeditor Martin R. Delany.[5] Following the convention, Whitfield's poetry
began to appear regularly in the *North Star*, and Whitfield himself soon became increasingly involved in various political movements led by Douglass
and Delany.[6] Whitfield's involvement with these men—particularly with
Delany—would later shape his career as both an activist and a poet.

While it is probable that Whitfield interacted with various African American political leaders at the Buffalo convention, there is little chance that he
met Whitman there. Despite the democratic and antiracist sentiments that
characterize much of *Leaves of Grass*, Whitman had little contact with African Americans before the Civil War. Whitfield's Buffalo barbershop, however, was a gathering place for men of letters and, as such, could have been a
draw to Whitman. William Wells Brown wrote in the early 1860s, "There has
long resided in Buffalo, New York, a barber, noted for his scholarly attain-
ments and gentlemanly deportment. Men of the most polished refinement
visit his saloon [*sic*], and, while being shaved, take pleasure in conversing
with him; and all who know him feel that he was intended by nature for a
higher position in life. This is James M. Whitfield."[7]

Whitman had already developed a sense of himself as a literatus at the
time of the Free-Soil convention (by 1848 he had published a handful of
poems and a few works of short fiction), but it remains an open question
as to whether or not his burgeoning identity as a writer would have been a
powerful enough motivation for him to seek out the literate company offered
in Whitfield's barbershop.[8] By the 1850s, however, both poets would develop
an interest in writing about life in the United States and, more specifically,
in creating poetry that could somehow embody the nation itself. Even if the
two men had met in Whitfield's barbershop to discuss their mutual interest
in writing poems that rendered the nation as verse, by 1848 neither had suf-

ficiently conceptualized his vision for American poetry to the degree that would have made for productive conversation. Nevertheless, their parallel projects to rewrite the nation as poetry were informed by the very concerns that brought both of them to the Buffalo Free-Soil convention.

The prospect of extending slavery into the western territories was cause for a variety of economic and moral concerns among the different factions of Free-Soilers with whom Whitfield and Whitman rubbed shoulders in the summer of 1848. More than anything else, the issue of slaveholding in the West brought to the fore an unresolved anxiety about how the United States defined its geopolitical boundaries with respect to race. Amid calls for the complete elimination of slavery and the less radical insistence that slavery be restricted to the southern states, an unspoken concern of many delegates at the convention was how, if at all, to reconcile a Eurocentric national identity with a resident African population. Beyond the scope of the Buffalo convention, the contentious debate over slavery led more than a few antebellum Americans to believe that the greatest source of national conflict during the mid-nineteenth century was not the forced enslavement of millions of human beings but the attempt to house two different and seemingly incompatible races in the same nation-state. Whitman himself wrote in an editorial for the *Brooklyn Times* ten years after the Free-Soil convention, "Who believes that the Whites and Blacks can ever amalgamate in America? Or who wishes it to happen? Nature has set an impassable seal against it. Besides, is not America for the Whites? And is it not better so?"[9]

Whitfield, albeit from the other side of the color line, expressed similar sentiments. He rejected the idea that racial amalgamation between African and European Americans would end the problems of racism and slavery in the United States, in part because he suspected an underlying desire on the part of those advocating amalgamation to eliminate any trace of black racial identity from American life. He harshly criticized what he called "the bleaching theory of Henry Clay," the proposal of the Kentucky senator "by which the negro race in this country is to be absorbed, and its identity lost in that of the Caucasian." He also came to distrust the integrationist agenda promoted by moderate abolitionists who looked forward to a time of equal citizenship for African Americans, writing in an 1853 letter to the editors of *Frederick Douglass' Paper*, "Dr. Johnson defined patriotism to be the last refuge of a scoundrel. But a *black patriot* in this country must be more fool than knave. The fact is, I have no country, neither have you, and your assumption that you are an *integrant* part of *this* nation, is not true."[10]

As Whitfield felt increasingly excluded from national life, he found solace in the radical position taken by Martin Delany and others that African Americans should leave the United States and establish an independent black republic in South America. Since the late eighteenth century, plans to relocate African Americans to such places as Africa, Canada, and the American West had come from across the political spectrum, including European Americans who wanted the nation to be exclusively for whites as well as black separatists who believed that African American autonomy could only be realized outside the United States.[11] In the same 1858 editorial where he postulated that "America [is] for the Whites," Whitman articulated both of these positions, arguing first that the United States is "better" suited to be a white nation and second that African Americans would only find independence and prosperity beyond U.S. boundaries. He wrote, "As long as the Blacks remain here how can they become anything like an independent and heroic race? There is no chance of it. Yet we believe there is enough material in the colored race, if they were in some secure and ample part of the earth, where they would have a chance to develope [*sic*] themselves, to gradually form a race, a nation that would take no mean rank among the peoples of the world."[12] Whitfield would have ceded to Whitman that black political equality could only be achieved outside the United States, but he would have taken issue with the notion that African Americans needed to "gradually" arrive at a state deserving the respect of other nations. Whitfield believed blacks to be inherently superior to whites, whom he described as "naturally inferior to [African Americans] in physical, moral, and mental power." He argued that this superiority was not self-evident only because of the impediments of chattel slavery and institutionalized racism, impediments that he called "a concatenation of obstacles, such as were never presented to any class of men before."[13] Based on these statements, it would seem that a conversation on racial politics between Whitman and Whitfield at the time of the Buffalo convention would have consisted of a volatile mix of agreement and disagreement, to say the least.

In the years that followed the Buffalo Free-Soil convention, Whitfield and Whitman continued to think about race relations in the United States at the same time that they began to experiment with turning the nation into poetry. Their mutual concern over the peaceful coexistence of blacks and whites in the United States influenced, in different ways, how their respective volumes of poetry took the forms that they did. Specifically, both poets came to realize that the dysfunctional character of multiracial America was an issue that had to be addressed by anyone who took up the challenge of antebellum tastemakers such as Emerson to realize the dictum that "America is a poem in our eyes."[14] For Whitman, the belief that African Americans did not belong in the United States led him to adopt the persona of a national bard who self-consciously acknowledged the contradictory aim of containing blacks and whites, slaves and masters, within a single country. This sense of contradiction as a defining feature of antebellum life influenced both the style and the subject matter of Whitman's poetry as he attempted to be the representative bard of a conflicted nation.

For Whitfield, the prospect of leaving the United States entirely and of creating an Afrocentric nation elsewhere in the world gave him a different perspective on the racial makeup of antebellum America. Whitfield came to believe that African Americans were central and not peripheral to the American experience, and that by leaving the United States they were not abandoning America so much as transplanting it to another location. The belief that the future of African Americans—and therefore, the future of America itself—lay somewhere other than the United States allowed Whitfield to think of himself as a representative American bard, as someone who, by publishing a book titled *America*, could speak for the very nation that rejected him.

The first section of this chapter lays out the similarities and differences between these poets' shared project to re-create the nation as a poetic text, paying special attention to how their different beliefs about antebellum race relations influenced them along the way. This first section also describes the artistry and rhetoric behind Whitfield's arrangement of the poetry in *America and Other Poems*, noting in particular how he foregrounds his calling as a bard by strategically incorporating commemorative poems throughout the collection. The second section provides a close reading of the poem "America," arguing that Whitfield's involvement in emigration politics informed how he recast his greatest social liability—his African racial heritage—as his principal asset for becoming the nation's representative poetic voice. Finally, the close reading of the poem "How Long" in the third section of the chapter shows how Whitfield's aspiration to speak to and for the nation as its bard is complicated by his allegiance to a smaller-than-national community of African Americans within the United States as well as to a transatlantic community of oppressed peoples.

IN 1850, FREE-SOILERS won a Pyrrhic victory in the war to keep slavery out of the American West. As part of the Compromise of 1850, Congress decided that slavery would be outlawed in California and that the right to hold slaves in other western territories would be determined by local governments. As a concession to slaveholding interests for limiting the expansion of slavery in the West, however, Congress also instituted the Fugitive Slave Law, which required northerners to return runaway slaves to their masters in the South. Whitfield and many other free northern blacks believed that the implications of the Fugitive Slave Law extended beyond the reenslavement of runaway slaves and that the new law amounted to, as Whitfield and others believed, "the virtual enslavement of every colored person in the United States."[15] As Martin Delany put it, with the Fugitive Slave Law in effect, free African Americans and runaway slaves alike felt that they were "liable at any time, in any place, and under all circumstances to be arrested, and upon the claim of any white person . . . sent into endless bondage."[16]

The fact that free blacks living in the North could feel so threatened speaks to more than just a concern that the Fugitive Slave Law would be cavalierly applied by rogue slave-hunters who would unlawfully capture and enslave free people of color; rather, it articulated the sentiment of many antebellum African Americans that the United States was fundamentally a white-only nation. Whitfield himself supported the idea expressed at the 1854 National Emigration Convention that "a people who are *liable*, under any pretext or circumstance whatever, to enslavement by the laws of a country, cannot be *free* in that country."[17] If a central yet unspoken question of the Buffalo Free-Soil convention of 1848 was whether or not blacks and whites could live together in the United States, for Whitfield, Delany, and many others, the Fugitive Slave Law answered that question decidedly in the negative.

The implications of the Fugitive Slave Law had a profound effect on Whitfield, tilting him toward a separatist agenda that informed both his politics and his poetry. At an 1853 convention for African American abolitionists, Whitfield signed a declaration of sentiments penned by Frederick Douglass asserting African Americans' "claim to be American citizens."[18] Within a few months, however, Whitfield wrote to *Frederick Douglass' Paper* saying that the Fugitive Slave Law was further proof that the only way for African Americans to secure their civil and human rights was to renounce any pretense to national citizenship, leave the United States entirely, and establish a black nation beyond U.S. borders.[19] Whether Whitfield made a radical change in position after signing this declaration with Douglass or was already, as Floyd Miller speculates, "at best ambivalent" toward Douglass's hope for an integrated America is unclear.[20]

What the extant historical records do indicate is that by mid-1853—around the same time that he published *America and Other Poems*—Whitfield threw his support behind Martin Delany's controversial proposal that African Americans emigrate from the United States. The previous year, in 1852, Delany had published *The Condition, Elevation, Emigration, and Destiny of the Colored People of the United States*, the philosophical treatise of what came to be known as the emigration movement. In the *Condition*, Delany argued that even though African Americans had done everything imaginable to earn their rights as citizens—from serving in the military to contributing to the national economy—their repeated denial of full and equal citizenship was proof that the United States was a nation exclusively for whites. The only rational solution, Delany argued, was to leave the United States and create a black nation elsewhere. Breaking with the policy of the overwhelmingly white-supported American Colonization Society, Delany rejected emigration to the U.S.-backed colony of Liberia on the grounds that African Americans had as much right to settle in the New World as Europeans did, and he advocated settlement in Central or South America instead.[21]

While he never entirely discounted the prospect of returning to Africa, Delany argued from a pragmatic standpoint that the more proximate regions of Central and South America facilitated the emigration of free blacks and runaway slaves alike. Unlike other African American emigrationists, Delany maintained that Canada was both politically and geographically too close to the United States to be considered a realistic option. Whitfield's extant political writings make it clear that he was well versed in the main points of Delany's emigrationist agenda, and in late 1853 Whitfield drew heavily from Delany's text during his participation in a six-month-long public debate over the merits of emigration that appeared in *Frederick Douglass' Paper*. Whitfield began this debate with Douglass himself after Douglass publicly disparaged the emigrationists' call for a mass exodus of black Americans from the United States, and the debate continued with William J. Watkins, the paper's assistant editor and a firm supporter of Douglass's plan for racial integration in the United States.

Watkins and Douglass considered emigration to be a divisive issue among African Americans and believed that the emigration movement threatened to undermine the more important goals of abolition and emancipation. Whitfield countered by citing Delany's argument that in order for African Americans to achieve what he called "a respectable position among the *great* nations of the earth," they would have to be a part of "the *ruling* element" of society and not live merely as second-class citizens.[22] Whitfield insisted that the combined legacies of slavery and racism made such a goal all but impossible in the United States and that emigration was the only sane alternative. The Whitfield-Watkins debate drew enough public attention that their essays were reprinted in other African American newspapers and later collected in pamphlet form. Whitfield himself quickly earned the reputation among opponents to emigration as "the principal defender of this vile scheme of expatriation."[23]

This staunch defense of emigration was on display in Whitfield's literary efforts as well as his political writings. In the same year that he publicly debated the merits of emigration in the pages of *Frederick Douglass' Paper*, Whitfield dedicated *America and Other Poems* to Martin Delany as what he called "a small tribute of respect for his character, admiration of his talents, and love of his principles." (Delany returned the favor by having a black revolutionary poet in his 1859 novel, *Blake*, recite lines from Whitfield's poetry.)[24] Along with dedicating his collection of poems to Delany, Whitfield also included a backhanded reference to his former affiliation with Douglass in a footnote to the poem "The North Star," explaining that "The North Star" is not only the name of the heavenly body that guides runaway slaves to freedom but also the title of "a newspaper edited by a fugitive slave," that is, Frederick Douglass (*America* 84). Since Delany's name was synonymous with the emigration movement at the time *America and Other Poems* was published, Whitfield was able to signal his political allegiances by dedicating the book to Delany and by relegating any reference to Douglass to an anonymous footnote.

Despite this very public display of political affiliation, however, Whitfield's poems themselves do not explicitly endorse the emigrationist agenda. Rather than write propaganda poetry for a specific cause, Whitfield instead took from the emigration movement a sense of irreconcilable conflict be-

tween white and black America and then used that conflict as the structuring principle for organizing *America and Other Poems*. By making emigration
politics the source of the volume's form but not its explicit content, Whitfield could give voice to the emigrationist worldview without alienating
abolitionists whose politics were more moderate. Less than a year after their
contentious debate in the pages of *Frederick Douglass' Paper* over the merits of emigration, for example, William Watkins quoted one of Whitfield's
poems in a speech he gave to commemorate the end of the British slave
trade, prefacing the poem with the words, "Let each one of us, then, unite
in the fervent aspiration of our own Whitfield."[25] That Watkins would still
feel enough affinity with Whitfield to refer to him as "our own" after nearly
six months of vigorous public debate speaks, in part, to Whitfield's concern
that emigration politics inform but not overwhelm his poetry.

Similarly, in an 1854 proposal he put forward for a pan-American periodical designed to be "the Organ of the Black and Colored Race on the American Continent," Whitfield argued that this periodical should not be used
exclusively for purposes of racial uplift. Instead, he stressed the importance
of literary value for its own sake, writing that "while such a periodical must,
from its very nature, be the most powerful and efficient of all anti-slavery in-
strumentalities, yet we would recommend that no piece be received merely
for its anti-Slavery qualities, but only for its merits as a literary production."[26] Apart from his strong commitment to political activism, Whitfield
had a deep and abiding faith in poetry and an almost Shelleyan belief that
poets are unacknowledged social legislators who, he wrote, have a "silent"
yet "pervading influence" that shapes "every relation of life."[27]

In contrast to Whitfield, who derived from the emigration movement
the notion of conflict as the defining feature of African American life while
keeping the specific tenets of emigrationism out of his poetry, Whitman, in
his early poems about slavery, wore his politics on his sleeve—politics that
he similarly expressed in prose for such publications as the *Brooklyn Weekly
Freeman*, a Free-Soil newspaper. All but one of the poems that Whitman
published between 1850 and 1855 were written to protest the Fugitive Slave
Law, the same piece of legislation that moved Whitfield away from Frederick Douglass's goal of racial integration and toward Martin Delany's plan
to emigrate from the United States.[28] Whitman's concern with the Fugitive
Slave Law in these early, pre–*Leaves of Grass* poems—whose conventional
style bears little if any relation to the free verse of his mature poetry—is not

with the violation of African American civil rights but, rather, the plight of white northerners who were beholden to return runaway slaves to their southern masters.

In general, Whitman saw the issue of slavery as a class conflict between white artisan laborers in the North and what he referred to as "aristocratic owners of slaves" in the South.[29] Whitman seemed to move away from the Free-Soil position expressed in these early poems, however, when he introduced the issue of slavery in the 1855 *Leaves of Grass* and announced that "the attitude of great poets is to cheer up slaves and horrify despots" (*LG55* xi). In the 1855 "Song of Myself," for example, Whitman shifts his sympathies away from white northern workers and toward slaves themselves. He imagines himself first as an abolitionist aiding a fugitive slave ("The runaway slave came to my house and stopped outside, / . . . / He staid [*sic*] with me a week before he was recuperated and passed north") and then as a runaway slave suffering the indignities of pursuit by slave-catchers: "I am the hounded slave . . . I wince at the bite of dogs" (*LG55* 19, 39).[30] This noticeable increase in empathy for African American slaves from Whitman's early political poetry to the poetry of *Leaves of Grass* has given pause to Whitman scholars in recent years.

A number of scholars have noted that the different tone in the pre-1855 Free-Soil poems and the mature poetry in *Leaves of Grass* says as much about Whitman's notion of what it meant to be an American bard as it does about his evolving attitude toward African Americans. It is in the midst of these meditations on slavery, as Betsy Erkkila and Martin Klammer (among others) have noted, that Whitman finds his voice as the representative national bard who contains the multitudes of a diverse and even contradictory nation.[31] In a provocative, pre–*Leaves of Grass* manuscript fragment from 1854 that is widely regarded as one of the key moments, if not *the* moment, when Whitman finds both his voice as the nation's representative poet and the loose free-verse style that can contain a fragmented nation, he writes,

> I am the poet of slaves and of the masters of slaves
> . . . .
> I go with the slaves of the earth equally with the masters
> And I will stand between the masters and the slaves,
> Entering into both so that both shall understand me alike.
>   (*NUPM* 1:67)[32]

Whitman's claim in these unpublished lines that he can somehow resolve the conflict between slaves and their masters bears little resemblance to Free-Soil politics, nor does it follow the conventional style of his Free-Soil poetry from the early 1850s. Instead, it sounds like the free-verse poetry of 1855 that welcomes the multitudes of the nation into the contradictory embrace of the American bard. The poet who wrote "I am the poet of slaves and of the masters of slaves" is, in short, the same poet who asks in "Song of Myself,"

> Do I contradict myself?
> Very well then . . . I contradict myself.
> I am large . . . I contain multitudes. (*LG55* 55, ellipses in original)

Thinking about slavery, it appears, was a necessary precondition for what Ed Folsom calls Whitman's "attempt to become that impossible representative American voice—the *fully* representative voice—that speaks not for parties or factions but for everyone in the nation, a voice fluid enough to inhabit the subjectivities of all individuals in the culture."[33] That this catholic embrace of a divided nation—slave as well as master, black as well as white—expresses itself in lengthy free-verse lines is part and parcel of Whitman's project for American poetry as he conceived of it in 1855. The primary form that the poetry of *Leaves of Grass* assumes is that of the free-verse catalog, the long descriptive list that, by virtue of its sprawling lines, is able to include all the diverse inhabitants of the nation in a single poetic gesture. The form of the Whitmanian catalog reinforced the idea that it was possible to contain such disparate populations as slaves and slavemasters into a single, unified nation, an idea that Whitman the Free-Soiler seriously doubted but that Whitman the American bard cherished.[34]

In only one poem does Whitman seem to register the potential chaos of the national contradictions that he otherwise embraces without question. In an uncharacteristically dark and ironic poem first published in the 1856 *Leaves of Grass*—a poem that contains the injunction "Let contradictions prevail! Let one thing contradict another! and let one line of my poems contradict another!"—Whitman is considerably more forthcoming about how his nation would appear if its latent contradictions were laid bare: "Let the theory of America still be management, caste, comparison!" he writes in a pair of lines that deny the United States its status as a bastion of liberty. "Let freedom prove no man's inalienable right! every one who can tyrannize, let him tyrannize to his satisfaction!" (*LG56* 317–18). As he sloughs off his otherwise enthusiastic embrace of national contradictions in this poem, Whitman also calls for a complete upheaval in the system of American slavery: "Let the slaves be masters! let the masters become slaves!" (*LG56* 319). By the end of the poem, Whitman records the complete downfall of his otherwise idealized democratic unity as he further condemns a multiracial nation whose unity has been exposed as a sham of contradiction: "Let the Asiatic, the African, the European, the American, and the Australian, go armed against the murderous stealthiness of each other! let them sleep armed! let none believe in good will!" (*LG56* 320). In this dark vision, the poet who one year earlier had claimed that the American bard can include the disparate elements of a multitudinous nation—"America is the race of races," he wrote in the preface to the 1855 *Leaves of Grass*, "the nation of many nations"—no longer believed that he could contain multitudes (*LG55* iv, iii). Instead, all he can do is powerlessly record the dissolution of his nation at the hands of irreconcilable and contradictory forces.

Whitman ultimately removed this poem from the final editions of *Leaves of Grass*, preferring instead to believe that if his poetry could imaginatively render an ideal world of perfect unity, then that unity would eventually follow as a material fact. This faith that poetry could solve the problems of the polity is central to Whitman's project of turning *Leaves of Grass* into a textualized nation. As David Reynolds has argued, "In the turmoil of the 1850s the very idea of America was at stake. . . . With central texts of American democracy losing stable meaning"—as the Constitution faced the threat of secessionism and the Declaration of Independence failed to enforce the creed that "all men are created equal"—"[Whitman] felt he had to create a new national text in which America was poetically reconstructed."[35] Reynolds's claim that Whitman wanted to turn a conflicted nation into a coherent book of poetry is a compelling description of how *Leaves of Grass* attempted to construct a unified textual America. It also accurately describes the conditions that led James Whitfield to versify the same nation in *America and Other Poems*. Two years before Whitman published the first edition of *Leaves of Grass*, Whitfield similarly crafted a national poetic text based on the contradictions that threatened to fragment the antebellum United States. His attitude toward those contradictions, however, led him to create a book considerably different from Whitman's. As did Whitman in *Leaves of Grass*, Whitfield also attempted a poetic reconstruction of a conflicted and even contradictory nation in *America and Other Poems*, but his goal was to high-light contradiction rather than to contain it.

The title poem of the collection, "America," introduces this sense of irrec-oncilable conflict through its parody of the patriotic song "America" ("My Country, 'Tis of Thee"). In his poem, Whitfield turns the invocation "My country, 'tis of thee, / Sweet land of liberty" into an accusation, writing,

> America, it is to thee,
> Thou boasted land of liberty, —
> It is to thee I raise my song,
> Thou land of blood, and crime, and wrong. (*America* 9)

By creating a poem parallel to the popular patriotic song, Whitfield intro-duces his readers to two Americas, the exuberantly celebrated (white) America of the song and the dismal (black) America of his poem. Follow-ing this poem, Whitfield divides the entire collection into four poetic se-quences, each of which consists of two or three pairs of poems whose con-trasting themes collectively give an image of America as a site of unresolved conflict. (See chart, "Poem Sequences in *America and Other Poems*.") He re-inforces the sense of conflict introduced in "America" by pairing, for ex-ample, a poem about a racist politician's oratorical prowess with a poem about a black poet's inability to access the power of language, a poem that celebrates the beauty of the world with a poem that reels in horror at human suffering, and a poem that commemorates U.S. independence on the Fourth of July with a poem that celebrates the end of the British slave trade on the First of August. This strategy of arranging poems into discrete and meaning-ful sequences—which is similar to Whitman's grouping of thematically re-lated poems into "clusters" beginning with the 1860 *Leaves of Grass*—is cen-tral to Whitfield's poetic reconstruction of the nation in *America and Other Poems*.[36]

BY ARTFULLY ARRANGING their poems into thematic units, Whitfield and Whitman were drawing on an emerging tradition in poetry publication. Neil Fraistat has shown that poets since antiquity have "recognized that texts are partly determined by . . . the selection and arrangement of poems into collections," and that following the advances in late-eighteenth- and early-nineteenth-century printing, poets became increasingly aware that a well-

Poem Sequences in *America and Other Poems*

organized volume of poems could create a "coherent perceptual field" that made the book as a whole add up to more than the sum of its parts.[37] Michael Hinds and Stephen Matterson have argued that U.S. poets in particular have a tendency to compose collections of poetry in ways that "[foreground] the formulation of America as a text." And while Hinds and Matterson identify *Leaves of Grass* as the Ur-text of the tradition among American poets who consider "the book [to be] a part of the unrealizably immense text of the nation," Whitfield's *America and Other Poems* not only predates Whitman's by several years; it also presents a much more elaborate attempt to render the nation as a poetic text.[38]

Through his arrangement of the poetry in *America and Other Poems*, Whitfield presents America, like the book that bears its name, as a nation deeply divided by race. In the first sequence of the book, two poems written to commemorate Christmas and New Year's celebrations frame a poem about John Quincy Adams's legislative battle against slaveholders in Congress and a poem about the 1839 *Amistad* slave revolt led by the African insurgent Cinque. While all four poems register a sense of hopefulness in the fight against slavery, they also speak to the conflicted status of African Americans who, as both a part of and apart from the nation, were unsure of their place in the national community. Fully integrated white members of society such as Adams can fight the injustice of slavery through legal and political channels, whereas black social outsiders such as Cinque must resort to extralegal measures in order to do so. This sense of conflict between the Adams and Cinque poems is reinforced by the holiday poems that come before and after them in the sequence: "Christmas Hymn" and "New Year's Hymn" both adopt an optimistic tone about the prospect of peace, but they alternately endorse the passivity of religious faith and the possibility of emigration as reasons for this optimism. While "Christmas Hymn" places its trust in a conventional notion of Christian long-suffering, the speaker of "New Year's Hymn" wonders whether he had better secure his destiny beyond national boundaries, writing, "Perchance, 'mid foreign scenes, we may / Forget the land that gave us birth" (*America* 21). Pairing "Christmas Hymn" with "New Year's Hymn" allows Whitfield to pose the same question raised by the Adams and Cinque poems: Are African Americans equal participants in American social institutions—either political or religious—or have they been forced to look outside these institutions for their salvation?

The overall hopeful tone of the first sequence of poems is contrasted in the sequence that follows it, which focuses on the conflict faced by a black poet whose desire to claim fellowship in a community of letters is challenged by the racism of his culture. The sequence begins with two related poems about the power of the poet to praise the beauty of the beloved and the grandeur of God, respectively. Each poem is, in many ways, an ars poetica that focuses as much on the poet's power with language as it does on the poem's subject matter. "To A. H." shows the poet reading the works of "many a bard of lofty mind" that he then skillfully draws on to fill his love poem with a variety of classical allusions, just as "Love" compares the poet's developing talent in poetry with his increasing faith in God (*America* 22). In the contrasting pair of poems from the sequence, Whitfield demonstrates how the power of language that he cherishes in "Love" and "To A. H." can be corrupted in a racist culture: "The Arch Apostate" laments that the erstwhile abolitionist Daniel Webster used his powers of oratory in Congress to support the Fugitive Slave Law, and "The Misanthropist" presents a portrait of a black poet whose ability to use language has been crippled by racism. "In vain thou bid'st me strike the lyre," he says in "The Misanthropist" to the muse that treats him so kindly in "Love" and "To A. H.," writing that it is impossible for him to "Break forth in patriotic fire, / Or soar on higher minstrelsy" because of racist appropriations of language such as those detailed in "The Arch Apostate" (*America* 48, 54). Pairing Webster's power over language with a black poet's powerlessness also recalls the poems of the previous sequence about John Quincy Adams's access to the formal networks of political power and Cinque's exclusion from these networks.

In the central poem of this sequence, "How Long," Whitfield draws on the tensions in the poems that frame it to say that if he were allowed access to the power of language, he could use it as a tool against oppression. "Oh for a pen of living fire," he pleads. "To rouse the people's slumbering ire, / And teach the tyrant's heart to feel" (*America* 39). Jonathan Culler has described such poetic entreaties as "bardic request[s]," arguing that poems in this vein "display their poetic calling and . . . mark the belief that language can sometimes make things happen."[39] Here and elsewhere in the book, Whitfield is eager to claim both the title of bard and the power of language, despite fearing that his readers will be reluctant to grant him those honors. In the preface he wrote for *America and Other Poems*, Whitfield anticipates the audience's resistance to his bardic pretensions and imagines a cool reception of his book: "'Another book of poetry,' exclaims the reader; 'and that, too, by

one of the proscribed race, whose lot has been ignorance and servitude'"
(*America* 2). Whitfield responds to this imaginary reader with a carefully
crafted mix of apology and self-assurance: "We do not claim that the poetry
is of the highest order," he concedes, "but we do claim that it would be cred-
itable to authors of greater pretensions than the humble colored man. . . .
There is the voice of true poesy speaking in it, which, though in the rough
it may be, and wanting the polish which education and refined opportunity
give, yet nature outgusheth in harmonious numbers, and her bard, all un-
tutored as he is, singeth sweetly, and giveth forth the conceptions of his soul
in 'words that breathe and thoughts that burn'" (*America* 2). While Whitfield may ask his reader to forgive a "humble colored man" for trespassing
on Mount Parnassus, he does not refrain from identifying himself as the bard
of nature, capable both of wielding archaic language forms ("outgusheth,"
"singeth," "giveth") and of creating words so powerful that they become
living entities of their own (they "breathe" and "burn," he writes, in a phrase
slightly misquoted from Thomas Gray).[40] The final sequences of *America and
Other Poems* similarly reinforce the message from the book's preface that,
despite the challenges he faces, Whitfield will persevere in performing the
duties of the bard.

In the third sequence, Whitfield pairs three poems that depict a world
of pain and horror with three poems that revel in the beauty of the world.
These six poems together illustrate the painful irony of living in a slaveholding nation that defines itself as a bastion of liberty, or what Martin Delany
described as the feeling of being "slaves in the midst of freedom."[41] The six
poems at the heart of this sequence are framed by dedication hymns for
African American churches that were known as centers of abolitionist ac-
tivity in upstate New York. This framing device puts a political edge on the
poems about beauty and horror, and it also reminds readers that Whitfield
was often called upon to perform the bardic duty of publicly commemorating important community events.[42] Throughout *America and Other Poems*
Whitfield leaves reminders of his bardic service as a commemorative poet.
Every poem in the first sequence, for example, commemorates someone or
something of cultural importance, just as the final sequence of the collection
includes a pair of poems about U.S. political independence and the end of
the Atlantic slave trade, poems that contrast the differing expectations of
whites and African Americans over what merits public commemoration.

The fourth sequence as a whole contrasts the disparate experiences of blacks and whites in the United States. This sequence centers around two poems that alternately present the poet as a community-oriented reformer whose poetry sounds a call for change ("Midnight Musings") and as an individualistic aesthete for whom the arts serve as a source of personal edification ("Ode to Music"). Surrounding these poems about the poet's conflicting loyalties to his art and to his community are pairs of poems that contrast how individuals and communities, both black and white, conceive of freedom. The first poem, "Self-Reliance," invokes an Emersonian image of an American individualist "Who cares not for the world's applause" but remains "to his own fixed purpose true" (*America* 69–70). The image of an individual freed from the bondage of popular opinion in "Self-Reliance" stands in contrast to the corresponding poem in the sequence, "The North Star," which is about a fugitive slave seeking freedom from physical bondage. Similarly, two other poems in the sequence contrast the anniversary of white Americans' freedom from colonial occupation ("Ode for the Fourth of July") with the moment when African slaves in the Caribbean celebrated the end of the British slave trade ("Stanzas for the First of August"). This pairing of disparate quests for freedom on August First and July Fourth reinforces the sentiment permeating the entire book that life in America is experienced in radically different ways for African Americans and their white counterparts.

Whitfield was commissioned to write "Stanzas for the First of August" in 1849 for the August First celebration held at the Michigan Street Baptist Church in Buffalo, New York (the same church, it bears noting, whose dedicatory hymn he included in *America and Other Poems*). The *North Star* published a transcript of this celebration in its issue of 10 August 1849, including the full text of Whitfield's poem. It appears from the report given by the *North Star* that African American abolitionists in Buffalo had self-consciously crafted their celebration so that it would mirror the celebrations that had taken place one month earlier on the Fourth of July. The Buffalo event had as much pomp and circumstance as any Independence Day celebration, including prayers, processionals, toasts, music by a brass band, a reading of the Act of Emancipation (rather than the Declaration of Independence), choral singing of the "Song of the Free" and "Be Free Oh Man, Be Free" (rather than the national anthem), and, of course, a poem written for the occasion by the bardic representative of the community, James M. Whitfield. Antebellum celebrants of the First of August knew that their holiday would always take a backseat to the Fourth of July in the national consciousness, but they also believed that the First of August better represented the spirit of American liberty than Independence Day itself. As the *North Star* reported, one of the toasts at the Buffalo celebration made this point explicitly when the Declaration of Independence was hailed as "the first promulgation of the theory of all men's right to life, liberty and the pursuit of happiness," only to be followed by the insistence that "the act of British West India Emancipation [was] the first reduction of that theory to practice."[43]

When Whitfield paired "Stanzas for the First of August" with "Ode for the Fourth of July" in *America and Other Poems*, he captured the spirit of ironic doubling that defined the Buffalo celebration. By taking his commemorative poem out of the context of public celebration and reprinting it in book form, Whitfield risked erasing the nexus of community values that had originally brought the poem into being. He risked, that is, turning the bardic utterance of a community's representative poet into the lyric utterance of a poet in solitude. It would have been impossible to fully re-create the public setting of 1 August 1849, but the structure Whitfield created for *America and Other Poems* nevertheless allowed him to evoke the acute sense of cultural conflict—the sense of standing united in opposition against a dominant national culture—that made celebrations of the First of August so meaningful for antebellum African Americans.

Whitfield's ability to bend the medium of print to his advantage and to retain the public context of his bardic duties is remarkable, but it is not wholly without precedent. Mary Loeffelholz has demonstrated that, despite being "smaller in scale than the national print sphere," nineteenth-century public poetry was often able to "communicate with and reimage" the world of print.[44] This migration of public poetry into printed texts takes a number of forms, one of which Loeffelholz refers to as the "anthology form" of single-author volumes of poetry: "literary works that in one way or another assemble discrete, formally demarcated, and formally diverse shorter poems . . . into a sequence marked by formal variation among its constituent poems."[45] There is a "formal reflexivity [to] anthology form," writes Loeffelholz, that allows a poet such as Whitfield to assemble the poems he had written for a variety of different public occasions into a format that could then serve as a commentary on the settings that had originally given them birth.[46] Just as individual poets took advantage of anthology form to reflect

on or critique the workings of the public sphere, the multiauthor anthologies of American poetry from the period—virtually all of which were as-
sembled with a nationalist agenda in mind—attempted to define the public
sphere as a site of national unity. When *America and Other Poems* was first
reviewed in the African American press, it was connected (albeit somewhat
erroneously) to this nationalist tradition of gathering poems into anthologies whose goal was to reflect this very unity.

Beginning in the late eighteenth century and continuing into the mid-
nineteenth century, a handful of American publishers gathered newspaper
and other ephemeral poems into book-length collections in an effort to
prove that the nation as a whole had developed a unified identity. As Alan
Golding observes, "This attempt to preserve a national literature simultaneously with its creation distinguishes the early American anthologists from
their British contemporaries. In the United States, unlike in England, the
survival of the national poetry canon depended largely on the anthologists'
success in preserving poetry."[47] For example, in the preface to the first published anthology of American poetry, *American Poems* (1793), Elihu Hubbard
Smith lamented that "the frail security of an obscure newspaper" was the
only haven for what he calls "some of the handsomest specimens of American Poetry." Thus he conceived of the anthology as an appropriate home
for the emerging literary tradition of the republic.[48] Almost fifty years later,
John Keese similarly wrote in his introduction to *The Poets of America* (1841)
that "the main part of our poetical literature . . . has usually come before
the public eye in small detached portions, with slight pretension to permanence." The design of poetry anthologies, he wrote, was "to repair [that] de-
ficiency."[49] Samuel Kettell, in his 1829 *Specimens of American Poetry*, echoed
this archival goal of "preserving a portion of what is valuable and characteristic in the writings of our native poets . . . for the cause of American literature," but he also made explicit that the preservation of poetry was tantamount to the construction of a national public sphere.[50] Kettell hoped that
his anthology would aid in "fostering a national spirit" and said that "the
development of the moral and intellectual character of a people" was directly related to the development of a national literary tradition, a tradition
that he characterized as "the inheritance of a race whose virtues have con-
secrated whatever they have left behind them."[51] Once it was collected into
anthologies, American poetry could serve as proof that the American public
had developed into a recognizable "race" and a unified "people." This same

poetry could then serve as a mechanism for ensuring that the reading public would continue to exist in a similarly unified form.

When a pseudonymous literary critic for *Frederick Douglass' Paper* made a case for including African American poetry in the canon of American literature, he cited Whitfield's *America and Other Poems* as a prime example of how to rescue black-authored poetry from obscurity and insert it into a unified national public sphere. "While American literature is rapidly growing into universal appreciation," the reviewer wrote in 1853, "the name of no colored American has as yet been blazoned upon its rolls of heraldry." The reviewer attributed this lack to the fact that African Americans who wanted to "secure for themselves a position in the rank of authors" often found their work confined to "the narrow limits of pamphlets or the columns of newspapers, ephemeral caskets, whose destruction entail[s] the destruction of the gems which they contain." After lamenting that "colored American literature exists only, to too great an extent, in the vast realm of probability," the reviewer looked optimistically to the example set by Whitfield and other African American poets who had recently published book-length volumes of poetry: "The hopes of the coming literary glory of colored Americans" rest, among other places, "in the earnest endeavors which many individuals among us, such as James M. Whitfield . . . are putting forth, in order to secure for themselves a position in the rank of authors."[52]

America and Other Poems may have invited comparison with the nationalist tendencies of antebellum poetry anthologies that similarly rescued poems from the "narrow columns of newspapers," but at its core Whitfield's book refuted the assumption that the national public sphere was a unified entity whose coherence was reflected in the anthology form. *America and Other Poems* is about conflict, not consensus; division, not unity. The public sphere that emerges in Whitfield's collection is presided over by a bard torn between the disparate elements of American life, from its competing celebrations for white and black holidays to its different standards for honoring white and black public figures. The poetry gathered into *America and Other Poems* reflects a public sphere of dissension and conflict; it carries into a printed text the public voice of a bard who had looked across the podium at a nation that he recognized only half of the time.

The stark contrast between the lives of black and white Americans that Whitfield used as the structuring principle for *America and Other Poems* was prescient of what sociologist W. E. B. Du Bois would describe in 1903 as

41

the "double-consciousness" of African Americans caught between the disparate worlds of white and black America. "One ever feels his two-ness," Du Bois wrote fifty years after Whitfield published *America and Other Poems*. "An American, a Negro; two souls, two thoughts, two unreconciled strivings; two warring ideals in one dark body, whose dogged strength alone keeps it from being torn asunder. The history of the American Negro is the history of this strife."[53] Du Bois's influential characterization of the African American experience was not available to Whitfield in 1853. He was, however, well aware of how Martin Delany and the emigration movement had conceived of African Americans as what Delany—and later, Whitfield himself—would refer to as "a nation within a nation."[54]

The emigration movement's belief that African Americans were a distinct population within and against a larger white nation gave Whitfield a conceptual framework for taking the poems he had published in the African American press and crafting them into a textual representation of the nation. Specifically, the binary structure of *America and Other Poems* shares the emigrationists' vision of the American continent as split between a white Northern Hemisphere and a black Southern Hemisphere. Delany in particular seemed to revel in the symbolic appeal of a black nation in the Southern Hemisphere that stood out in sharp relief against a white Northern Hemisphere. His vision of "a glorious union of South American States" as an alternative to the United States of (North) America presented South America as a racialized photo negative of the United States. Effectively inverting the percentage of whites to people of color in the midcentury United States, Delany wrote in the *Condition* that in Central and South America, "of [the] vast population but *one-seventh* are whites, or the pure European race," while the "colored population on this glorious continent" is overwhelmingly in the majority.[55]

Whitfield eagerly embraced this vision, writing as late as 1858 that it was "destined" for African Americans to populate the Southern Hemisphere of the New World. Delany's tableau of a color-coded New World captured Whitfield's imagination. Whitfield later wrote, echoing Delany's racialized image of the continent, that "the Saxon and the negro are the only positive races on this continent . . . and if the one is destined to occupy all the temperate regions of this hemisphere, it is equally certain that the other will predominate within the tropics."[56]

Admittedly, the implication that none of the other races in the Americas were "positive" enough to sustain settlements in the New World bespeaks an unresolved contradiction within the otherwise antiracist politics of the emigration movement, as does Whitfield's belief that African Americans would "absorb" the indigenous peoples of the Southern Hemisphere: Just as Anglo-Saxons have "absorbed" the other races in England, Whitfield reasoned, "the same result is being rapidly effected in South and Central America, by the absorption of all other races in the negro." Amid these and other attempts to rationalize the proposed colonization of Native American land by African Americans, Whitfield even went so far as to echo the language of U.S. expansionism. He wrote, "I believe it to be the destiny of the negro, to develop a higher order of civilization and Christianity than the world has yet seen. I also consider it a part of his 'manifest destiny', to possess all the tropical regions of this continent, with the adjacent islands."[57] The emigrationists never fully addressed the potentially dystopian nightmare for indigenous peoples that would almost certainly have resulted had their utopian plans been brought to fruition. Neither Whitfield nor Delany was ever given the opportunity to even attempt to resolve this conflict, however, as African American interest in emigration waned with the onset of the Civil War. Most emigrationists shifted their support to the Union cause and the abolition of slavery, and Delany himself became the first black field officer in the U.S. army in 1863.

For a brief and intense moment in the 1850s, however, the possibility of remapping the hemisphere into a white North America and a black South America fueled Whitfield's imagination as nothing else in his life ever would. Du Bois derived his model for double-consciousness from the then-new discipline of psychology, but Whitfield conceived of an America divided by race through meditations on geography. The tableau of a white North America and a black South America that the emigration movement advocated is, in essence, "double-consciousness" writ large on the text of the New World.

The title poem of Whitfield's collection, "America," inhabits this point of intersection between poetry, geography, and national identity—the point that, to recall, Emerson laid out as the central challenge of nationalist U.S. poetry when he said that "America is a poem in our eyes; its ample geography dazzles the imagination." As the following section of this chapter argues,

Whitfield's "America" invokes this relationship between geography and identity only to turn it on its head. Faced with the challenge of speaking as the bardic voice of a nation that saw no connection between national geography and African American identity, Whitfield joined with the emigration movement in reimagining an Afrocentric presence in American geography, and he did so in a way that made a black poet more rather than less likely to assume the role of American bard.

IN THE 1855 PREFACE to *Leaves of Grass*, Whitman writes that the American poet "incarnates [his nation's] geography and natural life and rivers and lakes." It is the duty of a national bard, he continues, to "attract his own land body and soul to himself" because "the proof of a poet is that his country absorbs him as affectionately as he has absorbed it" (*LG55* iv, xii). This "absorption," for Whitman, is more than just an internalization of national traits and characteristics; rather, it is a fusion of the American bard with the geographical substance of the nation, a fusion that connects a geographically delimited national space with the poet's physical body. "I inhale great draughts of space," he writes, and by so doing, he internalizes the entire expanse of the nation: "The east and the west are mine, and the north and the south are mine" (*LG* 123). Because Whitman believed that his book and his body were one and the same ("This is no book," he wrote; "Who touches this, touches a man" [*LG* 382]), he hoped that by connecting his body with the geography of the United States, he would turn *Leaves of Grass* into a textualized America, an incarnation in verse of the national flesh made word. Whitman was wholly in the American grain in drawing this connection between identity and geography.

Generations of European immigrants to North America, for example, solved what Perry Miller referred to as "the problem of American self-recognition" by maintaining that their identity as Americans was derived from the physical mass of the continent itself: "We may have come to the land by an act of will," Miller writes in the collective voice of European immigration, "but despite ourselves, we have become parts of the landscape."[58] Subsequent scholars of American culture have followed Miller in observing that Euro-Americans constructed a geographic notion of selfhood by defining themselves as "parts of the landscape."[59] Martin Brückner, for one, has recently argued that the early American response to the geography of the

New World "has one recurring plot line" wherein "the realities of the land overwhelm the individual author or fictional character to the point of re-configuring his or her sense of identity."[60] Similarly, in Whitman's model for what it meant to be an American bard—wherein a poet represent the nation by absorbing its geography—national identity is not a political construct but a latent force residing in the landscape. This overwhelming geographic force, according to Whitman, waits patiently for the poet who will "attract his own land body and soul to himself" and then, in that moment of intense communion with the landscape, transforms the poet into an American bard.

The identity that Whitman derived from the landscape as a representative national poet, however, differed markedly from the identity that Whit-field and other African American emigrationists took from the geography of North America. Whitfield and other members of the emigration movement did not operate under the assumption that the New World bestowed an identity upon its African American inhabitants by overpowering them with its vast geography. Rather, emigrationists such as Whitfield and Delany be-lieved that slavery in general—and legislation such as the Fugitive Slave Law in particular—presented African Americans with a political landscape that was confining and limited, not vast and overwhelming. As a result, the emi-grationists conceived of their relationship with national geography in a way that presented Whitfield with an alternative model for how to redefine the relationship between the black body and the American continent, and it was a model that made a black poet *more* qualified to "incarnate [his nation's] geography" than a white poet like Whitman.

One of the primary arguments that Whitfield, Delany, and other emigra-tionists made was that, as a "nation within a nation," African Americans occu-pied a circumscribed sphere that was smaller than the nation as a whole.[61] At the same time, though, the emigrationists claimed the geography of the en-tire globe in the name of African populations. As emigrationist Henry Bibb wrote, "The world is the Colored man's home, and any attempt of human legislation to restrict his boundary, or circumscribe his field of locomotion, is a gross violation of the fundamental principles of justice."[62] The emigra-tion movement's contention that African Americans had a right to settle anywhere in the world was predicated on the racialist argument that black bodies, more so than white, have an innate connection to geographic spaces across the globe, a connection that allows them to adapt successfully to any world climate. Delany wrote that people of African descent "are a *superior race*, being endowed with properties fitting us for *all parts* of the earth . . . prov[ing] our right and duty to live wherever we may *choose*; while the white race may only live where they can." While Euro-American raciologists contended that whites belonged in temperate regions and people of color in tropical zones, Delany claimed that African Americans "can bear *more different* climates than the white race. . . . The black race may be found, inhabiting in healthful improvement, every part of the globe."[63]

Delany further argued that this adaptability to world geography was proof that African slaves and their descendants bestowed upon North America the reputation it enjoyed in the nineteenth century as a prosperous and habitable nation. Indeed, he argued, Africans had given America its very identity. In the history of the colonization of the New World that Delany presents in the *Condition* (and which forms the foundation for many of Whitfield's pro-emigration articles in *Frederick Douglass' Paper*), he argues that were it not for the global adaptability of people of African descent, there would be no "America" as it was known in the nineteenth century. In the early years of the European colonization of North America, Delany writes, neither "the whites nor the Indians were equal to the hard and almost insurmountable difficulties, that now stood widespread before them."[64] Thus it fell upon the Africans to make the New World wilderness fit for human habitation. When Africans arrived, Delany writes, "the forests gave way before them, and extensive verdant fields, richly clothed with produce, rose up [as if] by magic."[65] Nineteenth-century Americans, who were accustomed to believing that the United States was a pastoral haven that stood between the industrialization of Europe, on one hand, and the savagery of "primitive" societies, on the other, would have recognized in Delany's description of the "extensive verdant fields" of seventeenth-century America what Leo Marx calls a nationalist ideology that imagined the United States to be "a well-ordered green garden magnified to continental size."[66]

Calling on this ideologically charged image of the-nation-as-garden, Delany locates a moment of forgotten history "fifty years previous to the sailing of Columbus in search of a new world" to attribute the creation of this idealized pastoral America to people of African descent. In 1442, Delany says, a Portuguese sailor took ten Africans to Lisbon, where "these Africans were set immediately to work in the gardens of the emperor . . . [and] were found to be skillful and industrious in agriculture." By showing Africans creating a pastoral masterpiece in Portugal — a neutral ground that was neither Africa nor America — Delany demonstrates not only that fifteenth-century Africans had the potential to create the continental garden that by the mid-nineteenth century was all but synonymous with "America," but that they could carry this garden with them wherever they went. Delany even goes so far as to argue that Africa itself was "America" anciently. "Like the present America," he writes "all the [ancient] world went to Africa to get a supply of commodities."[67] America, according to Delany, is not so much a place in the Western Hemisphere as it is a condition that responds to the presence of African bodies. By extension, then, Africans were not brought *to* America; rather, Africans brought America *with them*. And because Africans had previously brought America to the northern half of the New World in the seventeenth century, Delany reasoned, they could just as easily take it with them to the southern half in the nineteenth.

The intimate connection between black bodies and American geography that Delany argued for not only provided the ideological foundation for the emigration movement; it also left imaginative traces in Whitfield's poetry. Specifically, the implication of Delany's line of reasoning on a black poet's ability to incarnate American geography had a profound effect on Whitfield. In the model that Whitman puts forth in *Leaves of Grass* to claim that the American bard incarnates his nation's geography, the (white) poet's body is presented as a conduit for the national identity that lies latent in continental geography. The emigration movement, however, reversed the equation that made geography a source of national identity and argued instead that the presence of black bodies *invests* geography with identity. Because Africans created America in the first place, the reasoning follows, the American continent has a stronger connection to black bodies than to white. A black poet, by extension, is more qualified than a white poet to derive American poetry from American geography. As a member of a proscribed national subculture, a member of "a nation within a nation," Whitfield had little or no reason to claim that he could represent the nation. As a descendant of the people who had originally given the United States its identity as a nation, however, that claim had already been made for him. Just as Whitman would insist that, as "one of the roughs," the complaints against his coarse working-class demeanor were actually compliments on his affinity for the representative

American common man, so too did Whitfield turn the racial identity that would otherwise limit his citizenship into the basis for his innate connection to the political geography of the United States.

Nowhere is this redefinition of the relationship between race, geography, and national identity more evident than in the title poem of *America and Other Poems*, "America," which Whitfield wrote as a parody of Samuel Francis Smith's 1831 nationalist anthem of the same name. Whitfield was not the first poet to rewrite this hymn to American liberty that, by the 1850s, was a staple at July Fourth celebrations and other nationalist occasions. In the twenty years that had passed between the time that the song "America" was published and Whitfield parodied its opening lines in his own "America," other abolitionist poets had already written new versions of the song as a way to critique the failure of the United States to live up to its egalitarian ideals.[68] While most parodies of "America" center around the disjunction between the rhetoric of American liberty and the reality of American slavery, Whitfield's poem is unique in that it also focuses on what Robert Branham calls "the geography of white fantasy" that permeates the song's Puritan-origins imagery of the "Land where my fathers died, / Land of the pilgrims' pride."[69]

The popularity of the patriotic song "America" is due in part to the way that it gives voice to a belief in the inherent connection between U.S. national identity ("My native country"), human liberty ("Land of the noble free"), and American geography ("I love thy rocks and rills, / Thy woods and templed hills"). The song not only encourages its singers to let the sounds of freedom echo "From every mountainside"; it also suggests that America's physical topography itself joins in singing the songs of freedom:

Let music swell the breeze
And swing from all the trees
Sweet freedom's song.

As the voices of American singers blend with the sounds emanating from the national landscape, the song then makes the fantastic claim that the music of American liberty literally inheres in American geography. With the line "Let rocks their silence break, / The sound prolong," the idea that rocks themselves can burst forth into singing "Sweet freedom's song" thoroughly naturalizes the ideology of the United States as a land of freedom. The music of American freedom was not written by politicians and ideologues, the song suggests; rather, the music of American freedom is recorded in the stones of the continent itself.[70] It is this presumed connection between liberty, geography, and U.S. nationality—a connection similar to the one that Whitman makes in *Leaves of Grass* with his claim to incarnate his nation's geography—that Whitfield critiques in the title poem of *America and Other Poems.*

The song "America" begins with an appeal to the pilgrim fathers' geography of national origins. Whitfield's poem, however, complicates this attempt to link national identity to a single geographic space by recalling the transatlantic locations of the slave trade that problematize an African American's ability to connect identity to national geography. In so doing, Whitfield refutes the assumption that freedom and American geography are necessarily connected:

> It is to thee, my native land,
> From whence has issued many a band
> To tear the black man from his soil,
> And force him here to delve and toil;
> Chained on your blood-bemoistened sod
> Cringing beneath a tyrant's rod. (*America* 9)

Just as the singers of the song "America" address themselves to "My native country," in this passage Whitfield directs himself to "my native land." But as he recounts the history that made the United States the land of his nativity, he presents a narrative that differs in significant ways from the story told in the song about the freedom of New England's pilgrim fathers. Rather than describing American history as a pilgrimage from bondage to freedom as Puritans moved westward across the Atlantic from Europe to America, Whitfield makes the United States the point of origin for slave traders moving eastward across the Atlantic to bring Africans from freedom to bondage.

Whitfield reconfigures the geographic coordinates upon which U.S. history unfolds such that the traditional progress of freedom from the Old World to the New World is replaced with the voyage of slave traders from the New World to the Old World and back to the New World again. Whitfield's quagmire of pronouns in this passage reinforces his critique of the implied connection between geography, nationality, and liberty in the song "America": An African American poet calls America "*my* native land," but he also identifies a connection with Africa ("the black man from *his* soil") that, despite being his place of origin, is not his present location as speaker of the poem ("force him *here* to delve and toil"), a location that he then identifies with white people as "*your* blood-bemoistened sod." The belief in a one-to-one connection between geography and national identity at the core of the song "America" (and much of *Leaves of Grass*, for that matter) is complicated in Whitfield's poem through this demonstration of how difficult, if not impossible, it was for African Americans to extract a sense of identity from U.S. geography. From this point on, the poem engages in a complexly articulated double gesture as Whitfield highlights the fact that his African ancestry separates him from the model for geographic national identity expressed by the song "America" while at the same time arguing that this same ancestry enables him to remake the American landscape on his own terms. This double gesture, to reiterate, is the hallmark of the national outsider who would be the national bard: That which would exclude Whitfield from the nation is precisely what qualifies him to represent it.

After relating the shameful history of the slave trade, Whitfield then recalls a time when African Americans fought with white Americans against British colonial rule during the Revolutionary War. Rather than extend into peacetime the unity between black and white Revolutionaries that existed during the war, however, the white soldiers who were once "wounded, side by side" with black soldiers became what Whitfield calls "the framers of a code, / That would disgrace the fiends of hell" when they condoned slavery in the U.S. Constitution (*America* 11). Whitfield asks, "Was it for this, they shed their blood, / On hill and plain, on field and flood?" (*America* 10). The geographic vocabulary that Whitfield draws on to describe the setting of the American Revolution—"hill and plain," "field and flood"—is similar to the imagery in the song "America" of "thy rocks and rills, / Thy woods and templed hills." Whitfield continues to critique the failure of the American Revolution to grant full equality to African Americans by addressing the presumed connection between geography, nationality, and liberty. In a lengthy passage permeated with geographical imagery, he imagines how the fallen African American soldiers of the Revolution would have responded could they have seen the legacy of slavery that followed the war:

> Or could the shades of all the dead,
> Who fell beneath that starry flag,
> Visit the scenes where they once bled,
> On hill and plain, on vale and crag,
> By peaceful brook, or ocean's strand,

By inland lake, or dark green wood,
Where'er the soil of this wide land
Was moistened by their patriot blood,—
And then survey the country o'er,
From north to south, from east to west,
And hear the agonizing cry
Ascending up to God on high,
From western wilds to ocean's shore,
The fervent prayer of the oppressed. (*America* 12)

Whitfield fills this passage with the hills, plains, valleys, rivers, and mountains canonized by the song "America" and popular in what Perry Miller calls the "nativist inventor[ies]" of antebellum poetry wherein extensive descriptions of the landscape serve as definitions of national identity.[71] In Whitfield's poem, however, the "rocks and rills" and "templed hills" of the nation do not burst forth into songs of American freedom. Rather, as readers are presented with what in another context would be nationalist images of the American landscape, they instead "hear the agonizing cry" of oppressed slaves.

Whitfield follows this catalog of geographic scenes with a lengthy passage about the sounds of suffering that emanate from the national landscape: "The cry of helpless infancy / Torn from the parent's fond caress"; "The indignant wail of fiery youth, / . . . / Trampled by tyrants in the dust"; "The shriek of virgin purity, / Doomed to some libertine's embrace"; "The cry of fathers, mothers, wives, / Severed from all their hearts hold dear" (*America* 12–13). By directly linking these sounds of suffering with images of the national landscape, Whitfield revises the central assumption of the song "America" that the music of American freedom inherently resides in the nation's geography and instead shows how the cries of the oppressed are heard by anyone who honestly listens to the sounds of the landscape. The geographic images that in the song "America" minimize any sense of conflict over the U.S. commitment to freedom are reimagined in Whitfield's "America" as a testament to the ways that slavery and racism have created a disjunction between U.S. national identity and individual human liberty.

Whitfield reinforces this point in the form as well as the content of his poem. While most of the poem alternates between rhymed couplets (*aabbccdd*) and cross-rhymes (*ababcdcd*), at two key moments Whitfield introduces a distinct rhyme scheme that combines couplets and cross-rhymes into a six-line *abccab* pattern. In the first of these passages, which concludes the lengthy geographic survey cited above, Whitfield hears sounds different from those the song "America" purports to hear in the landscape:

> And then survey the country o'er, (*a*)
> From north to south, from east to west, (*b*)
> And hear the agonizing cry (*c*)
> Ascending up to God on high, (*c*)
> From western wilds to ocean's shore, (*a*)
> The fervent prayer of the oppressed. (*b*) (*America* 12)

The *a* rhymes present the total scope of the national landscape ("And then survey the country o'er" "From western wilds to ocean's shore"), while the *b* rhymes cover that landscape with the suffering of slavery ("From north to south, from east to west" "The fervent prayer of the oppressed"). The central *c* couplet reinforces that the sounds of the national landscape are not songs of freedom but cries of pain ("And hear the agonizing cry / Ascending up to God on high").

In the second passage where Whitfield uses this modified *abccab* rhyme scheme, he looks forward to a moment of divine retribution when the cries of the oppressors rather than the oppressed will be heard throughout the land. Just as the song "America" ends with a prayer ("Protect us by thy might / Great God, our King"), Whitfield's poem ends with a plea that divine vengeance be meted out on the slaveholding nation:

> [At] the promised time of God, (*a*)
> When his Almighty ire shall wake, (*b*)
> And smite the oppressor in his wrath, (*c*)
> And hurl red ruin in his path, (*c*)
> And with the terrors of his rod, (*a*)
> Cause adamantine hearts to quake. (*b*) (*America* 14)

The *a* and *b* rhymes in this passage appeal to a sense of divine justice: At the duly appointed "time of God" the "terrors of his rod" will be felt as his "ire shall wake" and cause the "hearts [of the oppressor] to quake." The *c* rhymes of this passage, which bring the "wrath" of God into the "path" of slaveholders, parallel the *c* rhymes of the previous *abccab* passage, but the parallelism is reversed: In the first of these formally distinct passages Whitfield describes the suffering of the oppressed, while in the second he describes the suffering of the oppressors. By creating a parallel between the *c* rhymes of these passages, Whitfield indicates that the present America of suffering slaves is not the same America of suffering slaveholders that will someday be. There is a sense here that the tables are turning and that a new America is about to come into being, an America whose identity does not passively arise from the stones and earth of the continent but, rather, as the conclusion of the poem indicates, derives from the agency of African Americans who are actively involved in the cause of human freedom.

The final lines of the poem confirm that a new American geography is in the process of creation, and that the songs of liberty promised by *this* America will not be sung by the rocks of the continent but by African American voices. Whitfield writes,

> We pray, and never mean to cease,
> Till weak old age and fiery youth
> In freedom's cause their voices raise,
> And burst the bonds of every slave;
> Till, north and south, and east and west,
> The wrongs we bear shall be redressed. (*America* 16)

Recalling an earlier moment in the poem when "From north to south, from east to west" all that could be heard was "The fervent prayer of the oppressed," Whitfield ends with an alternate vision of American geography wherein the African American voices raised in the cause of liberty create a geography of freedom as broad as the geography of oppression identified earlier: "Till, north and south, and east and west," he writes, "The wrongs we bear shall be redressed." Whitfield's poem does not ask its readers to wait for the voice of the landscape to sing them the songs of freedom (as does the song "America") but, instead, encourages them to make it a land of genuine freedom on their own. By making African American voices the precondition for creating a new America with a broad geography extending "north and south, and east and west," Whitfield's poem functions on the same logic as that of the emigration movement, namely, that African Americans do not *extract* national identity from geography, they *invest* geography with identity.

Melvin Dixon has argued that "Afro-American literature is replete with speech acts and spatial images that endow language with the power to re-invent geography and identity."[72] Whitfield's poetry is indebted to the tradi-tion that Dixon describes, but it also carries with it a distinctiveness that was born of the antebellum emigration movement. Specifically, Whitfield's poem is able to imagine that another America was possible in poetry because the emigrationists believed that they could create another America elsewhere in the world. Even though Whitfield's "America" neither ends with an ex-plicit endorsement of emigration policies nor identifies Delany's vision of a black republic in South America as the geography of liberty prophesied in the poem—Whitfield stays true to his belief that a poem not be valued "merely" for its political commitments "but only for its merits as a literary production"[73]—it is nevertheless the emigrationists' belief that people of African descent can transform the geography they inhabit that gives him the wherewithal to claim the kind of connection to the American landscape that would otherwise be all but imaginatively unavailable to him.

One of the ironies surrounding this effort to connect African Ameri-cans with the national landscape is that in order to do so, Whitfield must first ground himself in a worldview that does not derive its primary sense of identify from affiliation with the nation-state. Rather, it is a worldview that conceives of African Americans as what James Theodore Holly (a fel-low emigrationist) characterized as a "denationalized" community who, un-moored from their obligations to the nation, move freely throughout the globe.[74] In "America," Whitfield attempts to reconcile national identity with the alternately local and global coordinates that define African Americans either as a "denationalized" population within the nation or as a popula-tion for whom "the world is the Colored man's home."[75] However, in "How Long," the other major poem from *America and Other Poems*, Whitfield ex-plicitly rejects any allegiance to the nation-state and instead looks for soli-darity within the African American community, on one hand, and with simi-larly oppressed peoples across the globe, on the other. As the final section of this chapter argues, Whitfield's posture as a national outsider-*cum*-national bard in "America" is complicated in "How Long" by a complex set of alle-giances to people and places both local and global in scope.

BOTH WHITMAN AND WHITFIELD anchored their projects for Ameri-can poetry to American geography, albeit in different ways. Specifically, in

Whitman's desire to incarnate the nation and Whitfield's claim that African Americans have the power to create geographies of freedom, both poets drew on a long-standing tradition in early American culture to view the geography of the New World as a text into which is written the story of individual and community identity. From the Puritans' attempt to read a transcript of providential history in the "howling wilderness" of the American landscape to Emerson's insistence that "America is a poem in our eyes; its ample geography dazzles the imagination," Americans from the seventeenth to the nineteenth centuries believed (to greater or lesser degrees) that "the construction of the American subject was grounded in the textual experience of geography," as Martin Brückner puts it. Specifically, Brückner continues, Americans of the period were accustomed to reading "tales of how geography invariably transforms personal experiences into heartfelt characterizations of selfhood."[76]

In "How Long," one of the major poems in his collection, Whitfield adopts and then modifies this tradition whereby Americans find a source of individual and community identity in the text of national geography. Just as in "America" Whitfield borrows from the insights of the emigration movement to dismantle the assumptions about race, geography, and identity implicit in the patriotic song "America (My Country 'Tis of Thee)," in "How Long" Whitfield similarly redefines African Americans' relationship with the geography of the United States, and he does so in a way that directly complicates the tendency to treat geography as a source of identity. But whereas the poem "America" derives its critique from the emigrationists' belief that people of African descent carry with them the potential to transform the geographic regions they inhabit, in "How Long" Whitfield does not search for a single national geography upon which to anchor African American identity, whether that geography is in the United States or in a black-led nation in South America. Instead, "How Long" takes from the emigration movement the idea that black identity exists in a conceptual space alternately smaller-than-national and larger-than-national in scope: the circumscribed "nation within a nation," on one hand, and the expansive "world [as] the Colored man's home," on the other.

In the final section of "How Long," Whitfield adopts the convention of depicting the national landscape as a textual source of identity when he recounts the crimes of American slavery. He reports on the destructive influence of slavery as it "Spreads o'er this land" and sees in that landscape the "signs of fate and fear" that testify to the "moral darkness [that] spreads its gloom / Over the land in every part" (*America* 35, 37). Whitfield clarifies that the "moral darkness" and "dark omens" in the landscape are not blandly physical manifestations of American geography. Rather, these omens constitute a text that is as intelligible as a historical record: "And though no literal darkness spreads / Upon the lands its sable gloom," he writes, "Yet to the eye of him who reads / The fate of nations past and gone" these "dark omens" are clearly visible (*America* 36). He then proceeds to compare the "moral darkness" that he reads in the landscape with the biblical plague of darkness that Moses caused to descend upon Egypt during the Israelite captivity.

This typological comparison of American geography with biblical history—a comparison that treats the observation of the landscape as a venture in exegesis—is indebted to the tendency in early American culture to read the signs of one's destiny in the landscape, just as, in Sacvan Bercovitch's terms, "a believer unveils scripture."[77] Before treating the landscape as a typological text from which he can derive a biblical mandate for his identity as an American abolitionist, however, in earlier sections of the poem Whitfield introduces a variety of non-U.S. geographies that allow him to reframe the otherwise nationalist gesture of reading a geographic script of identity in an exclusively American context. In direct violation of the tradition that accords the American landscape the unique status of geographic sacred text, Whitfield treats other spaces on the globe as equally intelligible documents, and not merely as mute records that reinforce the exceptional character of U.S. national geography.

In the sections of "How Long" preceding the typological interpretation of the U.S. landscape that appears at poem's end, Whitfield scans the globe for landscapes where the "dark omens" of "slavery's gloomy night" are as readable as they are in the geography of the United States. His search leads him across the Atlantic to Africa and Europe, places that would otherwise be considered blank pages on the text of American identity but that in the poem's tour of the Atlantic rim become sites where Whitfield accumulates a variety of nonnational affiliations. When he looks toward Africa, for instance, he experiences a feeling of racial solidarity that connects him with other people of African descent whose ancestors were similarly brought to the United States as slaves. Just as Langston Hughes would write more than fifty years later of the "Ancient, dusky rivers" in Africa that provide black Americans with a foundation for personal and community identity, Whitfield summons an image of the West African river systems that he connects first with the institution of slavery and then with a black national subculture in the United States.[78] He writes,

> I see the Gambia's swelling flood,
> And Niger's darkly rolling wave,
> Bear on their bosoms stained with blood,
> The bound and lacerated slave. (*America* 30)

The Gambia River, which had been an outpost for Portuguese, French, and British empires in the eighteenth century, had by the nineteenth century earned a reputation as the seat of the West African slave trade. Similarly, it was in the delta of the Niger River that slavers would, as Whitfield writes, "furnish victims for that trade" that "breeds on earth such deeds of shame / As fiends might blush to hear or name" (*America* 30). In addition to functioning in the poem as metonymic reminders of the transatlantic slave trade, the Niger and Gambia rivers also serve as geographic shorthand for Whitfield's conviction that African Americans are a discrete and self-contained community whose identity as a people remains intact despite their having been repatriated into a slaveholding nation across the Atlantic. Specifically, in describing the rivers as having "bosoms stained with blood" and referring to African American slaves as the "children" of a mother continent, Whitfield depicts West Africans and their descendants as members of a racial family whose identity persists regardless of their current nation of residence (*America* 30). When identity is a question of genealogy rather than ideology, this Africa-as-motherland image indicates, being of African descent means belonging to a national family whose membership persists as a "nation within a nation" anywhere in the world.

Immediately following this image of a common African ancestry that unites black Americans in the United States, however, Whitfield shifts his gaze to Europe, where he recounts the aftermath of the failed revolutions that spread throughout the continent in 1848 and 1849. He dovetails his description of the Niger and Gambia rivers in the previous section with a picture of the Danube River in an elegy to the fallen Hungarian nationalists defeated by the Austrian empire in the Magyar revolution of 1849:

I see where Danube's waters roll,
And where the Magyar vainly strove,
With valiant arm, and faithful soul,
In battle for the land he loved. (*America* 30–31)

As Whitfield describes the turmoil of 1848–49, he does so with language
that parallels the European revolutionaries' commitment to "the land [they]
loved" with his earlier description of the affection that people of African descent feel for their home continent. This comparison of African slaves with
ethnic European insurgents is thematic as well as stylistic—thematic in that
both populations are depicted as suffering comparable defeats, and stylistic in that the parallelism between "I see the Gambia's swelling flood" and
"I see where Danube's waters roll" indicates a cultural continuity across the
Atlantic rim.

Whitfield was by no means alone in his expressions of sympathy for the
fallen European revolutionaries of 1848–49. Antebellum white Americans
overwhelmingly supported what they viewed as revolutions similar to their
own war of independence in 1776. (Indeed, Whitman himself included a
poem about the European revolutions in the first edition of *Leaves of Grass*
[*LG55* 87–88].) As Larry J. Reynolds has shown, the majority of white Americans not only expressed their support for the plight of ethnic Europeans
during this period of unrest, but they also "credited America with being a
political messiah to the world," a bastion of hope and liberty in a world of
tyranny and conflict.[79] In "How Long," Whitfield expresses the same sense
of support for the European revolutionaries that his white countrymen do,
but he does so without ascribing any messianic political triumphs to the
United States. Instead, the nation that claims to be a "grand asylum" for the
"trodden-down of every land" is home to "[w]orse scenes" of violence and
oppression than anything in Europe (*America* 32). Specifically, Whitfield
writes, the horrors occasioned by the Fugitive Slave Law are proof that the
United States stands with the imperial powers of Europe, and not with the
oppressed peoples of the continent. Passage of the 1850 law, which occurred
immediately following the failure of the European revolutions, leads Whitfield to conclude that the African slave trade, the quashed revolutions in
Europe, and the Fugitive Slave Law are proof that a midcentury apocalypse
is spreading across the Atlantic.

That Whitfield could equate African American slavery with European vassalage in this poem is consistent with opinions he expressed in prose as well. In a pro-emigration essay from 1853, Whitfield said that the sensation of belonging to "a nation within a nation" is not exclusive to nineteenth-century African Americans. "In every age of the world have been found classes of men oppressed by others," he writes, "marked by some peculiarity of race, color, language, or religion, existing within a nation, but forming no *'integrant part'* of that nation."[80] Martin Delany made a similar statement the previous year, writing that "in all ages, in almost every nation, [there has] existed a nation within a nation, a people who although forming a part and parcel of the population, yet were . . . but a restricted part of the body politic of such nations." He continued, "Such then are the Poles in Russia, the Hungarians in Austria, the Scotch, the Irish, and Welsh in the United Kingdom, and such also are the Jews."[81] It has become something of a commonplace to refer to the antebellum emigrationists, and Delany in particular, as the first black nationalists of the United States.[82] Statements such as these by Whitfield and Delany, however, testify that the emigration movement was just as likely to express a color-blind internationalism on behalf of denationalized peoples throughout the world as it was to tout the distinctive identity of African Americans. No emigrationist document expresses more eloquently than Whitfield's "How Long" this sense that black Americans belong to both a "nation within a nation" in the United States and a transnational community of marginalized peoples spanning the Atlantic rim.

In addition to drawing a parallel between the Gambia and Danube rivers, elsewhere in the poem Whitfield compares racial slavery with the trials facing European ethnic groups. In one particular moment he does so by directly alluding to the displaced Scottish bard of Sir Walter Scott's *The Lay of the Last Minstrel*. "Three millions drag their clanking chains," Whitfield writes of African American slaves, "'Unwept, unhonored, and unsung', / Doomed to a state of slavery" (*America* 34). In canto 6 of the *Last Minstrel*, Scott depicts an exiled bard who collapses into "the vile dust, from whence he sprung, / Unwept, unhonored, and unsung." Applying Scott's phrase to the conditions of American slavery allows Whitfield to draw an explicit comparison between black slaves and the *Last Minstrel*'s Scotsman in England who, like African Americans in the United States, "never to himself hath said, / This is my own, my native land!"[83] This allusion to Scott's poem forges a connection between a black subculture in the United States and a transatlantic community of similarly displaced populations by foregrounding the sentiment that neither population can lay claim to a stable national geography as a source of individual or community identity; that is, neither African American slaves in the United States nor oppressed ethnic groups in Europe can ever say, as Scott's minstrel does, "This is my own, my native land." Instead, the balance of Whitfield's poem indicates, both ethnic Europeans and African Americans can find refuge and solidarity in the national subcultures they belong to as well as an international coalition of similarly denationalized peoples.

Three years after Whitfield published *America and Other Poems*, Whitman added a new poem to the second (1856) edition of *Leaves of Grass* that, like Whitfield's "How Long," features the poet imaginatively traveling throughout the globe and reporting on the state of the world at midcentury. At first blush, Whitfield's "How Long" and Whitman's poem—which would eventually be titled "Salut au Monde!"—seem much more different than alike. "How Long," which retraces the path of the transatlantic slave trade, draws its imagery from the suffering of peoples along the Atlantic rim. Whitman's poem, by contrast, is an enthusiastic catalog of the sights and sounds of a prosperous world, with the United States at the center of unparalleled global productivity. In "Salut au Monde!" Whitman expands the circle of affection he had previously reserved for his fellow citizens to include nations and peoples from across the world. Whitman characterizes this communion with the globe as a transformative experience that turns an American bard into a citizen of the world:

> My spirit has pass'd in compassion and determination around the
>   whole earth,
> I have look'd for equals and lovers and found them ready for me in
>   all lands,
> I think some divine rapport has equalized me with them. (*LG* 120)

While the majority of "Salut au Monde!" moves its reader toward a mood of exuberant optimism about the state of the world, there is a darker undercurrent to the poem that similarly testifies to the worldwide oppression of the weak by the strong.

Whitman scholars have recognized for some time that the cosmopolitan ethos of "Salut au Monde!" complements the nationalism on display elsewhere in *Leaves of Grass*, seeing in it the fullest realization of Whitman's stated desire for an "internationality of poems and poets, binding the lands of the earth closer than all treaties and diplomacy" (PW 2:512). What has drawn less attention from critics, however, is that Whitman makes particular mention of populations in distress amid the celebratory atmosphere of the poem.[84] Alongside picturesque images that seem to be drawn from the pages of a travel brochure—such as "I hear the Spanish dance with castanets in the chestnut shade, to the rebeck and guitar"—Whitman also reports much more soberly, "I see all the menials of the earth, laboring" (LG 113, 118). He cites the oppression of women and the gendered division of labor, writing at one point about "women of the earth subordinated at [their] tasks." He mentions the victims of chattel slavery, recording "the wheeze of the slave-coffle as the slaves march on, as the husky gangs pass on by twos and threes, fasten'd together with wrist-chains and ankle-chains." In one section of the poem he addresses the peoples of Africa as "own'd persons dropping sweat-drops or blood-drops," lamenting that their "human forms" have been battered into "the fathomless ever-impressive countenances of brutes!" Whitman also mentions the suppressed European revolutionaries of 1848–49 as he hears "fierce French liberty songs" and "the cry of the Cossack" bearing witness to the persistence of tyranny around the globe (LG 119, 113). As in Whitfield's "How Long," the world geography of Whitman's "Salut au Monde!" is populated by "menials of the earth" who share a common burden of oppression.

Following the initial 1856 publication of "Salut au Monde!" however, Whitman revised and edited the poem in ways that minimize the impact of these images of worldwide suffering. Specifically, he removed lines that refer directly to minority groups in the United States while adding lines emphasizing that the United States would preside over a dawning era of international prosperity. While the poem initially ended with the cosmopolitan sentiment "I find my home wherever there are any homes of men," in later editions of the poem Whitman omitted this line and instead added that his imaginative journey throughout the world served an explicitly nationalist agenda:

Toward you all, in America's name,
I raise high the perpendicular hand, I make the signal,

To remain after me in sight forever,
For all the haunts and homes of men. (*LG56* 122; *LG* 120)

In the first edition of "Salut au Monde!" the poem was an all-inclusive tour of the globe that mentioned the United States as only one location among many. In later editions, the poem became an American salute to the world, with the United States becoming the stable frame of reference from which the rest of the world is viewed in contrast.

Whitman expressed elsewhere that world progress invariably hinged on the prominence of a single nation: "Any period one nation must lead," he wrote. "One land must be the promise and reliance of the future" (*LG* 266). In an unpublished political tract written in 1856, he specified that this nation was the United States: "Frontiers and boundaries are less and less able to divide men. The modern inventions . . . are interlinking the inhabitants of the earth together as groups of one family — America standing, and for ages to stand, as the host and champion of the same, the most welcome spectacle ever presented among nations."[85] The subsequent incarnations of "Salut au Monde!" bear out this sentiment that the United States would have a central role to play in the increasingly internationalized world of the nineteenth century. Nevertheless, the lines excised from the first "Salut au Monde!" hold out the possibility of a much more equitable internationalism, in terms of both a more modest role for the United States and a greater attention to world populations in crisis.

The earliest published version of "Salut au Monde!" is revealing not only in its expression of a cosmopolitan sentiment that tempers partiality for the nation, but also in the way that Whitman's coalition of oppressed peoples from across the world brings African American slaves together with working-class whites in the United States. One of the most telling lines to be removed from later editions of the poem is one in which Whitman directly addresses African American slaves along with servant populations in the Americas and Europe: "You peon of Mexico!" he hails, "you Russian serf! You quadroon of Carolina, Texas, Tennessee!" (*LG56* 120). In another pair of lines later excluded from the poem, Whitman places African American slaves alongside the working-class New Yorkers with whom he identified as "one of the roughs," writing, "I hear the Virginia plantation chorus of negroes, of harvest night, in the glare of pineknots, / I hear the strong baritone of the 'long-shore-men of Manahatta, — I hear the stevedores unlading the cargoes, and singing" (*LG56* 105). In a political tract written the same year as "Salut au Monde!" Whitman went to great lengths to characterize working-class white Americans as a dominated group whose interests were subordinated to those of an elite class of lawyers, businessmen, and politicians. Invoking the specter of European vassalage on American soil, Whitman asks at one point in the tract after detailing the denigration of labor in the United States, "Shall the future mechanics of America be serfs?"[86] Elsewhere in his political prose, to recall, Whitman blamed African American slave labor—and not the elitism of a rising professional class—for the "denigration" of free white labor. When he is able to see both black slaves and white workers in a transnational context, however, that sentiment is reversed.

Not only does Whitman's pairing of African American slaves and white workers in the 1856 version of "Salut au Monde!" represent a willingness to see a common tie between the "wage slavery" of working-class whites and the chattel slavery of African Americans, but the larger context of the poem also indicates that black slaves and white laborers join equally with "the menials of the earth" in a common resistance to oppression. Indeed, in the same political tract where he compares white workers to European serfs, Whitman writes with great optimism of a worldwide downfall of slavery, aristocracy, and oppression: "The times are full of great portents in These States and in the whole world. Freedom against slavery is not issuing here alone, but is issuing everywhere. . . . Landmarks of masters, slaves, kings, aristocracies, are moth-eaten, and the peoples of the earth are planting new vast landmarks for themselves."[87] As the various incarnations of "Salut au Monde!" indicate, Whitman was actively attempting to resolve—or, at least, to articulate—a complex set of loyalties to the United States, its national subgroups, and an international coalition of oppressed populations. Less than a decade after their missed meeting at the Buffalo Free-Soil convention in 1848, Whitman and Whitfield continued to share a similar set of concerns about race and slavery in both the nation and the world, concerns that informed each poet's sense of what it meant to be an American bard.

Whitfield would never fully realize his ambitions as a poet, however. His hope that *America and Other Poems* would "'put money in the purse' of the writer, that he may be able to cultivate, improve, and fully develop the talent which God hath given him" never materialized, and his career is marked more by regret than by success (*America* 2). *America and Other Poems* was well reviewed in a number of African American newspapers, and Whitfield himself was praised by other black writers as a "sable son of genius" and "one of the purest poets in America."[88] Nevertheless, his book was not as well received by the general reading public as Whitfield hoped it would be, and his dream of supporting himself as a poet never materialized.[89] Frederick Douglass once lamented that the glass ceiling of racism (along with Whitfield's obligation to support his three children) made it impossible for Whitfield to leave his career as a barber and pursue poetry full time: "That talents so commanding, gifts so rare, poetic powers so distinguished, should be tied to the handle of a razor and buried in the precincts of a barber's shop," Douglass wrote, "is painfully disheartening."[90] Even after *America and Other Poems* turned out to be a commercial failure, Whitfield had a second shot at a literary career. At the 1854 National Emigration Convention in Cleveland, Whitfield was chosen to be the editor of the *Afric-American Repository*, a review of literature and politics whose goal was to publish the best writing from North and South America alike. Extant historical records, however, indicate that the publication never got off the ground. Whitfield himself falls off the historical record in 1859 in Buffalo, only to appear again in 1861 in California. (Some have speculated that the two years were spent in Central America on a fact-finding mission for the emigrationists, but no hard evidence supports this.)[91]

Whitfield lived out the rest of his life in California and other western states—he died in 1871—working full time as a barber while gradually returning to poetry. Between 1867 and 1870, the *San Francisco Elevator*, a black-owned periodical, published a number of new poems and letters by Whitfield, and on two occasions he even had the opportunity to resume his duties in the office of the bard. In 1867 he was invited to write a New Year's Day poem to commemorate the signing of the Emancipation Proclamation, and in 1870 he delivered a poem that honored the ratification of the Fifteenth Amendment. The 1870 poem, a commemorative ode in honor of the constitutional amendment that extended voting rights to black men, is perhaps the most optimistic document he ever composed. In it, Whitfield calls the United States the most "favored land" on the planet, a place that "stands the first by land and wave, / Without a master or a slave."[92] For the New Year's poem, however, Whitfield was torn between celebrating the emancipation of African American slaves and reminding his readers of slavery's enduring legacy, writing that the memory of slavery

darkens each historic page,
And sends a discord through the lyre
Of every bard, who frames his song.[93]

Echoing the lament from *America and Other Poems* that slavery had handed him a "discordant lyre" upon which to craft his poetry, in this 1867 poem Whitfield continued to think that his work as a poet had been permanently fractured by racism. Nevertheless, there is reason to believe that the occasion for this particular poem also gave Whitfield a sense of how it would feel to be the bard of a unified nation. The published transcript of the poem (which included the oration that preceded it) records that "the hall was densely crowded with two thousand white and colored persons indiscriminately," and that Whitfield's poem "received marked applause from the audience during the delivery."[94] Such adulation might not have provided Whitfield with the financial support that he had hoped to secure with his poetry, but at the very least it gave him the opportunity to be the bard he had always known he was.

chapter two

POET OF A NEW AMERICAN RELIGION

I too, following many and follow'd by many, inaugurate a religion.
— *Walt Whitman, "Starting from Paumanok" (1891)*

In September 1879 Walt Whitman was visiting Denver, Colorado, as part of a trip to the western United States that included stops in Lawrence, Kansas, and St. Louis, Missouri. Almost twenty years earlier Whitman had written in the poem "A Promise to California" that he would travel to California because "these States tend inland and toward the Western sea, and I will also" (LG 108).[1] Restricted by limited finances and failing health, however, Whitman was unable to keep this promise and headed home to New Jersey without ever having seen the Pacific Ocean. If Whitman had continued on to the West Coast, however, he would most likely have made the journey via the Utah Territory. Many other California-bound literary travelers—such as Mark Twain, Richard Burton, and Horace Greeley—had similarly stopped in the Salt Lake Valley to get a firsthand look at the community that Leo Tolstoy is said to have called "the American religion."[2] If Whitman had passed through Salt Lake City and had there been given an audience with Mormon prophet John Taylor, Brigham Young's successor to the presidency of the Church of Jesus Christ of Latter-day Saints (Young himself having died two years earlier), Taylor might have followed Young's custom of giving his eastern visitors a sample of church literature that included both the Book of Mormon and a volume of poems written by Eliza R. Snow, a woman universally regarded as "the chief poet of the Mormon Church."[3]

Whitman had known about the Book of Mormon since at least the late 1850s, when he wrote a brief publication notice about a recent edition of the book for the *Brooklyn Daily Times*. "The present edition of the 'Book of Mormon,'" he wrote, "is an accurate reprint of the 3d American edition originally published at Nauvoo eighteen years ago, under the official sanction of the leaders of the Mormon Church. It is quite a curiosity in its way and should find a place in the library of every diligent book-collector."[4] The "curious" nature of the Book of Mormon that Whitman referred to stems from the story of its origins: Joseph Smith, the founder of the Mormon faith, claimed to have translated the book from golden plates that contained the history of a group of Israelites who emigrated to the American continent 600 years before the birth of Jesus Christ. Whitman's counsel that "every diligent book-collector" procure a copy of the Book of Mormon did not stem from his belief in the book's veracity. Rather, Whitman believed that the Book of Mormon belonged on U.S. bookshelves because it represented a realization of his hope that the New World would produce religious texts commensurate with the American experience. "Our chief religious and poetical works are not our own," he lamented, "nor adapted to our light" (LG 431). Whitman frequently expressed his hope that "native authors" would be "sacerdotal" in their approach to literature and provided his own work as an example of scripture for a new American religion, writing in *Leaves of Grass*, "I too, following many and follow'd by many, inaugurate a religion" (LG 22). He indicated the full scope of his ambition to be the poet of a new American religion in two informal notes he wrote during the late 1850s: In one he referred elliptically to "*Founding a new American Religion*," and in another he identified his mission to be "*The Great Construction of the New Bible*. Not to be diverted from the principal object — the main life work" (NUPM 6:2046, 1:353, emphasis in original).

While Whitman had known about the Mormons' "new American Bible" since at least the late 1850s, he did not know that the faith had a poet laureate in Eliza R. Snow. If Whitman had traveled to Salt Lake City in 1879, not only would he have received a copy of Snow's poems, but he might even have met the poet herself. In addition to being the most prominent of Brigham Young's polygamous wives, Snow claimed a significant amount of ecclesiastical authority among the Latter-day Saints. Apart from her formal authority over Mormon women as president of the "Female Relief Society" (over which it was said that "she reigns supreme"), Snow wielded informal authority over the entire church as an unofficial "third counselor" to Brigham Young, who was aided throughout his tenure as church president by two male counselors drawn from the patriarchal hierarchy of the church.[5]

Snow's religious authority emerged, in part, from her work as a poet, a work for which she received the distinguished title of "Zion's Poetess." "As the chief poet of the Mormon Church," one contemporary observer noted, "she enjoys a reputation such as would be impossible to any other woman among the Saints."[6] Indeed, while there were Mormon men who wrote poetry—including high-ranking men within the church hierarchy—it was Snow who was consistently called on to write commemorative verses for significant religious and cultural events in the Latter-day Saint community. In 1879 Whitman was only beginning to attract disciples who received him as a realization of Emerson's call that "the world still wants its poet-priest," but by as early as the 1840s the Mormons had already found their poet-priestess in Eliza R. Snow.[7] As "the high-priestess and poet-general of the Church," a number of nineteenth-century Mormons noted, Snow was said to have been "born with more than the poet's soul. She was a prophetess in her very nature."[8] The number of readers who also considered Whitman a prophet in his own right was growing during the late nineteenth century. Harvard professor Bliss Perry gave the derisive title of "hot little prophets" to the international group of scholars, writers, and activists whom William James said were "quite willing to admit that in important respects Whitman is of the genuine lineage of the prophets."[9]

In an essay from the late 1870s titled "The Gospel According to Walt Whitman," for example, Robert Louis Stevenson contended that Whitman's work was best characterized as prophecy rather than poetry. Stevenson went so far as to say that the prophetic temperament in Whitman was a primary feature of the poet's uniqueness among nineteenth-century authors: "Not as a poet, but what we must call (for lack of a more exact expression) a prophet, he occupies a curious and prominent position. . . . As a sign of the times, it would be hard to find his parallel."[10] Had he made it to the Utah Territory in 1879, Whitman would have been forced to concede that he shared this "curious and prominent position" with Eliza R. Snow, whose own career ran parallel to Whitman's project to write the poems of a new American religion. Admittedly, Whitman and Snow fulfilled their duties as American religious poets in quite different ways. Snow's poetry supported an organized religion that valued hierarchy and conformity, while Whitman believed that poets would replace priests in spreading a democratic gospel of individual self-determination. Whitman would seem to find his religious counterparts among the more progressive antebellum faiths than he would among the Latter-day Saints. The Shakers' belief that Jesus Christ had been reborn in female form, for example, shares Whitman's belief that "of male and female . . . either is but the equal of the other," just as the Oneida Perfectionists' advocacy of polyamorous relationships echoes Whitman's belief that sexuality opens a pathway to the divine (LG 24).

Regardless of the doctrinal differences between Mormonism and Whitmanism, both of these new American religions shared common ground in their respective attempts to reconcile their newness and their American-ness—their modernity and nationality—with the deep history of a sacred past over which the United States had no jurisdiction. For his part, Whitman was conflicted over his desire to create a modern secular religion rooted in American culture while maintaining his commitment to embrace the entire scope of world sacred history. In one poem he welcomed ancient religious traditions from the four corners of the globe:

> I respect Assyria, China, Teutonia, and the Hebrews,
> I adopt each theory, myth, god, and demi-god,
> I see that the old accounts, bibles, genealogies, are true, without
> exception. (LG 192)

Conversely, he prophesied in the preface to the 1855 *Leaves of Grass* that the purifying fires of modernity would consume every remnant of the sacred past. "There will soon be no more priests," he declared, insisting that a "superior breed" of U.S.-based "prophets en masse" would "arise in America and be responded to from the remainder of the earth" (LG55 xi). Whitman's image of himself as the poet-prophet of a new American religion, then, existed in tension with his allegiance to the sacred past of a larger world.

Snow and the Mormons experienced a similar tension when their adoption of ancient biblical practices—such as polygamy, communal living, and the theocratic rule of prophets—put them at odds with their host nation. The Mormons considered themselves the vanguard of a millennial faith that would usher in a future where the United States would play a prominent role in the apocalyptic events accompanying Christ's return to the earth. The majority of Americans, however, saw the Mormons' polygamy, theocracy, and communitarian lifestyle as evidence not that the Latter-day Saints were drawing on ancient tradition to prepare the world for an imminent millennium but that they had become like the "heathen" and "primitive" nations who were unwelcome in the modern world. One nineteenth-century commentator expressed this sentiment when he called Mormonism "a distinct, systematic, dispassionate contradiction of the American idea" and said that granting Mormons full fellowship in the United States would be "as impossible as . . . [accepting] an independent state of cannibals, infanticides, or widow-burners, which by some magic had been transplanted from the Marquesas, China, or Hindostan into the place now occupied by Georgia."[11] Another proposed removing the Mormons from North America entirely and relocating them to "some remote island beyond the jurisdiction of any Christian Government, for it is impossible that such a community should exist under any Government that is based on Christian principles."[12] Mormon polygamy and theocracy were reminders of a premodern past that most Americans were eager to forget. The Mormons, in contrast, believed that honoring these ancient beliefs made them the worthy heirs of a biblical heritage to which, in their opinion, the rest of the nation merely paid lip service. Snow herself said that this respect for sacred history qualified the Latter-day Saints to be "Columbia's noblest children" (*Snow* 256). It was from this perspective that the Mormons constituted the noblest and most representative of the nation's peoples that Snow extended her authority as "the chief poet of the Mormon church" to include the office of American bard.

The first section of this chapter compares Snow's efforts to be the poet of a new American religion with Whitman's, noting in particular the parallels between the Mormons' return of premodern spirituality to the modern world and Whitman's own desire for communion with the sacred past. Following this is a close reading of "Time and Change," the major poem of Snow's 1856 collection and her most ambitious attempt to explain how the Saints' recovery of such seemingly un-American practices as the theocratic rule of prophets made them more rather than less representative of national ideals. It is in "Time and Change" that Snow also dramatically foregrounds her work as a bard by embedding within the blank-verse narrative of the poem a pair of formally distinct Fourth of July commemorative poems that she uses as a meta-commentary on what it means for a population at odds with the nation to participate in national culture. The third section of this chapter situates Snow's representation of the Saints as quintessentially American—as "Columbia's noblest children"—within the complex conceptual geography of Mormonism, a geography whose defining feature was, on one hand, a cloistered sense of removal from the nation as a whole, and, on the other, an ambitious missionary effort that sent Mormon evangelists across the world to create a transnational network of Saints who, renouncing their home nations, pledged allegiance to a globally configured latter-day Zion.

The final section of this chapter addresses the issue of gender. Specifically, as Snow set out for herself the daunting task of addressing the United States from the fringes of national culture, she also faced the challenge of having her female voice heard by an androcentric nation. As was the case for many nineteenth-century women, Snow's access to the national stage was limited by a domestic ideology that attempted to place boundaries on a woman's sphere of influence. Sarah Josepha Hale wrote in 1837 that women poets are keenly adept at "inculcating reverence and love towards God," but when it comes to "awakening the spirit of national aggrandizement," she writes definitively that "here, woman has no place."[13] Even Lydia Sigourney, whose immense popularity during the mid-nineteenth century gave her as legitimate a claim to the title of national bard as any poet male or female, said that her muse was merely "a woman of all work, and an aproned waiter" in the kitchen of Mt. Parnassus. Sigourney echoes Caroline May's 1848 statement that the appropriate sphere of women poets is "home, with its quiet joys, its deep pure sympathies, and its secret sorrows."[14] It would seem that the patriarchal structure of Mormonism would have exacerbated the restrictions that an already sexist culture placed on Snow. She was not, for example, allowed to preach to promiscuous gatherings of Saints in such public venues as the Salt Lake Tabernacle.[15] But Snow nevertheless found ways to work within the doctrinal and social parameters of Latter-day Saint culture to legitimate her claim to speak both for her faith and for her nation. Specifically, Snow began her 1856 collection of poems with an epic invocation to a female as well as a male deity, a Mother in Heaven who governs the universe equally with a Father. While Emily Stipes Watts says that "the majority of American women poets have not felt . . . [able to] hail God as a great Camerado" as Whitman did, Snow both directly and intimately addressed a maternal goddess in a way that grounds her authority as both Zion's Poetess and an American bard.[16]

WHITMAN COMPLAINED TO his confidant Horace Traubel in the waning years of his life, "People often speak of the Leaves as wanting in religion, but that is not my view of the book—and I ought to know. I think the Leaves the most religious book among books" (*WWC* 1:372).[17] Beginning with his identification of *Leaves of Grass* as "the great psalm of the republic" in 1855, Whitman made his "scriptural ambitions," as Michael Robertson puts it, abundantly clear (*LG55* iv).[18] Robertson and others have noted that Whitman gave the 1860 edition of *Leaves of Grass* a biblical appearance by arranging the poetry into sequences where individual poems were numbered rather than titled (a design suggestive of the short chapters of books in the Bible), and by numbering each line of "Song of Myself" in a manner similar to the verses of scripture.[19] Traditionally, Whitman's lineage as the author of a poetic bible is linked to Emerson, who challenged Americans in 1850, "We too must write Bibles," and to Thomas Carlyle, who similarly predicted that a new bible would be written and that poets would soon replace priests.[20] Despite the insistence of Emerson, Carlyle, and others that a new era deserved a new bible, however, Lawrence Buell has observed that "the new Bible did not get written, unless one counts *The Book of Mormon*."[21] Buell's reluctance to seriously consider Mormonism as a context for understanding the culture within which Whitman's claim to be the author of a new American bible emerged is common among literary scholars of the past century, who often note in passing the parallels between *Leaves of Grass* and the Book of Mormon without considering how the two books bear similar witness to the cultural climate of a nation seeking to identify its distinctive religious character.[22]

A handful of nineteenth-century critics, however, were willing to entertain the notion that Whitman and the Mormons occupied opposite sides of the same coin. Less than a decade after Whitman's death, John Jay Chapman wrote that "Brigham Young and Joseph Smith were men of phenomenal capacity, who actually invented a religion and created a community by the apparent establishment of supernatural and occult powers. . . . By temperament and education Walt Whitman was fitted to be a prophet of this kind. He became a quack poet, and hampered his talents by the imposition of a monstrous parade of rattle trap theories and professions."[23] Similarly, one British literary critic wrote in 1860 that, once word of *Leaves of Grass* spread throughout England, "Whitman became as famous as the author of the Book of Mormon," while another reviewer noted five years earlier that, even though Whitman "has been received by a section of his countrymen as a sort of prophet . . . we are not disposed to accept him as one, having less faith in latter-day prophets than in latter-day poets."[24] This implied (and, indeed, backhanded) comparison between the men revered as prophets by the Latter-day Saints and Whitman as the poet-prophet of a new religion neatly summarizes the nineteenth-century assessment that a gullible young nation was so desperate to have a homegrown religion that it was willing to accept candidates as preposterous as Walt Whitman and Joseph Smith for the office of American prophet, and books as unlikely as *Leaves of Grass* and the Book of Mormon as their sacred texts.

The dismissive attitudes of both nineteenth- and twentieth-century commentators notwithstanding, the status of *Leaves of Grass* and the Book of Mormon as new American bibles testifies to more than just the overeager cultural nationalism of the antebellum era. Rather, each book in its own way redefined the relationship of the United States with the sacred history of the Bible, a relationship that Paul Gutjahr says, with a restraint bordering on understatement, "has pervasively marked American thought and culture."[25] It is difficult to overstate how central the Bible was to antebellum U.S. culture, which Lawrence Buell describes as "markedly religiocentric."[26] It is equally difficult to overstate the affront that a text like the Book of Mormon posed to a Bible-based nation. The Book of Mormon, which peopled the ancient American continent with Israelites, told a story about the sacred past that potentially appealed to U.S. cultural nationalism—Richard Burton wrote in 1861, "America . . . is a continent of the future; the Book of Mormon has created for it an historical and miraculous past."[27] But because that story lay outside the accepted framework of biblical history, it was difficult if not impossible for most Bible-believing Americans to regard the Book of Mormon as anything other than an insult to the sanctity of the Bible as the summum bonum of God's word.

Just as alarming to the biblical sensibility of nineteenth-century Americans as the new history that the Book of Mormon ascribed to the New World was the claim by Latter-day Saints that the book had come to Joseph Smith through divine means. That the Book of Mormon not only added a new chapter to sacred history but was said to have been revealed to a modern-day prophet resulted in what Nina Baym calls the "theological horror" of a religion that deigned to suggest that the history of God's dealings with humanity is continually unfolding rather than fixed in the pages of the Bible. As Baym writes, the pervasive belief among nineteenth-century Christians that "the life, death, and resurrection of Christ marked the last instance of direct divine historical intervention" of God in human affairs "explains the theological horror with which Islam and Mormonism were regarded, since the founders of both religions claimed to have experienced revelations of their own."[28] In 1852 a satire of Mormonism published in the *Lantern* treated with levity what most American Christians regarded as the Book of Mormon's very serious transgression upon the hallowed ground of biblical authority: "In Mormon City—the New Jerusalem—the Millenium [*sic*] is in full blast. . . . Old things have passed away. The old Bible is abolished, and the Young Bible is all in all."[29] The bite of this satire comes from more than just its playful combination of Brigham Young's surname with the notion that the Book of Mormon—identified here as the "Young Bible"—was a new American bible. The juxtaposition of the image of a millennial end of history in Mormon Utah with the widely held (if erroneous) belief that the Latter-day Saints had "abolished" the "old" Bible illustrates the opinion that, since the Mormons had embraced extrabiblical scripture, they had broken not only with mainline Christianity but with the accepted timeline of history itself.[30] As Jan Shipps has argued, "The coming forth of the Book of Mormon effected a break in the very fabric of history," a break that "wiped clean the slate on which the story of the past had been written."[31]

Even at his most secular, Whitman himself clung to the idea that the Bible necessarily maintained the integrity of a historical narrative on which both the United States and the world at large depended. In an essay titled "The Bible as Poetry," Whitman wrote, "No true bard will ever contravene the Bible" because "the principal factor in cohering the nations, eras and paradoxes of the globe . . . [is this] collection of old poetic lore, which, more than any one thing else, has been the axis of civilization and history through thousands of years" (*PW* 2:548). While denigrating the Bible's authority as the word of God—it is merely "old poetic lore" and not holy writ—Whitman still accorded to the Bible the primary role of lending unity to history. But if the Bible is, as Whitman says, the primary agent in bringing coherence to world history, then new bibles such as the Book of Mormon and *Leaves of Grass* violate a historical narrative that Whitman says "no true bard" should "ever contravene." Nevertheless, the efforts of both Whitman and Snow to be the representative bards of new American religions involved a negotiation with the sacred past that necessarily redefined their relationship with biblical history.

Throughout both his prose and his poetry, Whitman frequently rejected the sacred past in exchange for what he considered to be an even more sacred present. Assessing the "Dead poets, philosophs, priests," of the past, Whitman wrote that after "Regarding it all intently a long while, then dismissing it, / I stand in my place with my own day here" (*LG* 20). Preferring the possibilities of the present day to the legacies of the past, he wrote elsewhere, "Others adorn the past, / but you O days of the present, I adorn you" (*LG* 268). Because he believed, as he wrote in the 1855 preface to *Leaves of Grass*, that "what is past is past," Whitman advocated poetry and prophecy that would be "transcendant [*sic*] and new" (*LG55* iv–v). Generations of Whitman scholars have focused almost exclusively on Whitman's tendency to privilege the present over the past, saying that Whitman "[cut] himself loose from any past," that he wrote "seething poetry of the incarnate Now," and that the past in Whitman's poetry "had been so effectively burned away that it had, for every practical purpose, been forgotten altogether."[32] This image of Whitman as completely unmoored from the past has been tempered recently by scholars who have identified a richer dialogue with the past in Whitman's poetry.[33] The connection between religion and history in Whitman's poetry, however, has received little attention, despite the fact that the explicitly religious moments of *Leaves of Grass* highlight Whitman's attempts to link the American present with a global sacred past.

Although Whitman adopted a dismissive posture toward the past, he also believed, as he said in the preface to the 1855 edition of *Leaves of Grass*, that "America does not repel the past or what it has produced under its forms or amid other politics or the idea of castes or the old religions" (*LG55* iii). Alongside Whitman's glib comment that "what is past is past," then, exists a model for American sacred history that embraces the "old religions." "I do not despise you priests, all time, the world over," he wrote in "Song of Myself." "My faith is the greatest of faiths and the least of faiths, / Enclosing worship ancient and modern and all between ancient and modern" (*LG* 69). Whitman wanted his new religion to be "comprehensive enough to include all the Doctrines & Sects—and give them all places and chances, each after its kind" (*NUPM* 6:2046).[34] He wanted to encompass every religious manifestation from every age and place, promising that he would "enter into the thoughts of the different theological faiths—effuse all that the believing Egyptian would—all that the Greek—all that the Hindoo, worshipping Brahma—the Koboo adoring his fetish stone or log—the Presbyterian—the Catholic with his crucifix and saints—the Turk with the Koran."[35] Whitman wanted his new American religion to achieve two competing goals: He wanted it to break completely with a sacred history that he deemed to have limited usefulness for the modern era, and at the same time he wanted it to serve as a tribute to the religious heritage of the world. Whitman's conflicting models for sacred history emerged from a similar desire on the part of the Latter-day Saints to disassociate themselves from nineteenth-century religion while connecting to the sacred past. The Mormons' belief that they were living in what they called "the dispensation of the fullness of times" at a moment when their prophets were carrying out "the restoration of all things" allowed them to think of themselves as both an entirely new faith and a very old religion that had embraced the forgotten practices of sacred history.

Eliza R. Snow's own conversion to Mormonism was indebted to her conviction that a restoration of the sacred past was an essential step toward an imminent millennium. Before becoming a Latter-day Saint in 1836, Snow was a member of Alexander Campbell's Disciples of Christ congregation, a primitivist sect that, like a number of others in early nineteenth-century America, rejected contemporary Christianity in exchange for what they called "a restoration of the ancient order of things."[36] While the Disciples attempted to revive what they considered to be the pure Christian doctrines of the first century A.D.—including such practices as communal living, apostolic authority, and Pentecostal ecstasies—the Mormon prophet Joseph Smith preached what he called "the restoration of all things," a project that involved not only a renaissance of first-century Christianity but also a recovery of such pre-Christian practices as the ministry of prophets, the building of temples, and, most conspicuously, the practice of polygamy. Even though the Mormon restoration was selective in what it restored (polygamy and prophets were restored while Levitical feasts and offerings, for example, were not), Smith suggested that the Mormons would eventually restore everything recorded in biblical history, including the ancient practice of animal sacrifice that the crucifixion of Christ was supposed to have made irrelevant.[37] Mormonism appealed to Snow and other early converts because it claimed to be a restoration of *every* era of biblical history and not merely of the first century of Christianity. This "reunion with the deep past," as Richard Bushman calls it, confirmed for the Latter-day Saints that the age they were living in was so close to a millennial end of history that the future began to bend into the past.[38]

Indeed, the Mormon "restoration of all things" was grounded in a belief that a return to the past is a necessary precondition of an imminent millennium. As Klaus J. Hansen says, "When Smith spoke of the 'restoration of all things' in the last days, he expressed a cyclical view of history in which the end—his own generation—would be like the beginning."[39] Snow reflected this sentiment in a poem where she writes of "The restitution of all things" (the language is from Acts 3:21), which she said would

> Restore the earth to its primeval state,
> And usher in the long-expected reign
> Of Jesus Christ. (*Snow* 19)

The Mormon desire to recover the sacred past reconceptualized the traditional model by which Christian history is supposed to influence the lives of believers. In conventional Christian historiography, the life of Christ represents what Terryl Givens calls a "cardinal eruption of the divine into the human," which produces "a spate of mythic reverberations" throughout history as Christians see typological parallels between their own experiences and the experiences of the sacred past.[40] While Jane Tompkins has argued that religious parallels in nineteenth-century Christian sentimental literature prove "that human history is a continual reenactment of the sacred drama of redemption," the Mormons' *literal* belief that they had entered the sacred time of the deep past led them to feel that their lived experiences were not repeated acts in a centuries-old play but, rather, in Givens's terms, "the ongoing substance rather than the shadow of God's past dealings in the universe."[41] It is from this perspective that Snow criticized those who "vainly thought" that

> The history contain'd the essence of
> The things declar'd—that the rehearsal of
> Those blessings had transferr'd the blessings down:
> As though a hungry man could satisfy
> His appetite upon the bare *belief*
> That other starving people had been fed. (*Snow* 17, emphasis in original)

Snow's comparison of food to sacred experience neatly articulates the Mormons' desire to relive rather than merely reread sacred history. Just as "a hungry man" cannot be fed on the knowledge of another's meal, neither could the Mormons be content with a "rehearsal" of sacred history or a "transferr[al]" of blessings from a past era to their own. As patriarchal prophets like Abraham and Moses, Joseph Smith and Brigham Young felt that they had access to the blessings of the past not by reading about the ancients but by living as they did.

By reliving the sacred history of an earlier era, though, the Mormons appeared to their contemporaries to have returned to an undesirable past that had supposedly been superseded in the modern nineteenth century. The Mormons' belief in the absolute ecclesiastical and political authority of prophets, their communal living, and their polygamous marriages were seen as a step backward on the scale of historical progress that was said to have culminated in democracy, the free-market economy, and Protestant morality. As what John L. O'Sullivan called in 1839 "the great nation of futurity," the United States found it difficult to tolerate populations that looked backward instead of forward.[42] Snow, however, believed that ancient practices such as polygamy were central to the restoration of all things that necessarily preceded the millennium. In an autobiographical sketch written in the 1870s, Snow says that when she first heard about polygamy, she was torn between the moral beliefs of the recent past and her conviction that she was living in a premillennial era that embraced sacred history: "The subject [of polygamy] was very repugnant to my feelings—so directly was it in opposition to my educated prepossessions, that it seemed as though all the prejudices of my ancestors for generations past congregated around me. But when I reflected that I was living in the Dispensation of the fulness [sic] of times, embracing all other Dispensations, surely Plural Marriage must necessarily be included."[43] In her defense of polygamy, Snow shares the two attitudes toward the past that Whitman adopted when he made the contradictory pronouncements in the 1855 preface to *Leaves of Grass* that "what is past is past" and "America does not repel the past": She was willing to dismiss the recent past as irrelevant, but only because she believed that her American religion did not repel the deep history of the sacred past, no matter how repellent the practices of ancient biblical history might appear to a modern nation.

There are moments in *Leaves of Grass* when Whitman resolves his conflicted relationship with the sacred past by appealing to a model of history similar to the Mormons' "restoration of all things." Whitman believed that recovering the discarded past was one of his obligations as an American bard. "The greatest poet," he wrote in the 1855 preface to *Leaves of Grass*, "drags the dead out of their coffins and stands them again on their feet. . . . he says to the past, Rise and walk before me that I may realize you" (*LG55* vi, ellipsis in original). While the biblical imagery of Whitman summoning the past just as Christ raised the dead is only implied in this passage, else-where in *Leaves of Grass* Whitman explicitly says that his duty as a poet-prophet—and, even more audaciously, as a poet-messiah—is to "realize" the distant past. In "Passage to India," for example, Whitman identifies himself as "the true son of God, the poet" and says that he will bring about a millen-nial future by restoring the sacred past (*LG* 319). "Passage to India" begins as an ode to modernity with the poet "Singing the great achievements of the present," but the poem soon adopts a retrospective mood as Whitman promises "to sound, and ever sound, the cry with thee O soul, / The Past! the Past! the Past!" (*LG* 315). Elsewhere in the poem he completely subordinates the present to the past:

> For what is the present after all but a growth out of the past?
> (As a projectile form'd, impell'd, passing a certain line, still keeps on,
> So the present, utterly form'd, impell'd by the past). (*LG* 315)

He writes that the past contains within it the seeds of possibility for both intellectual and spiritual growth:

> Passage indeed O soul to primal thought,
> Not lands and seas alone, thy own clear freshness,
> The young maturity of brood and bloom,
> To realms of budding bibles. (*LG* 320)

Rather than being the exclusive product of modernity, then, Whitman's new bible is born of a time when the primordial energy of the sacred past pro-duced the world's "budding bibles." Whitman can claim the ability to write a new bible (to be "the true son of God, the poet") not because he has effected a break with the past but because he can return to the moment in sacred his-tory when the original bibles were new.

Elsewhere in *Leaves of Grass* Whitman reinforces the idea that his new religion is an outgrowth of the old religions. In an underexamined passage of "Song of Myself" Whitman says that he composed his book by accumu-lating pages from the "budding bibles" of the past:

> Taking myself the exact dimensions of Jehovah,
> Lithographing Kronos, Zeus his son, and Hercules his grandson,
> Buying drafts of Osiris, Isis, Belus, Brahma, Buddha,

In my portfolio placing Manito loose, Allah on a leaf, the crucifix
  engraved,
With Odin and the hideous-faced Mexitli and every idol and image.
  (*LG* 67)

When Whitman writes in the first line of this passage that he is "Taking myself the exact dimensions of Jehovah," he seems again to identify himself as a modern poet-god whose goal is to replace the deities of the past. As the following lines indicate, however, Whitman is not taking Jehovah's measurements in order to assume his divine garb. Instead, Whitman is measuring the size of a page of sacred text upon which Jehovah is described so that he might tip this page into the binding of his new American bible. In addition to this page devoted to the Israelite god, Whitman includes lithographed images from the sacred narratives of ancient Greece; drafts of pages that contain the gods of Egypt, Assyria, and India; loose sheaves of paper for the Algonquian and Islamic deities; an engraving of the Christian cross; and portfolio pages of gods from the Norse and Aztec traditions. Whitman's new bible does not rise from the ashes of old bibles that are burned away in the consuming fire of modernity. Rather, *Leaves of Grass* is a composite of the leaves from older bibles. While elsewhere Whitman makes the audacious claim to be both the prophet and the messiah of a new American religion, in this passage from "Song of Myself" he adopts the more modest role of the poet-printer who constructs his book from discarded sheets of holy writ and then writes his poems as a palimpsest on the sacred past.

In the 1855 preface to *Leaves of Grass*, Whitman explains his rationale for gathering the texts of the sacred past into his own new bible. He writes that American poets should open themselves to "the eternity which gives similitude to all periods and locations and processes and animate and inanimate forms, and which is the bond of time, and rises up from its inconceivable vagueness and infiniteness in the swimming shape of today, and is held by the ductile anchors of life, and makes the present spot the passage from what was to what shall be" (*LG55* xi). Just as Whitman believed that the Bible "has been the axis of civilization and history through thousands of years," he thought of his own sacred text as having a similar power to create a "bond of time," and that in order to cement this bond, he had to restore what had happened in "all periods and locations" of sacred history. Accordingly, Whitman's new American bible can acknowledge its newness without repelling the past because it "makes the present spot the passage from what was to what shall be."

While Whitman appears at times to be a religious restorationist whose allegiance to the sacred past bears a striking similarity to that of the Latter-day Saints, it is important to note that Whitman was a much more catholic restorationist than the Mormons were. Whitman was eager to make connections to every conceivable tradition of sacred history, whereas the Mormons centered their restoration exclusively on a narrative of biblical history. Whitman was impatient with attempts to reconstruct history that focused on a few well-known historical communities to the exclusion of the lesser-known (though, in his eyes, equally important) groups. He wrote, "Do you suppose that History is complete when the best writers and [sic] get all they can of the few communities that are known, and arrange them clearly in books? . . . Nobody can possess a fair idea of the earth without letting his or her mind walk perfectly easy and loose over the past" (NUPM 5:1926). Whitman's willingness to include non-Western religions in his restoration project—his willingness to "walk perfectly easy and loose over the past" without regard for a Bible-centered narrative of sacred history—stands in stark contrast to the Mormons' exclusion of nonbiblical religions in what they claimed was a restoration of *all* things. As Robert Louis Stevenson wrote in "The Gospel According to Walt Whitman," Whitman "is not against religion; not, indeed, against any religion. He wishes to drag with a larger net, to make a more comprehensive synthesis, than any or than all of them put together."[44]

What is ironic, then, is that as the Mormons restored such biblical practices as polygamy and the theocratic rule of prophets, they were perceived by their contemporaries as having more in common with Islamic and other "pagan" traditions than with the Judeo-Christian tradition that supposedly formed the basis of American civilization. Whitman may have wanted to place "Allah on a leaf" of his new American bible, but most Americans could not tolerate the idea that a religion resembling Islam could flourish in the United States. The title alone of Catharine Waite's sensational *The Mormon Prophet and His Harem* (1867) suggests the manner in which anti-Mormon texts drew parallels between the polygamy and postbiblical prophecy of both Mormonism and Islam. Even before polygamy became public knowledge, the Illinois state senate accused Mormons of practicing "the Mohometan [*sic*] faith under a name little varied from the original, the tendency [of which] strikes at the very foundation of our society."[45] Islam was not the only point of comparison that Americans used to dismiss Mormons from national fellowship. In 1862 the *North American Review* rationalized the U.S. refusal to grant statehood to the Utah Territory on the grounds that the Mormons had more in common with the "savages" of the earth than they did with the citizens of the United States. "If Utah is admitted with its polygamy," they wrote, "why may not some island of the sea, which America may come to possess, claim, with its Pagan rites and its feasts of human flesh, to be received as a sovereign State into the Union?"[46]

This figurative imposition of racial difference onto the Mormons was made literal in a widely circulated description of the Mormon "racial phenotype" composed by Roberts Bartholow, an assistant surgeon in the U.S. army who visited Utah briefly in the late 1850s. Bartholow argued that Mormon polygamy was creating a new race of people in the American West: "The yellow, sunken, cadaverous visage; the greenish-colored eye; the thick, protuberant lips; the low forehead; the light, yellowish hair, and the lank, angular person, [that] constitute an appearance so characteristic of the new race, the production of polygamy, as to distinguish them at a glance."[47] Depicting the Mormons as an amalgam of the various "undesirable" races of nineteenth-century America—the "yellow" skin of Chinese immigrants, the "thick, protuberant lips" of African Americans—allowed white Americans to think of the Mormons as having more in common with the non-Western world than with the West. Other observers from the period similarly remarked that "the Mormons are spoken of as a distinct race of beings," and that "the child of Mormon polygamy was simply a white negro."[48]

It should come as no surprise that the Mormons' restoration of the prophets and polygamists of the distant past would make them seem out of step with their countrymen and -women, both racially and temporally. "Deep time," writes Wai Chee Dimock, "is denationalized space."[49] The dominant culture of a modern nation regularly depicts minority populations as existing in a different temporality, with race frequently serving as the visual sign of one people's modernity and another's barbarity.[50] This sense of Mormons as profoundly—if not racially—different from the majority of Americans continued as Mormonism grew from a national to an international concern. Reporting on German perceptions of race in America, a correspondent to

Frederick Douglass' Paper wrote in 1853, "Their interest seemed to be about equally divided between Negroes, Indians, and Mormons. On hardly any subject have I been more questioned than concerning the Mormon[s], a people with whom I have very little acquaintance. If I had a live one to exhibit I could make a small fortune among these speculative, philosophic, meditative Deutschen."[51] The Mormons might have been a philosophical curiosity to the Germans, but they inspired a much different response from their countrymen and countrywomen, a response that included mob violence, an extermination order issued by the state of Missouri, and the forced evacuation of the Latter-day Saint settlement in Nauvoo, Illinois, at a time when Nauvoo rivaled Chicago in size and prosperity.[52]

After two decades of local opposition in Ohio, Illinois, and Missouri, national opposition to the Mormons began in earnest after the church's 1852 announcement that they were solemnizing polygamous marriages, a decision that made "the Mormon question" into what historian R. Laurence Moore calls "one of the most drawn out and highly publicized events in all of American history."[53] Following the successful model for reform fiction provided by Harriet Beecher Stowe's *Uncle Tom's Cabin* (1852), four anti-polygamy novels were published between 1855 and 1856. The most popular, Maria Ward's *Female Life Among the Mormons* (1855), sold 40,000 copies within a few weeks.[54] Following the Civil War, antipolygamy measures grew exponentially—as did the number of anti-Mormon novels, which swelled to almost 100—until Utah's final bid for statehood in 1896 required that Mormons renounce the practice of plural marriage.[55] These sensational novels defined polygamy as a corruption of the sanctity of the domestic space and, by extension, the civil society for which the home served as the foundation. As long as nineteenth-century domestic writers depicted the monogamous home as the center of a spiritual, emotional, and economic nexus that defined both the nation and the civilized world, polygamy was a threat both to national unity and to civilization itself. Nancy Bentley writes, "In the end, anti-polygamy writers established a new common sense: to tolerate such a redefining of 'home' meant perforce the undoing of the national polity," which meant that Mormon polygamists were necessarily denied "any possible place in American nationhood."[56] When Stowe herself wrote the foreword to Fanny Ward Stenhouse's *"Tell It All": The Story of a Life's Experience in Mormonism* (1874), she further linked what the 1856 Republican Party platform called their opposition to "the twin relics of barbarism: slavery and polygamy."[57]

The language of the Republican Party platform illustrates how the Mormons' belief that they were restoring sacred history was perceived by their contemporaries to be a recovery of the savage past: Not only is the bondage of polygamous wives compared to the bondage of African American slaves, but both practices are seen as the "relics" of a barbaric past. By classifying polygamy as a "relic" from the past rather than a feature of the modern era, Americans placed Mormons at a distant spot on the historical timeline that they used to define the United States as the pinnacle of modern progress. Echoing his contemporaries' belief that Americans had made greater progress than any other nation, Whitman called the United States "The crown and teeming paradise, so far, of time's accumulations" (LG 310). In *Democratic Vistas*, Whitman said that the spot occupied by the United States at the top of the historical pecking order banished anyone from the nation who drew inspiration from the past: "The models of persons, books, manners, &c., appropriate for former conditions," he wrote, "are but exiles and exotics here" (PW 2:395). Polygamy and theocracy, for example, may have been "appropriate for former conditions," but those who revive such practices in modern America were unwelcome "exiles." Eliza R. Snow felt acutely that she was an exile from the nation of her birth and expressed this sentiment frequently in her poetry. In one such poem, she praises the United States above all other nations and then notes that, despite her affection for the country, she could not claim it as her home:

> But O, I find no country yet
>   Like my Columbia dear;
> And oftentimes *almost* forget
>   *I live an exile here.* (*Snow* 81, emphasis in original)

Such poems appear throughout Snow's oeuvre. In a lengthy blank-verse narrative titled "Time and Change"—the centerpiece of her 1856 volume of poems—Snow depicts Mormon exile through a creative adaptation of the doctrine of the restoration of all things. "Time and Change" attributes the exile of the Saints from the United States to their controversial belief that the ancient biblical past had been restored in modern America. Snow also uses the poem to argue that the faith of the Mormons in the restoration of sacred history makes them more rather than less committed to "Columbia dear" and, by extension, that the Mormons' poet laureate herself is more rather than less qualified to be the bard of the nation as a whole.

WHEN "TIME AND CHANGE" was first published in pamphlet form in 1841 and circulated throughout the Mormon community, the local church-owned newspaper encouraged young Latter-day Saints to "commit [the poem] to memory, and thus transmit it as a useful and pleasing lesson to future time." It was a difficult request, given that the poem is over 600 lines long, but it nonetheless emphasizes the importance of Snow's poetry to the early Mormon community.[58] "Time and Change" takes its readers through what would have been a familiar historical narrative that begins in the Bible and continues with the history of the Protestant Reformation in Europe, the Puritan emigration to New England, and the American Revolution. It concludes by critiquing the recent failures of the U.S. government to protect Mormon settlements in Missouri and Illinois from mob violence, and then it prophesies the millennial reign of Jesus Christ in an American Zion founded by the Latter-day Saints. Like any number of historical poems written in the antebellum period, "Time and Change" confirms what Nina Baym calls the "extraordinary historical mission" of the United States by "placing the new nation in world history."[59] But while the purpose of most antebellum historical poetry was to define the United States as the world's final premillennial civilization, in "Time and Change" the millennial Zion that arises on American soil is only provisionally identified with the United States. According to the poem, if the United States repents of its opposition to Mormonism, it will be allowed to share in the blessings of Zion; if it does not, those blessings will pass to another, worthier civilization, namely, the Mormons.

Such a narrative of the tenuous position of the United States at the top of the historical pecking order was not uncommon. Most Americans were overwhelmingly confident that the United States would be the dominant world power when a literal or figurative millennium brought about the end of history: "That holy millennium of liberty," as Whitman himself wrote in an 1846 editorial for the *Brooklyn Daily Eagle*, "is to be worked out through the people, territory, and government of the United States."[60] Nevertheless, social critics from temperance advocates to abolitionists frequently reminded American readers that the United States could fall from grace as easily as had previous civilizations. Within this tradition of social reform literature that uses the specter of historical change to sway its readers, "Time and Change" argues that American decline is imminent unless the United States not only ceases its persecution of the Mormon Church but embraces its leaders as prophets. Snow raises this specter of imminent change through her personification of the forces of history in the figures of "Change," whom she describes as having the power to decide whether a civilization will rise or fall, and "Time," a record-keeper who physically contains the passage of history in the "cumbrous fold" of his robes rather than writing it down in textual form (*Snow* 239). While Change would seem to be the more important of the two figures, Time is identified as "our great hero," largely because of the way that his record-keeping serves as a metaphor for the Mormon doctrine of the restoration of all things (*Snow* 248).[61]

In depicting Time as preserving a record of history in the fabric of his clothing rather than the words of a written text, Snow proposes that the past is neither mediated by language nor frozen in stasis but, rather, that it has the immediacy and intimacy—the tactility, even—of a garment. For the early Mormons, the appeal of depicting Time in this way is obvious: The image of a garment saturated with the sacred past suggests that the robes of prophecy and polygamy can be removed from the earth centuries before the birth of Christ and then replaced centuries later without a hint of anachronism. In the conclusion of the poem, Snow explicitly connects the image of the robes of Time with the doctrine of the restoration. She writes that before Zion emerges as the millennial civilization that will outlast the end of history, Time will spread his "rich, primeval robes" across the earth and thereby return to the world everything that has taken place since the creation (*Snow* 260). At the end of history, she writes, Time's

> deep folded drapery will be
> Unroll'd; and, in the waiting presence of
> Heaven's legally commission'd council, all
> His vestments search'd. (*Snow* 239)

Snow continues that the "coming forth" of Time's records

> will comprehend
> "The restitution of all things, spoken
> By all the holy Prophets since the world
> Began." (*Snow* 241–42)

By equating the deeds of Time with the Saints' latter-day restoration of all things, Snow submits that the Mormons' revival of such biblical practices as prophecy and polygamy is both an inevitable function of the historical process and a necessary precondition for an imminent millennium.

Despite this conscious invocation of the restoration of all things, mention of polygamy is noticeably absent from the poem (no doubt because the doctrine of plural marriage was only discussed in whispers when the poem was originally published in 1841 and would not become public knowledge until the 1850s). The restoration of prophetic authority, however, takes center stage. According to the historical narrative Snow sets forth in "Time and Change," civilizations are only able to protect themselves from destruction at the hand of Change by heeding the warning of prophets. "The registry of Time," she writes, shows that "a Prophet *is* / And *always has been*, the forerunner of" the deeds of Change (*Snow* 243, emphasis in original). Thus Snow emphasizes that the Mormons, like Time himself, remember with perfect clarity that the biblical era was a time when "Prophets were / No comic sights—no strange phenomena" (*Snow* 241). This passing mention that the Mormons were considered "strange" and "comic[al]" for espousing what seemed to nineteenth-century Americans to be an outdated belief in prophets is the only reason that the poem gives for why the Latter-day Saints were in conflict with their fellow countrymen and -women. The actual reason for these conflicts was a complex mix of religion, politics, and territorial claims. But by reducing the issue to a simple question of religious liberty—specifically, of the Mormons' right to believe in living prophets—Snow is then able to introduce the figure of "Liberty" as a historical personification on a par with Time and Change. And in making this connection between American Liberty and the restoration of prophetic authority, Snow is also poised to make the case that the Latter-day Saints are exemplary citizens rather than national outcasts.

After depicting Liberty as having escaped the "dread oppression" of seventeenth-century Europe and migrated across the Atlantic to North America, Snow writes that Liberty is newly threatened and posits that the only way to ensure the U.S. position at the vanguard of world history is to protect Liberty from Change (*Snow* 253). (The renewed threat to Liberty is, of course, the persecution of the Latter-day Saints.) According to the internal logic of the poem, preserving Liberty against a "momentous revolution" at Change's hand requires sacrificing Liberty's freedoms to the dictates of prophetic counsel, because it is only, to recall, by heeding the warnings of the prophets that the wrath of Change can be abated (*Snow* 238). The implications for the United States are obvious: If protecting America from the ravages of Change requires national obedience to prophets, the country need not only tolerate Mormon theocracy but subscribe to it. As such, the Mormons' belief in prophets should make them "Columbia's noblest children" (as Snow calls them later in the poem), rather than exiles from the nation (*Snow* 256).

The claim that Snow makes at this point—that the Mormons deserve to be revered for precisely the reasons that they have been reviled—predates by almost fifteen years Whitman's posture as "one of the roughs," a common criminal who speaks for the common man. In adopting the persona of the national outsider as national bard, however, Snow backs herself into a corner. By privileging the Mormons' faith in prophecy, she presents what many nineteenth-century Americans would have regarded as a seemingly irresolvable contradiction: Liberty can only be preserved by ceding a portion, if not all, of one's personal freedom to prophetic authority. In a nation where prophets were considered the relic of a past that had long since been superseded by democracy's promise of individual self-determination (as well as Protestantism's promise of an unmediated relationship with God), it would have struck many Americans as wholly inconsistent to say that the personal freedoms of an entire nation depend on the absolute authority of a man who claimed to speak with God.

The conflict between liberty and divine authority that Snow's poem raises is one that most nineteenth-century Americans lived with on a daily basis, whether they acknowledged it or not. The problem of how to reconcile personal liberty with divine authority lay at the heart of two competing models of U.S. national identity: first, that the United States is God's chosen nation, a New Israel that typologically relives the biblical narrative of divine guidance, and second, that the United States is a modern nation that has broken with an authoritarian past in the name of democracy and individual rights. Most Americans were blithely unaware of the implications of this contradiction. In 1846, for example, the rationale for the Mexican War was both that God had divinely ordained the United States to become a continental nation and that the forces of democracy were duty-bound to liberate Mexico from the despotism of European rule.[62] The nation at large could hold this contradiction at bay as long as the idea of the United States as a modern Israel remained a metaphorical abstraction. When the Latter-day Saints took it literally that the chosen people of the biblical past had been reborn in North America, however, the simmering conflict between democracy and divine authority came to a boil.

One of the effects of "Time and Change," then, is to foreground the conflict between the divine and democratic models of nineteenth-century U.S. national identity. Specifically, the poem demonstrates that one of the responsibilities of the national poet is to craft poems that resolve ideological conflicts such as this. At two key moments in "Time and Change," Snow calls attention to the bard's duty to work with the materials of national history in a manner similar to that of the state historian who, in the words of Edward Said, "manipulat[es] certain bits of the national past, suppress[es] others, elevat[es] still others" in an effort to tell what Priscilla Wald calls the "official story" of the nation.[63] The first of these moments occurs when Snow's narrative of history arrives at the American Revolution and the founding of the United States. Until this point, Snow has spent more than 300 lines recounting the biblical past of prophetic authority and about 100 lines on the story of Liberty's emigration from Europe to North America. After presenting two disparate historical paths—one sacred, one secular—leading to the same moment of national origins, Snow stages a scene where she, in the office of the national bard, disrupts the form of the blank-verse narrative and composes a patriotic ode that brings together these separate narratives of historical progress. Poets laureate and national bards are often tasked with interpreting the past in ways that smooth over potentially contradictory moments in the nation's history. Snow was uniquely poised to do precisely this because she earnestly believed that the Saints' theocratic government, which she referred to on a number of occasions as a "perfect government," would provide the best protection for individual liberty (*Snow* 478, 644).

At around line 460 of "Time and Change," Snow inserts a commemorative ode into the blank-verse narrative that allows her to perform the duty of the national bard, writing that the memory of the Revolution "Awoke the minstrel's sweetly sounding lyre, / To chant far-echoing strains to Liberty!" (*Snow* 255). In self-consciously mentioning the instrument of the bard and then altering the form of her narrative poem to that of a public ode (she shifts from iambic pentameter to dactylic tetrameter and from unrhymed verse to an *aaab* rhyme scheme), she takes upon herself the obligation of the national poet to craft an identity for the nation out of potentially conflicting historical narratives. The poem that she produces, titled simply "Ode," is a patriotic celebration of the American Revolution that depicts "Religion, sweetly smiling . . . beneath / The tolerating spire of Liberty" (*Snow* 256). In language that draws equally upon the discourses of religion and personal freedom—language, that is, designed to connect two potentially disparate narratives of national history—the poem praises "Sacred Liberty" and the "Righteous vengeance" with which it was defended by the "sons of freemen" during the Revolution (*Snow* 255).

Snow's decision to insert a commemorative ode within the blank-verse narrative of her poem was consistent with the formal experimentation taking place elsewhere in antebellum poetry culture. Mary Loeffelholz has noted how poets from the period experimented with similarly "nested" poetic forms that embedded "lyrics or ballads inside [the] dramatic or narrative frame" of a longer, usually blank-verse, poem structure. One of the effects of nesting shorter poems within longer ones, Loeffelholz argues, is to model "the conditions of the liberal public sphere" such that the climate of public debate is reflected in a single poem that contains disparate poetic forms.[64] It was within the antebellum public sphere, to recall, that conflicting versions of national history defined the United States as either a modern Israel or a bastion of Enlightenment values. Given the bard's duty to commemorate national history in a way that minimizes such conflicts, nesting this patriotic ode within a blank-verse historical narrative was Snow's way of unifying two disparate versions of national identity into a consistent whole.

When "Time and Change" was first published in 1841, Snow was already well aware of her responsibility as a public bard, as Zion's Poetess. By the 1850s and 1860s, her responsibilities would increase manyfold. She recalled later in her life that, for every Independence Day on 4 July and every celebration of the Saints' arrival in the Salt Lake Valley on 24 July, she was "expected to furnish one song, and sometimes more than one, for each of these occasions."[65] Jill Mulvay Derr and Karen Lynn Davidson, the editors of a comprehensive volume of the more than 500 poems that Snow wrote during her lifetime, note that Snow always wrote with a sense of her bardic duties in mind: "Her poems were social instruments, usually intended to be read, posted, or sung in public. . . . She considered poetry an entrée into public discourse rather than a venue for personal disclosure and reflection."[66] Not only did Snow understand herself to be a bardic rather than a lyric poet, but she was also keenly aware that her commemorative poetry spoke with a fractured voice: Every 4 July she wrote as the poet of the nation, and every 24 July as the poet of national exiles. Writing from the fringes of national culture, Snow aimed her bardic addresses at a moving target that was sometimes a unified nation and, at other times, a community of outsiders. There is another moment in "Time and Change" when Snow self-consciously assumes the office of the bard as a way to highlight the fractured nature of her poetic calling, a moment that involves the same kind of formal variation as does the poem-within-a-poem titled "Ode."

Thirty lines after the first nested ode interrupts the blank-verse historical narrative of "Time and Change," Snow embeds another formally distinct poem: a four-stanza lament titled "Ode for the Fourth of July" that, like the ode preceding it, differs from the blank verse narrative in its meter and rhyme scheme as well as its material appearance (both nested poems are titled with a gothic script that diverges from the roman font in the rest of the larger poem). This second poem-within-a-poem is also prefaced by the announcement that "the lyre awakes," which similarly alerts readers to an impending public performance from the bard (*Snow* 256). But "Ode for the Fourth of July" is not the performance of a bard whose goal is to reconcile the conflicts of national identity from the state-sanctioned pulpit of a July Fourth celebration. It is, instead, the performance of an outsider bard who uses public poetry to challenge rather than enforce communal values, to dispute national consensus rather than affirm it.

Despite adopting the form of a commemorative ode, the content of the nested "Ode for the Fourth of July" explicitly rejects the notion of a shared national identity grounded in common history. Rather, the entire first stanza of the poem is a pitched invective against the idea of collective memory.

> Shall we commemorate the day,
> Whose genial influence has pass'd o'er?
> Shall we our hearts' best tribute pay
> Where heart and feeling are no more? (*Snow* 257)

Refusing to share with her countrymen and countrywomen a common nostalgia for the glorious national past, Snow prefaces the ode with the comment that the muse of history will

> Awake the lyre, but not to chant such deeds
> Of noble patriotism as twin'd the wreath

Of never-fading laurels round the heads
Of our forefathers. (*Snow* 257)

Rather than compose a patriotic ode, she writes that the awakening lyre responds instead to the muse of exile as it sings of "when oppression pour'd / Upon a persecuted people" in the West (*Snow* 256). "Yes, the lyre awakes," she writes,

And in low notes of plaintive eloquence
Breathes forth a tone of suffering and distress.
Ah! hear Columbia's noblest children sing
Of *rights usurp'd*—of grievance unredress'd!
    (*Snow* 256, emphasis in original)

Despite this lengthy promise that the lyre will sing the woes of a persecuted people, "Ode for the Fourth of July" is curiously short on specific details about either the cause or the nature of this people's sufferings. In sacrificing detail to invective, the poem obliquely recounts the trials of a people suffering "beneath oppression's galling chain" who have "had to fly" from their home nation (*Snow* 256–57). Similarly, there is no explanation for what these persecuted people have done to be considered "Columbia's noblest children" other than that "Columbia's glory is a theme / That with our life's warm pulses grew" (*Snow* 256–57). Since "Time and Change" was initially published as an in-house poem circulated among the Mormon community, the referent of this "persecuted people" would have been obvious. But Snow's reluctance to provide specific details suggests more than just her confidence that the readers of her poem would know the history of Mormon persecution. Indeed, other historical poems in her 1856 volume provide a level of detail to indicate that her purpose in writing was as much journalistic as it was literary. (A review of Snow's 1856 volume of poems in the *Latter-day Saints' Millennial Star*, for example, specifically praised Snow for writing historical poems that "are so vivid and truthful that, with a little effort on the part of the reader, the scenes she portrays seem to pass in lifelike reality before him.") [67]

Answering the questions that "Ode for the Fourth of July" leaves unanswered—Who are these persecuted people? Why have they been persecuted? and Why are they "Columbia's noblest children"?—requires readers to remember the blank-verse portion of "Time and Change" that explains how people in the modern era are "prone to ridicule" those who continue to believe in prophets (*Snow* 247). And since prophets provide the only protection against the national decline brought on by Change, believing in prophets is also what makes the Mormons more rather than less likely to earn the title of "Columbia's noblest children." In requiring her readers to recall the previous sections of the poem to answer these questions, Snow forces an intratextual reading between the blank-verse narrative of "Time and Change" and the iambic tetrameter of "Ode for the Fourth of July" that makes the form of the Revolutionary ode contain the content of biblical history. The two competing narratives of American origins — Revolutionary liberty and divine biblical authority — are brought together through an intratextual link between these formally distinct sections of the poem. Unlike the first nested poem-within-a-poem, however, the effort here is not to resolve the contradictions of national history; rather, it is to lay them bare. "Ode for the Fourth of July" challenges the rest of the nation not only to remember its foundational principles as a divinely ordained nation but also to embrace the deep biblical past on which those principles are based. In demanding her readers to jump from one section of the poem to another and to move from one poetic form to another, Snow ultimately requires them to think across one historical period to another in a manner that recalls the doctrine of the restoration of all things. Readers of the poem must, in essence, embrace the idea that the past will flow into the present just as biblical sacred history finds its way into a celebration of the Fourth of July.

Using the Fourth of July as an occasion for social critique was already an established tradition by the time Snow wrote "Ode for the Fourth of July" in 1841.[68] Apart from making the common gesture of celebrating the nation's origins while criticizing its current shortcomings, however, Snow's decision to write a Fourth of July poem has further implications. "Time and Change" was originally published the week of 6 April 1841, corresponding with the anniversary of the founding of the Church of Jesus Christ of Latter-day Saints in 1830.[69] Just as Frederick Douglass would deliver his 1852 address "What to the Slave Is the Fourth of July?" on 5 July in order to highlight the differences between how whites and African Americans celebrate their independence, Snow's publication of a July Fourth poem on the birthday of Mormonism suggests that the moment of national origin she is commemorating is not that of the United States but of a new Mormon empire. The implication is clear: Another civilization has stepped onto the stage of history and the American era is coming to an end.

Snow's claim that the Latter-day Saints were rising to world-historical prominence is a bold one, and while this claim would have only been well received by her coreligionists, many other Americans would still have been willing to grant to her that the Mormons were indeed creating a new society unlike anything they had ever seen before. Whitman himself wrote in an article for the *Brooklyn Daily Times* in the late 1850s that the Mormons were the "founders of a new empire, apostles of a new faith, [and] pioneers of a new civilization."[70] Defining the relationship between this "new civilization" and the nation that presided over its birth was a challenge that Snow took up elsewhere in her poetry. Specifically, she sought to define how the Mormon "kingdom," as some nineteenth-century commentators referred to it, differed from American democracy not only in its political philosophy but also in its relationship with the other nations of the world.[71] In "Time and Change" Snow is principally concerned with proving that the Mormons be recognized as a representative national population because of their belief that a restoration of premodern spirituality will save the United States from historical decay. However, in other poems, as the following section of this chapter demonstrates, she renders the nation secondary to the more essential commitments she feels toward the local Mormon community in the American West and a global network of Latter-day Saint missionaries and converts throughout the world.

ONE OF WHITMAN'S bohemian cohorts from Manhattan, novelist Fitz-Hugh Ludlow, shared with Whitman the opinion that the Latter-day Saint settlement in the Utah Territory was not just a subset of the United States but an entirely "new empire," a place so different from the surrounding nation that the act of crossing the boundary into Utah was tantamount to entering another world. In his 1870 narrative of his travels through the West, Ludlow writes of the shock he experienced when he and his companions realized that they had entered the Utah Territory without noticing that they had left the United States proper: "I had not expected to recognize Utah by any unerring sign; to know when I came to it by a polygamistic flavor in the atmosphere," he writes dryly, "but I own that the sensation of entering Mormondom without knowing it was somewhat singular."[72] Ludlow's sense that the dividing line between "Mormondom" and America was a threshold of such significance as to give him pause was a sensation shared by the Mormons and their American neighbors alike. One nineteenth-century commentator observed that "the Saints . . . talk of 'going to the States' as if they belonged to another nation," and as late as the 1950s, sociologist Thomas F. O'Dea referred to Mormon Utah as a "near nation."[73] In one poem Snow herself disowned her U.S. citizenship and pledged her allegiance to the Mormon theocracy in the West, writing, "I claim no country, nation, kingdom, creed, / Excepting Zion:—that I proudly name."[74]

It was easy for both Mormons and non-Mormons alike to think of Latter-day Saint settlements as autonomous entities when places like Nauvoo, Illinois, and Kirtland, Ohio—and, ultimately, the entire Utah Territory—functioned as independent city-states with their own commerce, educational systems, militias, and currency. (Brigham Young at one point even attempted to develop a separate alphabet for the English language for the Mormons to use.)[75] Despite this estranged relationship with their home nation, however, the Mormons often reached out to the United States. Even though Fitz-Hugh Ludlow insisted that "nothing can bring the Mormon and the national ideas together," he still allowed that an enduring sense of national loyalty on the part of the Latter-day Saints made it "hard for Uncle Sam's prodigals to forget the old man," and that in the Utah Territory there continued to be "a sneaking thrill for the liberty pole and the spread eagle."[76] Snow herself wrote about her persistent patriotism when she recalled the day in 1847 that her wagon train reached the Salt Lake Valley: "Soon after our arrival in the valley a tall liberty-pole was erected, and from its summit (although planted in Mexican soil), the stars and stripes seemed to float with even more significance, if possible, than they were wont to do on Eastern breezes."[77] Snow's belief that the American flag flew more freely when hoisted in the company of the Saints—in essence, that the Mormons had carried the spirit of America with them into exile—informed many of her verses. In a number of poems, Snow characterizes the Mormons as "the champions of our country's cause" and encourages the nation to look to Utah for an example of American ideals (*Snow* 217). "Fair Columbia," she writes, "look away to the West," for "The white-crested Eagle has fled to the mountains, / The Genius of Liberty follow'd us here" (*Snow* 87, 265). Many Mormons shared this belief that, at heart, the Latter-day Saint movement was wholly American. When Mormon apostle John Taylor asked in 1855, "Who are the Mormons?" in a short-lived New York City–based newspaper called *The Mormon*, his reply was adamant: "Americans! Patriots!"[78]

Legal historian Sarah Barringer Gordon has written that the Mormon .settlement in the Utah Territory occupied "an ambiguous and changeable place" that allowed it, on one hand, to be considered a loyal appendage to the nation proper and, on the other, to be regarded as a law unto itself.[79] Complicating the Saints' ambiguous nationality even further was the vast and wide-reaching Mormon missionary system, which as early as the 1840s led the Saints to experience a stronger sense of kinship with converts and potential converts throughout the world than they did with their American compatriots. In the years preceding the Civil War, Mormon missionaries went as far as India, Hong Kong, New Zealand, Palestine, Europe, and the Pacific islands in search of converts, and missionary periodicals were set up in New York City, Liverpool, Copenhagen, Paris, Hamburg, and Geneva to disseminate information to converts traveling to the United States.[80] So successful were the efforts of these missionaries that, by the 1860s, 35 percent of the population of the Utah Territory was foreign-born.[81] Upon seeing this initial success, Brigham Young prophesied, "Thousands of the Saints will gather in from the nations of the earth. This will become the great highway of the nations. Kings and emperors and the noble and wise of the earth will visit us here."[82]

While the greatest influx of converts came almost exclusively from northern Europe and the British Isles, the belief that the gathering of the faithful was a global event remained a fixed component of nineteenth-century Mormon life. Indeed, just the impact of a dedicated cohort of missionaries serving in the far-flung reaches of the globe was enough to cement the image of Mormonism as a worldwide faith. One antebellum Mormon newspaper furthered the image of the Latter-day Saints' global presence by publishing a recurring column titled "To all our Presiding Elders throughout the World," which extended an invitation to missionaries abroad to write in with information concerning "the country where you reside, its inhabitants, customs, manners; its arts, sciences, productions, curiosities, and religion; or any other thing that you may deem interesting." In response to this solicitation came articles about life in Cuba, the Sandwich Islands, the Crimea, and China, as well as numerous European nations.[83] Among non-Mormons as well existed the perception that the Saints were creating an international coalition of believers. In a *Life* magazine illustration from the turn of the century titled "Mormon Elder-berry, Out with His Six-Year Olds, Who Take after Their Mothers," for example, there appears a black-garbed, bearded polygamist surrounded by nine children whose mothers, based on the appearance and dress of the children, come not only from the European countries of Scotland, the Netherlands, Ireland, England, and France, but also from China, Africa, Japan, and Native North America.[84] Even though such multicultural plural marriages were nonexistent, the perception that Mormon missionaries were converting people from across the world was difficult to dispel. Indeed, according to the *Manchester Guardian* in 1856, the Mormons' "immense and well-concerted missionary system . . . already wields an influence over the whole globe."[85]

At the core of Latter-day Saint doctrine lies a charge to spread the gospel of the restoration to the entire world. Joseph Smith wrote that the preaching of the word would not stop "till it has penetrated every continent, visited every clime, swept every country, and sounded in every ear," and Mormon scripture has God himself declaring that his purpose for the latter days is "to gather out mine elect from the four quarters of the earth, unto a place which I shall prepare, an Holy City . . . and it shall be called Zion, a New Jerusalem."[86] Eliza R. Snow believed such prophecies. She dedicated her 1856 collection of poems "To all the Saints of God, no matter where / Your countries lie, or what your nations are," and in one poem she sent tidings "To the Saints of all countries and isles of the sea" (*Snow* vii, 225). She also records in her journal that she told a group of young Latter-day Saints that they would have to prepare themselves to live in the international community that would be the result of this missionary effort. "Situated as you are in the 'City of the Saints,'" she told them, "the place destined for the gathering of people from every nation, kindred, tongue, and people; you must expect to associate with people of widely different dispositions and understandings, and whose habits and manners have been formed under every variety of circumstances."[87] That Snow would encourage young Mormons not only to be aware of convert populations throughout the world but to prepare to live with them side by side speaks to her understanding that the goal of Mormon missionary work during the nineteenth century involved more than preaching the word and saving souls. Rather, missionaries were to bring bodies to

Zion, the hub for convert immigration referred to in Mormon circles as "the center of all centers."[88]

Early Mormons such as Snow lived in what historian Richard Bushman calls a "sacred geography [that] had no equivalent elsewhere in the United States." "Mormon space," Bushman writes, "consisted of these two elements: first, the convert population streaming along the lines of gathering from all over the globe, and second, the central city of Zion."[89] The conceptual geography of Mormon Zion connected a relatively small community of believers in the American West with an expansive network of missionaries and their converts (both actual and potential) across the world. Inhabiting a space that alternately expanded to fill the globe and then contracted down to the boundaries of a single city further complicated the Mormons' already tenuous relationship with the United States. In particular, it complicated the idea that the Saints were the principal inheritors of American values (or "the champions of our country's cause," in Snow's terms). In many of Snow's poems, she questions whether the Saints' status as "Columbia's noblest children" put them squarely in the American grain or if their habitation in Zion, with its sacred geography linking the "City of the Saints" with a global missionary effort, somehow replaced their need for affiliation with a nation-state. This issue frequently surfaces in Snow's 1856 collection of poems in the form of two images: The first is of the Saints' exile in the Rocky Mountains, and the second is of the summons that Mormon missionaries make to the peoples of the world. In a brief prose interlude in the 1856 volume, for example, Snow writes of the Latter-day Zion as "a City of Refuge, beyond the reach of the ruthless mobocrat, and far from the unhallowed rage of the heartless persecutor," a city where the Saints of God will "sound His praises till they shall reverberate from mountain to mountain, and echo to the most distant nations of the earth" (*Snow* 202).

This recurring pair of images—the city of refuge and the global gathering—is often accompanied by the image of a flag. The nature and character of this flag, however, shifts from one poem to the next: Sometimes the flag is the Stars and Stripes, and at others it is an ensign unique to the Saints. In one poem, Snow describes the Mormon's Zion as a quintessentially American place where live "our country's braves" and "Where Columbia's glorious banner" (i.e., the American flag) "Waves o'er mountain-top and dell" (*Snow* 263). In the same poem, Zion is also a gathering place for the imminent arrival of converts from across the globe ("And we soon shall hail as neighbors / Those who dwell in lands afar"), as well as a place for "outcasts / From the country whence we came" (*Snow* 263–64). As other, similar poems suggest, it is around the image of the flag that Snow seems to be working out whether the United States presides over this latter-day Zion or whether the Saints' affinity for their fellows both in the Rocky Mountains and across the earth exceeds their loyalty to the nation. The refrain of another poem, "National Song," for example, introduces the same image, albeit under the banner of an entirely different flag:

> Lo! here in the midst of the snow-cover'd mountains,
>   We call to all nations — all people forsooth;
> Come, come to our Standard, the Deseret Standard,
>   The Standard of Freedom, Salvation, and Truth. (*Snow* 261)

As in other poems of this type, Snow identifies a central location in "the midst of the snow-cover'd mountains" (a location that elsewhere in the poem she explicitly identifies as a site of "exile") and from this space makes a "call to all nations" (*Snow* 262). Rather than "Columbia's glorious banner," however, the flag here is "the Deseret Standard," which has all the characteristics associated with the Stars and Stripes — "Freedom, Salvation, and Truth" — but it is the flag of "Deseret," the name that Brigham Young initially gave to the Utah Territory before it was changed to Utah by the federal government.

Other poems follow this same pattern, with Snow placing a flag — sometimes that of the United States and other times not — over a Rocky Mountain Zion that looks outward to the rest of the world. In "Celebration Song for the Fourth of July," the flag flying over the Utah Territory is clearly the Stars and Stripes:

> The banner which our fathers won,
> The legacy of Washington,
> Is now in Utah wide unfurl'd,
> And proffers peace to all the world. (*Snow* 217)

In "Anniversary Song," written to commemorate the Saints' arrival in the Salt Lake Valley on 24 July, however, it is "Zion's Banner" and not the American flag that waves in the mountain breezes:

Zion's Banner—Freedom's Ensign,
  Broad and gloriously unfurl'd,
Waves amid the Rocky Mountains—
  Heavenly beacon to the world. (*Snow* 203)

When Snow flies the American flag in such poems, she suggests that the Latter-day Saints are continuing the national mission that began with the Puritans, and that the Mormon Zion is merely another "city on a hill" that the "redeemer nation" of the United States holds up as an example to the world.[90] Flying "Zion's Banner" or "the Deseret Standard," however, suggests that the "new empire" of Mormonism that commentators (including Whitman) referred to in the late 1850s had not only separated itself from its parent nation but had also adopted the form of a polity quite different from that of the nineteenth-century nation-state. The Mormons' "new empire" does not organize its people according to the geographic borders of a single, unified nation but, instead, imagines a nexus whose lines of affiliation work their way through the earth with little or no regard for the political boundaries of organized nation-states.

Whitman would have recognized elements of his own somewhat conflicted nationalism in these poems, particularly in Snow's reluctance to credit the United States with reigning over the influx of immigrant converts who were building Zion in the American West. In "Passage to India," for example, Whitman similarly imagined a spiritual rejuvenation of the globe that involved people from across the world coming together in support of a common cause. But just as Snow was hesitant to have the American flag preside over a worldwide gathering of Saints, so too does "Passage to India" register a sense of uncertainty about the role that the United States would play in the global spiritual awakening Whitman prophesied. In "Passage to India," Whitman commends his nation for building the transcontinental railroad, saying that the railroad not only fulfilled Christopher Columbus's dream of a direct westerly route from Europe to Asia but also laid the groundwork for a spiritual unification of the globe that (according to Whitman) was the real reason behind Columbus's voyage. He writes that the transcontinental railroad made it possible for the different nations of the world to be "hook'd and link'd together," an accomplishment he credits with being "God's purpose from the first":

The earth to be spann'd, connected by network,
The races, neighbors, to marry and be given in marriage,
The oceans to be cross'd, the distance brought near,
The lands to be welded together. (LG 316)

Whitman writes that the transcontinental railroad performed the feat of "Tying the Eastern to the Western sea," of creating "The road between Europe and Asia" that Columbus set out to find (LG 317). In so doing, Whitman ascribes a prominent role to the United States as both the physical and spiritual center of the world. But in using language that credits the United States with fulfilling the dream of the sailor from Genoa ("Ah Genoese, thy dream! thy dream! / . . . / The shore thou foundest verifies thy dream"), he also threatens to make the United States a mere afterthought of "God's purpose from the first" (LG 317).

Columbus's goal, to recall, was to find an open passageway, not a continental landmass. By calling America the realization of Columbus's dream to link the East and the West, Whitman turns the United States into a stop on a larger journey, a road rather than a destination. In Snow's poetry and "Passage to India" alike, the United States—represented by the American flag and the transcontinental railroad, respectively—alternates between being central and incidental to a spiritual convergence of people from across the globe. When Snow and the Mormons conceptualized Zion as a local community of Saints who welcomed a global influx of converts, the nation retained a ghostly presence as the ambiguous flag waving over the Rocky Mountains. In some poems, Zion merely tolerates America; in others, Zion *is* America. Similarly, as Columbus's dream of a connecting link between Europe and Asia, in "Passage to India" the United States alternately appears as and then disappears from the center of the world. Befitting the persona that both poets adopted of a national outsider who would be the national bard, both Snow and Whitman alternated between a belief in the American mission that bordered on zealotry and a skepticism regarding U.S. prominence in the world that bordered on treason. What remains consistent in both poets is a tension between the nation itself and potentially denationalizing forces both within and beyond national boundaries.

RUFUS GRISWOLD, literary tastemaker and editor of the influential anthology *Poets and Poetry of America* (1842), predicted in 1853 that the representative American poet whom literary nationalists were anxiously awaiting would be a woman from the western United States possessed of a "prophetic" sensibility. Griswold opined that American women, and not men, were writing the poetry that had the most distinctive national characteristics: "Those who cherish a belief that the progress of society in this country is destined to develop a school of art, original and special, will perhaps find more decided indications of the infusion of our domestic spirit and temper into literature, in the poetry of our female authors, than in that of our men." Having identified the gender of the American poet, Griswold then located the region from whence she would come: "It is in the West, too, where we look for what is most thoroughly native and essential in American character." This woman poet from the West who was "destined" to write representative American poetry, according to Griswold, would also possess a "prophetic recognition" that would allow her to "[see] the divine relations of all things."[91] Even though Snow's 1856 volume of poetry appeared only a few years after Griswold made his prediction—and despite the fact that she was a woman from the West who was said to possess "a lofty and prophetic as well as poetical inspiration"—it should come as no surprise that Griswold did not regard Snow as the ideal American poet.[92] Trained as an orthodox Baptist minister, Griswold was no doubt expecting that his American bard would rise from the ranks of mainstream Christianity. (This same line of thinking similarly led Griswold to write a censorious review of *Leaves of Grass* in 1855 condemning the "obscenity" and "beastly sensuality" of Whitman's poetry.)[93]

Regardless of the fact that Snow's religious affiliation set her apart from the majority of other antebellum poets, the question of whether her gender made it more or less difficult for her to perform the duties of a national bard affected her standing both within and without Mormon culture. (Griswold, it bears noting, was decidedly in the minority with his opinion that a woman would be universally accepted as America's national poet, and he might only have said this to encourage sales of his book.) Snow's gift for "prophetic recognition" would have been rejected by most, if not all, mainline American Christians, who believed that prophets were a relic of the ancient past. Her powers of prophecy should even have received a cool welcome from her own coreligionists, who believed that the ability to prophesy on behalf of the entire church was the exclusive privilege of a single male prophet, such as Joseph Smith or Brigham Young. Even though Snow was referred to as a "priestess" and a "prophetess" by many Latter-day Saints, the realm of her ecclesiastical authority was, by and large, limited to Mormon women. As the leader of the churchwide women's organization, she was once referred to as the "president of all the feminine portion of the human race," a title that limited her sphere of influence within the church just as it attempted to expand that influence beyond the borders of the Utah Territory.[94]

In one very significant exception, however, Snow's "prophetic . . . inspiration" was enthusiastically embraced by the entire church. That exception is an 1845 poem titled "The Eternal Father and Mother," which would prove to be so popular in the Mormon community that, soon after its initial publication, it was set to music and quickly became one of the Saints' most beloved hymns.[95] In the poem, Snow presents a vision of a heaven that is governed equally by a father and a mother god, submitting that it is only with the "mutual approbation" of both a heavenly father and a heavenly mother that human beings may find eternal life (*Snow* 2). While it is unclear whether Snow originated the Mormon doctrine of a Mother in Heaven or learned of it from Joseph Smith, she popularized the belief to such a degree that by 1893 the president of the church identified Snow's poem as the source of the doctrine, calling it "a revelation, though it was given unto us by a woman— Sister Snow."[96] That Snow was credited with originating the doctrine of God the Mother in a religion that did not grant women the right to receive revelation for the church as a whole speaks, at least in part, to her skillful use of domestic imagery: The doctrine of a heavenly mother boldly asserts the existence of a female divinity, but Snow's poem safely weds her and places her in the domestic sphere.

By making the goddess a wife and mother, Snow was careful not to challenge the Mormon patriarchy even as she reimagined the centuries-old tradition of a father god whose sole authority governs the heavens. The sanctity of the home—as well as the traditional role of women in the home—remains intact for Snow even though in other poems she continues the reasoning begun in "The Eternal Father and Mother" that the presence of a Mother in Heaven increases the potential of women on earth. In an 1855 poem titled "Woman," Snow writes that the biblical injunction that a wife be a "help-meet" to her husband does not denigrate women to second-class status, but she suggests instead that women stand alongside men in both earthly and heavenly affairs: "'Help-meet' for man—with him she holds a key / Of present and eternal destiny." Snow was solidly on the conservative end of the burgeoning women's rights movement of the 1840s and 1850s, and thus she relied on the language of the domestic sphere to make the few gains for women that she was willing to claim. She writes in "Woman" that a wife is the "Queen of her household," a position of honor that portends the royalty that will be hers in heavenly courts above. Reigning in queenly dignity in the home, she writes, "constitutes the germ of what will be / In the high courts of immortality."[97] Snow could be a strong advocate for women, even if that advocacy was constrained by the parameters prescribed by her religion. In the poem "Woman," for example, she criticizes antebellum feminists' desire to claim the equal rights for women that she was only willing to consider within a domestic and religious context: "If 'rights' are right when they are rightly gain'd / 'Rights' must be wrong when wrongfully obtain'd."[98]

Despite her reliance on domestic imagery and her elevation of wife- and motherhood to divine status, Snow herself was childless, and it was an open secret that she was Brigham Young's wife in name only. (A visitor to the Utah Territory wrote of Snow in the 1860s, "I am led to believe that she is not a wife to Young in the sense of our canon; she is always called Miss Eliza.")[99] After Snow died in 1887, her childlessness was referenced by a prominent church leader who, rather than denigrate Snow for not having fulfilled her maternal duty, commented instead, "Inasmuch as the deceased was deprived of bearing children, she is entitled to be called Mother among this people, just as much as George Washington is to be called Father by the people of the United States."[100] That Snow was compared to George rather than Martha Washington in her status as the mother of the Mormon people not only suggests the position of authority she had attained among the Saints but also testifies to a larger tendency in the nineteenth-century United States wherein the supposedly private sphere of women's domestic life could be made to influence a public sphere dominated by men. Elizabeth Petrino and others have referred to this tendency as the hallmark of a worldview which held that "the home [was] a place from which women could exert almost as much control in the world as men."[101]

Whitman himself drew on the discourses of what has been called "domestic feminism" in imagery that he used to describe the health and well-being of the nation.[102] He frequently used the image of a mother—what Betsy Erkkila calls "the image of a divinely charged matriarch"—to depict the United States.[103] Whitman described America as "a grand, sane, towering, seated Mother" and hailed the nation as "the Mother of All" throughout the *Drum-Taps* poems (*LG* 387, 230). Whitman used mother imagery to provide a model of unity for an otherwise fractious nation, and he issued himself the challenge to "Make a picture of America as an IMMORTAL MOTHER, surrounded by all her children young and old—no one rejected—all fully accepted—no one preferred to another. For as to many sons and daughters the perfect mother is the one where all meet, and binds them all together, as long as she lives, so The Mother of These States binds them all together as long as she lives" (*NUPM* 1:435). He wrote in another note from the late 1850s that he wanted his poems "to bring in the idea of Mother—the idea of the mother with numerous children—all great and small, old and young, equal in her eyes—as the identity of America."[104]

Eliza R. Snow would have had a difficult time imagining the United States as an all-inclusive mother who embraced her Mormon children with equal love. A number of editorial cartoons from mid-nineteenth-century newspapers depict the Mormons—along with other racial, ethnic, and religious minorities—as unwanted national children. In one such cartoon, America is depicted as a frazzled housewife being overrun by her unruly Mormon, African American, Native American, Irish, and Chinese children; in another, the nation is a mother bird who feeds all the hatchlings in her nest except two disfigured little chicks labeled "Mormonism" and "Catholicism."[105] Whereas Whitman could use the image of a "divinely charged matriarch" to suggest the unity and equality of an idealized American democracy, Snow had difficulty thinking of herself and her people as part of a happy national family. Instead, she used the image of the divine family in "The Eternal Father and Mother" to comment on the Mormons' exile from their national home.

"The Eternal Father and Mother" is told from the perspective of a childlike narrator who addresses a Father God and Mother Goddess from her earthly exile, laments her separation from them, and asks when she will return to their presence. (Reminiscent of Wordsworth's "Ode: Intimations of Immortality from Recollections of Early Childhood," Snow describes the domestic heaven from whence she came as the location of her "primeval childhood," writing that in mortality she has "wander'd / From a more exalted sphere.") On its own, the poem recounts an individual's longing for a spiritual home. When Snow placed the poem at the front of her 1856 volume and identified it as the "Invocation" of the collection, however, the theme of celestial exile became a gloss on the larger story of Mormon exile, which reappears throughout the collection as a whole. Other poems in the volume, for example, draw on domestic imagery to recall that the Saints "forsook the home of childhood" when they left the United States to build Zion, and that in the Utah Territory they are "far, far away from the land of our home, / And, like strangers, in exile we're destin'd to roam" (*Snow* 3, 68).

Recasting "The Eternal Father and Mother" as the "Invocation" of the collection allowed Snow to draw an implicit comparison between the social drama of national exile and the divine drama of mortal exile. One Latter-day Saint reader said as much in 1877 when he commented that "The Eternal Father and Mother" illustrates not only "the vast system of Mormon theology, which links the heavens and the earth," but also the "drama of Mormonism itself." The same reader also said that the poem provides "a rare view of the spiritual type of the high priestess of the Mormon Church."[106] That Snow herself would have wanted "The Eternal Father and Mother" to achieve these two goals—that is, to convey both the "drama" of Mormon exile and her own authority as the poet-priestess of the Latter-day Saints—is evident in her using the poem as the "Invocation," particularly given that an epic invocation is expected to introduce the larger themes of the poem as a whole and establish the poet's ability to command the muse.

As a domestic-sentimental poem, "The Eternal Father and Mother" seems an unlikely choice for the "Invocation" of a poetry collection that attempts to tell the epic story of a people, but Snow's choice was neither accidental nor cavalier. Snow was well aware of epic conventions, particularly that of the epic invocation. One of the poems in her 1856 collection is an epyllion about early episodes in the life of Mormon prophet Joseph Smith, which begins with a four-stanza "Introductory Invocation" that conforms to a number of epic conventions (*Snow* 15). If Snow had used this "Introductory Invocation" as the general invocation of the entire collection, it would have framed the volume as the heroic struggle of the prophet and his people. By using "The Eternal Father and Mother," however, she shifts the emphasis to a domestic realm over which she as a "Mother among this people" was authorized to preside.

In casting "The Eternal Father and Mother" as an invocation, Snow departs from the expectations of the genre while still retaining many of its goals. She replaces the blank verse or heroic couplets of a traditional invocation with a trochaic meter that shapes the rhythm of the poem around the domestic words "Father" and "Mother." Similarly, she does not command her heavenly muse to sing as an epic poet might but, instead, adopts a tone befitting that of a humble child making modest requests of her parents. In a series of reserved and decorous questions, she opens the poem by asking God the Father when her mortal exile will be over and when she will return to her heavenly home: "When shall I regain thy presence," she asks, "And again behold thy face?" Her address to both the Father and Mother at the end of the poem is similarly that of a respectful child:

> When I leave this frail existence—
>> When I lay this mortal by;
> Father, Mother, may I meet you
>> In your royal court on high? (*Snow* 2)

The one-sided conversation that Snow carries on with her heavenly parents owes its genesis to the conventions of literary sentimentalism as well as to the epic poet's address to the muse. Kelly Richardson, among others, has argued that nineteenth-century sentimental poetry depends on the apostrophe as a central literary device because the apostrophe's address to an absent listener "allows the speaker both to remember an absent person . . . [and] to create a place so that person can be addressed and thus be made present."[107] Snow's sentimental imagery stands in sharp contrast to Whitman's depiction of a divine mother pregnant with the bibles and messiahs of the religion of the future, as in poems such as "Thou Mother with Thy Equal Brood," where he describes an American goddess that is "all-supplying, all-enclosing worship—thee in no single bible, saviour, merely, / Thy saviours countless, latent within thyself, thy bibles incessant within thyself" (*LG* 385). Snow's vision of a Mother in Heaven may hew more closely to nineteenth-century expectations of domestic womanhood than does Whitman's image of an overabundant fount of matriarchal energy, but her creative use of the sentimental apostrophe within the conventions of the epic invocation allows her to claim a significant amount of authority as a female poet nonetheless.

Snow's use of the apostrophe registers a sense of separation and loss, coupled with the hopefulness that the loving bonds of family life can ultimately overcome that loss. Through the apostrophe, she is able to communicate the feeling of exile that lies at the heart of the "drama of Mormonism." But the direct address of the epic invocation also displays the power and authority of a poet who can bend the muse to her will. Snow's invocation of a divine family—and, in particular, a domestic goddess—as the muse of her collection endows her with the authority she requires as a female poet in a patriarchal religion and an androcentric nation. Nineteenth-century collections of poetry by women often came with prefaces by male editors whose authority was necessary to establish the woman poet's credibility.[108] By calling upon the muse of a mother god in her invocation to the collection—rather than, say, asking her prophet-husband, Brigham Young, to put his seal of approval on the volume—Snow garnered her authority from a female source. (In her subsequent volume of poems, which was published in 1877, she altered her strategy dramatically and opened the collection with a dedicatory poem titled, "To Brigham Young, President of the Church of Jesus Christ of Latter-day Saints.")[109]

It is no small thing that Snow included the name of the Eternal Mother in the title of the poem as it appeared in the 1856 collection. When the poem was originally published in a Latter-day Saint newspaper in 1845, it bore the title "My Heavenly Father." In its subsequent publication as a hymn, it was referred to in 1855 by its first line, as "O my Father thou that dwellest" and, later, only as "O My Father."[110] That her muse was a divine goddess as well as a patriarchal god was a point that Snow underscored in the 1856 collection. The authority Snow claims by invoking a divine female muse does not come easily in the poem, however. Given that so much of "The Eternal Father and Mother" is dedicated to the speaker posing questions to her Father and Mother in Heaven, Snow had to be careful about depicting the form in which a response would come from these divine beings. Instead of having a clear voice from heaven answer her questions—as would be the prerogative of a male Mormon prophet—she writes that an ambiguous "secret something" has whispered to her the truths about her distant heavenly home:

> Yet oft-times a secret something
>   Whisper'd, "You're a stranger here;"
> And I felt that I had wander'd
>   From a more exalted sphere. (*Snow* 2)

This whispered "secret something" gives the image of a parent speaking gently to a sleeping child, an image that, again, reinforces both the domestic setting and the family ties between heavenly parents and their children. While this gentle whispering confirms that God is a loving parent who communicates freely with his earthly children, Snow also notes that without "the Key of Knowledge" restored to Mormon prophets in the latter days, she would not be able to understand the meaning of these divine whisperings. She writes,

> I had learn'd to call thee Father,
>   Through thy Spirit from on high;
> But, until the Key of Knowledge
>   Was restor'd, I knew not why. (*Snow* 2)

Of the two forms of spiritual knowledge presented thus far—the secret whisperings she hears directly from heavenly parents and the Key of Knowledge that opens the heavens to the prophets of the restoration—Snow appeals to neither as the source of her inspiration that there is a Mother in Heaven. Rather, she calls upon her own sense of reason to deduce that a domestic heaven would be incomplete without an Eternal Mother espoused to the Eternal Father:

> In the heavens are parents single?
>   No: the thought makes reason stare:
> Truth is reason: truth eternal,
>   Tells me I've a mother there. (*Snow* 2)

Snow modifies the apostrophe she had heretofore employed as the poem's central poetic device when she ceases to pose questions to God and instead addresses herself with the rhetorical question, "In the heavens are parents single?" Rather than risk blasphemy by depicting the voice of God speaking to a woman on matters of doctrine, she settles for the lesser sin of trusting reason over revelation.

Snow deducts from the principles of God's literal parentage and the similarity between earthly and heavenly homes that reason would demand the existence of a mother god. Appealing to reason as an appropriately feminine form of knowledge would seem to contradict the nineteenth-century expectation that women's poetry come from the emotions rather than the intellect. As Caroline May wrote in her 1848 introduction to *The Female Poets of America*, a woman's "inspiration lies more in her heart than her head."[111] Revelation is an extrarational form of knowledge denigrated in a secular society but privileged in a religious one. Reason, then, is the only recourse for a woman in a religious culture that grants the right to receive revelation on questions of doctrine exclusively to a male prophet. Attaining the knowledge of a mother god through feminine reason allowed Snow to access the religious authority of male prophecy by inverting the cultural authority of women's sentimental poetry. Snow could be revered as a priestess and a prophetess, but only when she respected the boundary that male prophets had drawn around the powers of prophecy and revelation. It is ironic, then, that by eschewing revelation for reason—which was regarded at the time as a largely if not an exclusively male faculty—she found a place for herself as a woman and a poet.

Another irony surrounding Snow's use of "The Eternal Father and Mother" as the invocation of her 1856 collection is that the action of the poem takes place entirely in solitude as the speaker prays, meditates, and reasons alone, despite the fact that, as "the chief poet of the Mormon church," one of Snow's primary responsibilities was to compose poetry for public occasions. That the poem that introduces a book of public poetry would be so intimate in its expression is fitting, somehow, to the experience of a woman who had sacrificed her life to build up the kingdom of God on the earth. Had Snow never converted to Mormonism, she might have developed a private lyric voice like that of many antebellum women poets rather than the public voice that came to dominate the vast majority of her poetry. Indeed, until the day in 1831 when she met the Mormon prophet Joseph Smith, Snow could have written her life story as a composite biography of the prototypical antebellum American poetess. Born in 1804 in the small town of Becket, Massachusetts, Snow was the granddaughter of Revolutionary War veterans and the daughter of austere Protestant parents. She demonstrated a precocious ability for poetry at a very young age, writing her homework assignments in verse and publishing poems in local newspapers under such fanciful pseudonyms as Narcissa and Pocahontas.[112]

Before becoming Zion's Poetess in 1838, Snow wrote a number of poems that express her affinity for the moments of private meditation when she could compose in quiet solitude. In one poem, she wrote of enjoying the hours of "soft stillness and silence [that] awaken the Muse," calling such moments

a time [and] a place that the minstrel should choose
While so sweetly the moments in silence pass by
When there's nobody here but Eliza and I.[113]

The church to which she had dedicated her life was generous enough to eventually give Snow a room of her own where she could write and reflect in private. A visitor to Utah described Snow's room in Brigham Young's Salt Lake City mansion as "overlooking the Oquirrh mountains, the Valley, the River Jordan, and the Salt Lake; a poet's prospect, in which form and color, sky and land and water, melt and fuse into a glory without end."[114] Looking out across the Salt Lake Valley as the desert blossomed like a rose, there were moments when "Eliza and I" could still, in the words of Emily Dickinson, "[shut] the Door— / To her divine Majority" before the services of Zion's Poetess were required of her again.[115]

chapter three

THE FIRST WHITE ABORIGINAL

*This was Whitman. And the true rhythm of the
American continent speaking out in him. He is the first white aboriginal.*

—D. H. Lawrence, Studies in Classic American Literature *(1923)*

For the first half of 1865, Walt Whitman was working as a clerk at the federal Bureau of Indian Affairs in Washington, D.C. He appears to have enjoyed the job, which offered him a steady paycheck, a flexible work schedule, and the opportunity to meet with the Native American delegates who had came to negotiate treaties and land deals with the federal government. Native Americans had been appearing regularly in Whitman's poetry and prose since the early 1840s, but not until his time at the Indian Bureau did he have extended contact with indigenous peoples. These delegations of visiting Indians left a strong impression on the poet who had previously written that Native American history and culture are "the proper subjects for the bard or the novelist."[1] The Native delegates who captured Whitman's attention were those he considered the most "traditional" or "authentic" in appearance, those, that is, whom he described as "so different, so far outside our standards of eminent humanity." "Most have red paint on their cheeks," he wrote in a composite sketch of such Indians. "Many wear head tires of gaudy-color'd braid, wound around thickly—some with circlets of eagles' feathers. Necklaces of bears' claws are plenty around their necks. . . . All the principal chiefs have tomahawks or hatchets, some of them very richly ornamented and costly." A friend to whom Whitman sent this description concurred that, in essence, the only good Indian is an exotic Indian, writing, "An Indian is only half an Indian without the blue-black hair and the brilliant eyes shining out of the wonderful dusky ochre and rose complexion" (*pw* 2:577–80).

While Whitman experienced the Bureau of Indian Affairs as a living panorama of exotic images, it was a place of tension and anxiety for the Native delegates themselves who had come to negotiate complex

John Rollin Ridge (Yellow Bird)

legal and territorial issues with the United States. No one felt this anxiety more acutely than John Rollin Ridge, who had come to the bureau in the spring of 1866 with a delegation of Cherokees hoping to find a resolution to a decades-old conflict that had left the Cherokee Nation fragmented and factionalized. Ridge was particularly anxious because the conflict he had come to resolve was a direct result of decisions made by members of the Ridge family thirty years earlier. As leaders in the Cherokee Nation during the era of Indian Removal, Ridge's father and grandfather believed that tribal survival required capitulating to the U.S. government, and they had yielded to U.S. demands that the Cherokees leave their homeland in the state of Georgia. The Ridges and a minority of Cherokees voluntarily moved west of the Mississippi in 1836, to be followed two years later by the rest of the Cherokee Nation in what has come to be known as the Trail of Tears. While the Ridges maintained that they had the Cherokees' best interests at heart in signing a treaty for removal to present-day Oklahoma, a rival faction within the Cherokee Nation called the treaty a betrayal. After Ridge's father, grandfather, and uncle were murdered by opponents to the removal treaty, Ridge himself killed a removal opponent in retaliation and fled to California in 1850. Ridge's dream of returning to the Cherokee Nation to assume the leadership role that he considered his birthright was dashed when the agents at the Indian Bureau signed a treaty with the delegation sent by Ridge's rivals instead.[2]

Whitman was no longer working at the Bureau of Indian Affairs when Ridge arrived in Washington, D.C., in 1866. Had he been given the opportunity to meet with Ridge as he had met with other Indian delegates, Whitman would probably not have considered Ridge to be one of "those great aboriginal specimens" whom he had admired for their "unique picturesqueness" (PW 2:578–79). Ridge, who attended a private academy in Massachusetts as a youth and worked as a political journalist throughout his adult life, had adopted many Euro-American customs in both speech and dress. And even though Ridge was the author of well-received poems and essays about Native American culture—which he published under his Cherokee name, Yellow Bird—Whitman would not have regarded him as one of the "noble specimens of savage and hardy Nature" whose appearance he considered "impressive, even artistic" (NUPM 2:880; PW 2:578). Whitman was drawn to the Indians at the bureau who projected the "inherent and athletic royalty of the man of the woods and mountains," Indians who looked at the world with "the great eyes of the superior birds & animals." Ridge would no doubt have seemed too civilized, too *human* even, for Whitman, who said that the Indians he admired not only had the eyes of "birds & animals" but were themselves "magnificent and beautiful animals" (*NUPM* 2:880–81; *PW* 2:578).

Whitman might have agreed with the friend to whom he sent his description of the Native delegates that someone as Americanized as Ridge was merely "half an Indian." He would not have been alone in this opinion: One of the official documents circulated at the bureau regarding Ridge's claim for leadership of the Cherokee Nation referred to members of the Ridge faction—many of whom had married whites and embraced Anglo-American culture—as "white Indians."[3] It is ironic that Whitman would have considered Ridge to be "half an Indian," given that Whitman himself had, albeit in a different context, cultivated the image of a "white Indian." When D. H. Lawrence called Whitman "the first white aboriginal" of American literature in 1923, he reinforced the persona that Whitman had already labored to establish of a white poet who had attuned himself to what Lawrence called "the true rhythm of the American continent."[4]

Whitman reveled in comparisons of his life and work with the aboriginal energy of the New World, believing that any connection to the original inhabitants of the continent would bolster his claim to be America's representative bard. He so enjoyed the complaints of a reviewer of the 1855 *Leaves of Grass* that his poems "resemble nothing so much as the war-cry of the Red Indians" and that the poet himself "reminds us of [Shakespeare's] Caliban flinging down his logs, and setting himself to write a poem" that he included the review in an appendix to the subsequent edition of his book.[5] In the 1840s a fellow newspaper editor said that Whitman was "what you call a civilized but not a polished *Aborigine*. . . . [And] it has been asserted by one of his brother Editors that he is a lineal descendent from some Indian tribe."[6] Similarly, in the late 1850s the bohemian author Henry Clapp reportedly called out to Whitman amid the conversations at Pfaff's bar, "Come, Whitman, you savage, open a page of nature for us."[7] Whitman was no doubt invested in romanticizing the Native Americans he saw at the Bureau of Indian Affairs because he, too, wanted to share in their perceived exoticism. Whitman, who described his poetry as a "savage song" that he issued forth in a "barbaric yawp," was eager to project an image of having renounced civilization and embraced savagery (*LG* 276, 78). When the secretary of the interior dismissed Whitman from his job at the Indian Bureau on the grounds that

Leaves of Grass did "not come within the rules of decorum & propriety pre-scribed by a Christian Civilization," Whitman must have been heartened by the insinuation that the federal government was too civilized a place for someone as uncivilized as he considered himself to be.[8]

Had the two poets met in 1866, Ridge would have received Whitman's assessment of him as "half an Indian" with equal parts approval and offense. The son of a Cherokee father and a white mother, Ridge was just as proud of his Cherokee ancestry as he was of his successful assimilation of Euro-American cultural norms. He was, in this respect, part of what one anthro-pologist has referred to as the "planter class of mixbloods" in nineteenth-century Cherokee society, an elite minority of well-to-do Cherokees who, while sharing "a fierce loyalty to common ancestry" with their full-blooded counterparts, nevertheless embraced "English [as] its first language, evan-gelical Christianity its religion, and acculturation its code."[9] As such, Ridge was committed to the apparently contradictory goals of preserving indige-nous culture *and* spreading American civilization throughout the continent.

This line of thinking may seem today to be problematic at best and de-structive at worst, but during his lifetime Ridge would chastise the Ameri-can government for its treatment of Native peoples in the same breath that he encouraged Indians to look to Western civilization for their salvation. In an epistle to his cousin written during the 1850s, for example, Ridge in-sisted that there was no "prouder object" to which he could dedicate his life than "civilizing and improving these mighty remnants of the Indian race—bringing all these scattered tribes one by one into the fold of the American Union." In the same letter, however, Ridge also wrote of his desire to expose U.S. mistreatment of Native Americans, claiming that he was similarly com-mitted to bringing "justice to a deeply wronged and injured people by im-pressing upon the records of the country a true and impartial account of the treatment which they have received at the hands of a civilized and Christian race!"[10]

Whether Ridge honestly believed that he could achieve these seemingly contradictory aims is a question that both his detractors and his support-ers have been asking since the nineteenth century.[11] Regardless, there are moments when Ridge's desire to defend indigenous peoples while uphold-ing the civilizing mission of the United States produces a visionary strain in his poetry that, like a similar strain in Whitman's, imagines a space where harmony can exist between whites and Natives where there had only been conflict before. Out of what Roy Harvey Pearce has called the "American obsession with the problem of the civilized vs. the savage"—an obsession born of a need to define a "civilized" national identity within and against the presence of "savage" Indians—both Whitman and Ridge experimented with strategies for unifying Euro-American and Native American cultures in ways that would allow them to serve as the representative voice of the nation.[12] Neither poet was very systematic in his thinking on the subject (and each made serious missteps along the way), but both nevertheless remained invested in the idea that the United States could be remade in the image of a "white aboriginal." Each poet had moments when he embraced an orthodox narrative of the U.S. destiny to reign over the American continent, but each poet also expressed real faith that a blending of Euro-American and Native American cultures would transform both the nation and the world.

The first section of this chapter compares Whitman's efforts to present himself as a "savage" white man who had rejected the trappings of civilization with Ridge's desire to harmonize U.S. and Native American culture, focusing in particular on the imagery in Ridge's early poetry of "wild half-breeds" and "civilized Indians" who model both the pitfalls and possibilities of cultural amalgamation. The second section argues that the international climate of gold-rush California provided Ridge with an expanded vocabulary of images to illustrate how the mingling of peoples (beginning with whites and Natives and extending to populations from across the globe) would challenge received notions of race and national identity. According to the stereotype of the vanishing Indian—which held that Native Americans would inevitably move westward into oblivion as the U.S. frontier extended toward the Pacific Coast—Ridge was expected to leave his Cherokee homeland for something similar to Hiawatha's "happy hunting grounds" in the distant West.[13] Instead, as Ridge moved westward to California, he found a space where the convergence of disparate cultures fulfilled his vision of cultural amalgamation that began with the image of the American bard as a white aboriginal. This vision, as explained in the third section of the chapter, is most forcefully articulated in a poem, the first line of which is "Hail to the Plow!," from late in Ridge's career that depicts California—which was considered by many (including Whitman) to be a quintessentially American space—as having been unmoored from its host nation and transformed into the central node of an emerging global society. "Hail to the Plow!" was, like most of Ridge's later poems, read in public on a commemorative occasion to an audience who thought of Ridge as a representative of the triumph of civilization over savagery. At a number of key moments in the poem, Ridge directly confronted his audience's assumptions about Native peoples in hopes of redefining the values of both the audience members themselves and the larger national culture they represented. Such moments are where Ridge most actively assumes the role of the "white aboriginal" as American bard.

ONE OF WHITMAN'S few published accounts of his experience with the Bureau of Indian Affairs is a short article from the *Washington Evening Star* describing the time he met with a Sioux delegation. The article is written in the third person (it was published anonymously), and as such gives the impression that Whitman himself was the dignitary that the Sioux had traveled hundreds of miles to meet:

> Yesterday afternoon, Walt Whitman, who was walking down the avenue, stepped in, by invitation of the Agent, and made them [the Sioux delegation] a short impromptu visit. "Tell them", said the agent to the interpreter, "that the poet-chief has come to shake hands with them, as brothers." A regular round of introductions and hearty hand-claspings, and "How's!" followed. "Tell them, Billy", continued the agent, "that the poet-chief says we are all really the same men and brethren together, at last, however different our places, and dress and language." An approving chorus of guttural "Ugh's!" came from all parts of the room, and W. W. retired, leaving an evidently captivating impression. (*NUPM* 2:881)

Not only does Whitman's account of his meeting with the Sioux overinflate his importance in the eyes of both the Indians and the bureau agents, but it also, and perhaps more importantly, gives him the opportunity to slide a little further into savagery as he momentarily trades in the title of American bard for that of "poet-chief." The figure of the poet-chief complements that of the white aboriginal in that both personae allow Whitman to function as a mediating influence between whites and Indians, a link between two otherwise disparate worlds. The government agent and the interpreter might do all the talking in this anecdote, but the "captivating impression" that Whitman leaves on both whites and Indians alike suggests that the presence of the "poet-chief" himself constitutes the real medium for communication between the two groups. That Whitman's message as poet-chief is to remind those in attendance of their common humanity—"we are all really the same men and brethren"—furthers the notion that he is uniquely capable of bridging the gap between civilization and savagery.

Elsewhere in his writings, however, Whitman could express considerably less faith in his ability to help whites and Native Americans find common ground. At one point he shrugged his shoulders at the "inexorable" law of history that foretold the demise of indigenous and other nonwhite peoples: "The nigger, like the Injun, will be eliminated," Whitman said to his confidant Horace Traubel. "It is the law of races, history, what-not: always so far inexorable—always to be" (*wwc* 2:238). Even though he considered the "elimination" of Native Americans to be a historical inevitability, he also expressed regret over this impending genocide and spoke in tones of genuine sorrow on behalf of "the poor aboriginals, so to call them, [who] suffer, go down, [and] are wiped out" (*wwc* 6:423). Such statements reveal that Whitman experienced what Ed Folsom calls a "a tortured ambivalence about the role America's natives would play in the development of the country's character. . . . The Indians, Whitman knew, had been abused and treated unjustly, but he also subscribed to the notion of progress and social evolution and believed that it was inevitable and ultimately valuable that America extend itself from sea to sea."[14] Whitman attempted to ameliorate this ambivalence the only way he knew how: by setting aside a space in his poetry that would serve as a perpetual tribute to the lives and legacies of the first Americans. In the 1880s Whitman proposed a "poem of the aborigines" in which he planned to include "every principal aboriginal trait, and name" (*nupm* 1:275). The poem never materialized as such, but many of Whitman's other poems reflect his feeling that indigenous peoples form an important part of his comprehensive vision of American life.

In this desire to give Native Americans a central place in his poetry, Whitman was also participating in the antebellum debates over the role that Indian themes would play in an emerging nationalist literary tradition. Writers and critics in the United States since the early nineteenth century had proposed that Indian stories would be an important, if not defining, element of a distinctive body of national literature. Whitman himself had written in the 1840s that "the remnants of Indian legends . . . would be the true and legitimate romance of the continent," a uniquely American romance that would silence the criticisms of "those of the Old World [who] frequently tell us we have no fit themes for poetry and imagination here."[15]

Whitman's belief that an American bard should include Native themes in his poetry was in keeping with the opinions of writers and critics who argued that Native American stories belonged not to the indigenous cultures where they had originated but to the white people who had only recently settled the continent.

One commentator noted in 1849, for example, that all of the "Iliad [*sic*] material" of American literature could be found in the experiences of indigenous peoples, and that it was the "unquestioned right" of white Americans to draw on those experiences when writing their own national poetry. Indians, this critic wrote, embody "all the distinct and characteristic poetic material to which we, as Americans, have an unquestioned right."[16] Soon after white Americans began to claim the history of indigenous peoples as their own, the presence of actual Indians was no longer considered necessary. In an 1825 essay titled "The Literary Spirit of Our Country," for example, a young Henry Wadsworth Longfellow argued that the rise of American poetry depended on the demise of Native Americans. It would only be, he wrote, "when our native Indians, who are fast perishing from the earth, shall have left forever the borders of our wide lakes and rivers" that "our land will become, indeed, a classic ground."[17]

Whitman's ambivalent attitude toward Native Americans can be seen in his mixed response to the idea that a dying race of Indians was leaving behind the stories that would serve as the foundation of an emerging U.S. literary tradition. He wrote in one poem that as "the red aborigines" passed from existence, the only reminder that a civilized nation was once home to "savage" and "primitive" people would be the Indian names that white Americans would give to rivers and towns: "they melt, they depart, charging the water and the land with names." In another poem, however, he proposed that Native Americans were not "waiting for civilization" as the uncivilized remnant of the nation's prehistory but, rather, were "past it and mastering it" (*LG* 27, 65). In registering this ambivalence about the relationship of Native peoples to white America, Whitman might have cost himself the popular and critical attention that a writer such as Longfellow achieved when, in *Hiawatha*, he embraced virtually without reservation the antebellum dictum that national poems should chronicle the passing of the Indians. That *Hiawatha* towered over *Leaves of Grass* in popularity when the two books were published within months of each other in 1855 is a testament, among other things, to the two poets' different perspectives on the place of Indians in American literature. Longfellow wrote in an elegiac mode that consigned Native peoples to extinction, whereas Whitman attempted to resurrect the Indian into the persona of the white aboriginal and the language of poems that he described as "wild and untamed—half savage."[18] (Such language, to recall, was compared in an early review to "the war-cry of the Red Indians.") Indeed, when Whitman was pressured by some of his supporters to present himself as a fireside poet of the Longfellow variety—complete with groomed and curled hair—he insisted that he was more of a "savage" Indian than a Boston Brahmin: "There are some of my friends who are determined that I shall not be represented as a savage with a tomahawk, so they curl me up—agonize me" (*WWC* 4:227). Whitman's sense that an American bard should not only write about Indians but also in some way *become* an Indian put him in an interesting position with respect to his antebellum contemporaries: He shared their colonizer's appetite for indigenous stories, but he was also willing to cede a significant portion of his ontological territory to Native Americans.

Whitman, at least to some degree, appreciated that the effort to place Native Americans at the center of U.S. letters would also have a transformative effect on the white people who coveted their stories. As Monica Kaup and Debra Rosenthal have argued, "If the white nationalist imagination appropriates indigenous identity, the conquest also cuts both ways: 'indigenization' hybridizes the European [settler]."[19] Throughout his career, Whitman sought to hybridize the office of American bard. Ed Folsom has noted that Whitman saw himself, metaphorically at least, as "the issue of the marriage of the trapper and the red girl" recorded in "Song of Myself" when he chronicled his visionary trek to the western frontier:[20]

> I saw the marriage of the trapper in the open air in the far west, the
>   bride was a red girl,
> Her father and his friends sat near cross-legged and dumbly smoking,
>   they had moccasins to their feet and large thick blankets hanging
>   from their shoulders,
> On a bank lounged the trapper, he was drest mostly in skins, his
>   luxuriant beard and curls protected his neck, he held his bride by
>   the hand,

She had long eyelashes, her head was bare, her coarse straight locks
   descended upon her voluptuous limbs and reach'd to her feet.
   (LG 36)

As the imagined offspring of a white frontiersman and a Native American woman, Whitman identified himself with the nineteenth-century cultural type that William Scheick describes as "the figurative half-blood, [the]
half-blood in spirit or temperament."[21] Whitman was not the only writer
to populate his texts with figurative half-bloods. Cooper's *Leatherstocking
Tales*, for one, feature a white hero whose knowledge of Indian customs en-
sures his survival on the frontier. But there are meaningful differences between Cooper's Hawkeye and the persona of the poet-chief. Both Whitman
and Cooper experimented with appropriations of indigenous culture, but
Whitman was willing to internalize Native American identity to a degree
that Cooper—who was quick to describe Hawkeye as "a white man who has
no taint of Indian blood"—was not.[22] When Whitman publicly asked Emerson when "a savage and luxuriant man" would vitalize American literature,
for example, he was not referring to further literary treatments of Indians
but, rather, to poets themselves who had been transformed by dwelling on
the same continent with indigenous peoples (LG56 352).

Whitman's laudable attempts to remake the American bard in the image
of the nation's first inhabitants, however, ultimately carried little conse-
quence for him either personally or politically. He could step into or out of
the persona of the white aboriginal at his convenience, just as he could safely
imagine what life would have been like as the child of a white frontiersman
and a Native American woman. In contrast, a writer like John Rollin Ridge,
whose father was Cherokee and his mother white, lived with the reality of
his biracial identity on a daily basis. And even though Ridge was not always
the victim of overt racism, his mixed-race heritage profoundly affected both
his sense of self and his views on the future of American society.[23] During
Ridge's time as a journalist in the 1850s and 1860s, few topics captured his attention more than what he and other nineteenth-century thinkers referred
to as "amalgamation": the "mixing or blending," as *Webster's* 1913 dictionary
has it, "of different elements, races, societies."[24] While editing the *Sacramento
Daily Bee* during the late 1850s, for example, Ridge frequently ran stories
about interracial relationships involving not only whites and Native Americans but also African Americans, Mexicans, and Chinese immigrants.[25] In

one such article, Ridge echoed the racist assumption that intermarriage between whites and people of color was a necessary precondition for "civilizing" the world: "Wherever the white race goes, amalgamation takes place. It has progressed with the march of civilization on this continent, and it *will*, with the certainty of an inevitable law, solve the destiny of the races."[26] As a member of an elite class of mixed-race Anglo-Cherokees—whom he referred to as "the most respectable and intelligent portion of the Cherokee people"—Ridge had, in many ways, internalized a belief in the superiority of Euro-American culture.[27] (Whitman appears to have shared this belief, as when he commented that the most prominent Native Americans in U.S. society benefited from "being of mixed blood, having a dash of white, not pure Indian" [*wwc* 6:400].)

But Ridge was also capable of thinking about race in ways that did not exclusively privilege whiteness. He wrote in one article that intermarriage between whites and Natives was not so much a solution to the U.S. "Indian Problem" as it was an overture to a worldwide racial amalgamation that would eventually result in a complete elimination of racial and even national categories: "A universal amalgamation of the races seems to be going on," he wrote. "It is possible that the present identity of nations and tribes will some day be entirely lost in the commingling and absorption of specific elements."[28] Rather than merely "whitening out" indigenous populations, Ridge believed that the "commingling" of races would ultimately redefine— and even render irrelevant—racial and national identity. Just as Whitman wanted to indigenize national identity with the figure of the American bard as a white aboriginal, Ridge took this same idea one step further by proposing that everyone, eventually, would be a "half-breed" of some sort. If Whitman the poet-chief thought of himself as the bard most suited to preside over an indigenized national identity, then Ridge, as a mixed-race Anglo-Cherokee who foresaw "a universal amalgamation of the races," positioned himself to be the poet of an even more radically conceived "half-breed" nation.

As someone who felt that he was personally experiencing the early stages of this "universal amalgamation of the races," Ridge found himself in the awkward position of having to reconcile his vision of a future where racial intermixture was the norm with the present-day reality of an ever-increasing gulf between whites and Native Americans. Ridge seemed to believe that, in the interim, he could retain a strong connection to his Indian heritage while embracing an entirely orthodox vision of American progress. Lucy Maddox has argued that such a position would have been hopelessly naive in a period when "the almost universally shared assumption [was] that there were only two options for the Indians: to become civilized, or to become extinct."[29] Nevertheless, many of Ridge's written statements indicate a desire to support indigenous peoples while still pledging allegiance to the civilizing mission of the United States. Ridge wrote passionately about revising the ill-informed assumptions that white Americans held about Indians in general and the Cherokee in particular. He wrote, "I want to write the history of the Cherokee Nation as it *should* be written and not as white men will write it and as they will tell the tale, to screen and justify themselves." Similarly, in 1855 he wrote of his desire to create a pan-tribal "newspaper devoted to the advocacy of Indian rights." "If I can establish such a paper," he wrote, "I can bring into its columns not only the fire of my own pen, such as it may be, but the contributions of the leading minds in the different Indian nations.... Men, governments, will be *afraid* to trample upon the rights of the defenceless [*sic*] Indian tribes when there is a power to hold up their deeds to the execration of mankind."[30] When this newspaper failed to materialize, Ridge remained true to his initial commitment by writing and publishing articles on Native American history, culture, and politics for mainstream periodicals.[31]

At the same time that he carried out this campaign to defend Native American rights in the press, however, Ridge was unabashed in his support of Manifest Destiny and made no apologies for his belief that the United States had a central role to play in "civilizing" the American continent, writing in one newspaper article of his hope "to see Uncle Sam the dominant lord of every square sod of ground, from Panama to the Arctic Pole, on the soil of North America." "Young America has a mission to accomplish," he continued, "and you might as easily write and preach the whirlwind into composure as seek to check him in the career marked out for him by an eternal and unswerving destiny."[32] Even Ridge's position on Native American rights was not that the various Indian nations retain their sovereignty, but that they be granted statehood and taken into the American fold.[33] Similarly, while Ridge dreamed of a "universal amalgamation of the races" that would completely redefine racial and national identity, he often imagined that this amalgamation would take place in a decidedly uneven manner. He spoke optimistically that "the races of mankind [are] progressing, slowly but surely, toward the grand ultimatum of a common destiny." But in describing what would be required to achieve that "common destiny" Ridge often privileged some races over others: "The time is rapidly approaching when the world will be inhabited by a few leading races," he wrote, "speaking each a language not hard to be understood by the other . . . while all other distinctive languages, peoples and governments will go down into the gulf of the past."[34]

Determining whether Whitman's desire to incorporate an indigenous identity into his public persona was a colonizing or a hybridizing gesture is difficult because of his ambivalence toward Native Americans. Likewise, the complex set of opinions that Ridge held on U.S. expansionism, Indian rights, and racial amalgamation makes him similarly difficult to pin down. Depending on the angle from which he is viewed, Ridge can come across as either an assimilationist, a subversive, or a tortured soul. A journalist who knew him during the 1850s and 1860s is one of the many people who have struggled to understand how Ridge could think of himself as an equal participant in both Western civilization and Cherokee tribal culture. After telling the story of how Ridge had "raised the war-whoop" on his father's and grandfather's opponents in the Cherokee Nation, this journalist recalled one of Ridge's most famous poems, an ode to California's Mount Shasta that compares the snow-covered mountain with the civilized rationality of Golden State politics. Pausing to wonder at a man he referred to alternately as a "brilliant journalist" and a "fiery Cherokee," he invited his readers to share with him the curious spectacle "of the refined editor of the Marysville Democrat, author of that most lofty poem addressed to Mount Shasta, raising the war whoop." Stymied by the enigma of a man who seemed to coexist in the disparate worlds of civilization and savagery, this journalist could do little more than marvel at "the gifted representative of the Cherokee nation."[35]

By the same token, just as the publishers of Ridge's one novel, *The Adventures of Joaquin Murieta* (1854), were marketing the author as "a Cherokee Indian, born in the woods . . . and familiar with all that is thrilling, fearful, and tragical [*sic*] in forest-life," Ridge distanced himself from the persona that was being attached to him as an Indian who had been "reared in the midst of the wildest scenery."[36] In the late 1850s Ridge criticized a fellow Native American writer whom he believed had uncritically embraced the stereotype of the "savage Indian." In an article titled "Hiawatha by a Live Indian," Ridge described how "George Copway, the celebrated Ojibway [*sic*] Chief, is on a tour throughout the Atlantic States, reading Hiawatha, in full costume. He meets with immense success."[37] In another article written later that same year, Ridge overtly expressed his contempt for Copway, betraying a subtle sense of disdain in his initial comment that Copway's "immense success" depended on the spectacle of a "Live Indian."[38] Rejecting the notion that a Native writer could only be successful by parading about in "full costume" (as Copway did) while still allowing his readers to think that he had been "reared in the midst of the wildest scenery" (as the preface to *Joaquin Murieta* has it), Ridge attempted to present himself as inhabiting a space between white "civilization" and Native American "savagery."

Ridge's effort to present himself as an intermediary between white and Native society—along with his sense of the difficulties involved in doing so—is on display in some of his earliest poems. One such poem is "The Stolen White Girl," a loosely autobiographical love poem written during his early twenties about a "wild half-breed" and the "beautiful bride" that "he stole . . . away from the land of the whites" (*Ridge* 72–73).[39] The poem takes quite a few liberties with the actual story of Ridge's marriage to a white woman from Arkansas, but in the process of creating a romanticized version of his interracial marriage, Ridge reveals some of his first thoughts on what would be required of someone attempting to live in both white and Native worlds. In the poem, Ridge depicts what was in reality a rather uneventful courtship as a quasi-captivity narrative featuring a "wild half-breed" who thunders across the prairies on horseback while apparently wearing little more than a "belt round his waist" and a "knife at his side." A representative passage from the poem reads,

> The prairies are broad, and the woodlands are wide
> And proud on his steed the wild half-breed may ride,
> With the belt round his waist and the knife at his side.
> And no white man may claim his beautiful bride.
> Though he stole her away from the land of the whites,
> Pursuit is in vain, for her bosom delights
> In the love that she bears the dark-eyed, the proud,
> Whose glance is like starlight beneath a night-cloud. (*Ridge* 72–73)

"The Stolen White Girl" gives the impression that the poem's "half-breed" character has been civilized by his white parentage to the point that he is willing to enter a legitimate union with a white woman—she is his "bride" and not merely his lover or even his victim—but that his Indian heritage had also kept him alluringly "wild." Unlike the title character of Whitman's novella *The Half-Breed*, whom Whitman described as a "strange and hideous creature," the "half-breed" of "The Stolen White Girl" is a dynamic figure who embodies all of the romance of the frontier.[40] In this respect, Ridge uses the poem to suggest the positive aspects of his biracial identity, of simultaneously coexisting in two disparate cultures. Being of mixed racial heritage, Ridge suggests, gives him the best of both worlds: It grants him the social approval of a legal marriage as well as the outlaw cachet of living on the fringes of respectability.

No accounts of Ridge's own marriage to a white woman indicate anything to the effect that his wife was stolen from her home or that her white family attempted to reclaim her from captivity. Indeed, not only had whites been intermarrying with Cherokees since the late eighteenth century, but the relative wealth and prominence of his family would have made a union with Ridge a not undesirable option for many frontier families.[41] On one level, then, the tension at the heart of the poem—namely, that the "girl of the 'pale face'" and "her Indian mate" are violating a social taboo by running off together—appears to be wholly a product of Ridge's imagination (*Ridge* 74). At the same time, however, Ridge would have no doubt heard the story of his Cherokee uncle and white aunt being burned in effigy on their wedding day by the local white townspeople, just as he would have known of the debates raging in the popular press over the perceived evils of intermarriage between whites and Cherokees.[42] He might even have been aware of how the marriage between his Cherokee father and white mother was covered in the press. The *Maryland Gazette*, for example, reported in 1824 that Ridge's maternal grandfather was "afflicted to distraction at the degradation of his daughter" on the day of her wedding, just as others among her relatives suffered "affliction, mortification, and disgrace" when they learned that a member of their family had "marr[ied] an Indian and [been] taken into the wilderness among savages."[43]

Amid the sensationalistic aspects of "The Stolen White Girl," then, Ridge shows a burgeoning awareness of how the image of an Indian "half-breed"—and, in particular, a "half-breed" who is entering another interracial relationship—could be used to suggest the pitfalls as well as the possibilities of cultural commerce between whites and Native Americans. On one hand, Ridge uses the interracial relationship in "The Stolen White Girl" to present a picturesque chiaroscuro that begs readers to set aside the politics of miscegenation in exchange for an aesthetic appreciation of the multiracial pair: "The contrast between them is pleasing and rare," Ridge writes, as "Her sweet eye of blue" complements his "majestic and darker" complexion (*Ridge* 73). But just as the poem would have an aesthetic sensibility trump the social taboo of interracial marriage, however, Ridge also includes a set of images that remind readers of the proscriptions against miscegenation. Specifically, "The Stolen White Girl" features a bower-of-bliss scene with the young lovers retreating "Far down in the depths of the forest" to escape the disapproving eyes of society (*Ridge* 73). In a similar poem, titled "A Cherokee Love Song," Ridge also depicts a Cherokee man inviting a white woman to "place thy small white hand in mine" as the two retreat to a secluded island where they can consummate their love in secret (*Ridge* 43–44). In both poems, an interracial couple has to find a space outside normative society—on an island, deep in the forest—in order to be together, suggesting that, contrary to what Ridge wrote about an impending "universal amalgamation of the races," American society was not yet ready to accept such relationships as the norm.

Another example of the young Ridge contemplating the challenges involved in brokering between whites and Natives is a curious poem that, rather than depicting a romanticized "half-breed" challenging the sexual taboos of interracial marriage, ambiguously identifies a narrator that could be either a white man trying to connect with Native culture or a Native American whose immersion in white society has distanced him from his indigenous heritage. In an untitled poem that begins with the line "Far in a lonely wood I wandered once," Ridge presents a narrator who happens upon what he believes to be an Indian burial ground while walking in the forest.[44] The narrator reports that "my footstep paused before / A mound of moss-grown earth" wherein lay buried the last remnants of a "noble race" that "many years agone . . . / Had roamed these forest-wilds." Indulging in a nostalgia for the previous inhabitants of the continent that would have resonated with most white writers of the antebellum period, Ridge's narrator avails himself of the aesthetic of the vanishing Indian, the same aesthetic that informed the belief of Longfellow and others that dead Indians would give birth to American culture. Indeed, in his address to the Indian buried at his feet the narrator of the poem notes that a thriving civilization has transformed the land that once belonged to the now-deceased Indian and his people:

> A thousand cities
> Stand, where once thy nation's wigwam stood,
> And numerous palaces of giant strength
> Are floating down the streams where long ago
> Thy bark was gliding. All is changed.

Grieving the passing of the Indians while celebrating the growth of the United States, Ridge's narrator would have found good company among the antebellum literary nationalists who were similarly eager to mourn over the beautiful corpse of a romantically dead Indian. At the same time, a number of oddities in the poem make ascribing Ridge's tone of mourning and nostalgia entirely to the aesthetics and politics of the vanishing Indian difficult.

First among these oddities is a passage wherein the narrator chooses to memorialize the dead Indian by vowing to protect his gravesite from cultivation by white farmers:

> My hand shall not disturb
> The slightest stem that takes its nutriment
> From thee. The white man's share may plough some other
> Mounds where Red men sleep, round which no mourner
> Stands in watch to guard the relics of a friend;
> But no rude step, and no rude hand shall e'en
> Despoil the beauty of this silent spot.

The narrator does not explicitly identify himself as a Native American in this passage, but in referring to "the white man" as a separate third party and calling the remains of the deceased Indian "the relics of a friend," the narrator presents the possibility that he, too, is an Indian. But the poem is ambiguous and evasive on this point and does not definitively identify the narrator. The fact that Ridge signed the poem with his Cherokee name, "Yellow Bird," does as much to solve the mystery of the narrator's identity as it does to raise further questions about a scene that, potentially, depicts an Indian mourning for another Indian.

Specifically, the narrator of the poem is wholly unaware of who or what is buried in the gravesite at his feet. When he comes across the burial mound he remarks,

> I wondered,
> For a while, what mortal here had found
> A resting place?

Not knowing who or what might be interred in the burial mound, the narrator invents a history for what he presumes to be the body of a deceased Indian: "Then thought I, 'This must be the grave of one / Who ranked among the warriors of the Wilderness!'" The narrator then imagines, in language evocative of the vanishing Indian, how the death of this "warrior of the Wilderness" would have played out:

> And when he saw his country
> Doomed, his tribe o'erthrown, and his strong arm
> Grown weak before his pale-faced foes; and when
> He knew the hour was come, in which his soul
> Must leave the form it once had moved to noble
> Deeds, and travel to the hunting-grounds, where erst
> His fathers went, he here had dug his grave,
> And singing wild his death-song to the wind,
> Sunk down and died!

If the narrator is indeed a Native American, his ignorance concerning the gravesite—as well as his eagerness to imagine a history for it—is puzzling. It suggests either that the Indian buried at his feet came from a tribe or nation that the narrator himself does not belong to, or that the narrator has lost touch with his indigenous heritage to the point that he can only know his ancestors through the Euro-American stereotype of the vanishing Indian. Ridge's own biography would support both of these possibilities. Ridge wrote the poem when he was living in Osage Prairie, Arkansas, after he and his family had left the Cherokee homelands in Georgia. Thus the burial ground identified in the poem could belong either to the Osage or to another tribe of Plains Indians. Similarly, by the time that Ridge wrote the poem in 1847, he had spent most of his youth in white-run schools where he had been taught by Christian missionaries to believe that "the Indian cannot be preserved in his savage state. . . . His manners, his customs, his superstitions and his language, must be exchanged for the pursuits of industry, the habits of the white man, and the faith of the christian."⁴⁵ Given the close parallels between the narrator of "Far in a lonely wood" and Ridge's own biography, the narrator's offer to protect the deceased Indian's grave from being plowed under by white farmers is a rather bold gesture, particularly in light of recent Cherokee history.

The official reason that white Americans gave for removing the Cherokees from Georgia was that they were failing to properly cultivate the land. The federal government argued that white farmers, armed with the techniques of modern agriculture, were in a position to "improve" the valuable land of the Cherokee Nation in ways that the Cherokees themselves had theretofore been unable to accomplish. This line of reasoning deeply wounded the Cherokees, who believed that they had been exemplary among Native Americans in their efforts to adopt white farming techniques.⁴⁶ Indeed, in his valiant (and albeit somewhat racist) opposition to Indian Removal, Ralph Waldo Emerson specifically cited the Cherokees as exemplars of the possibility that Native Americans could successfully "redeem their own race from the doom of eternal inferiority [by] borrow[ing] and domesticat[ing] in the tribe the arts and customs of the Caucasian race."⁴⁷ In having the narrator of "Far in a lonely wood" protect an Indian burial ground from white farmers, Ridge suggests that not only does he want to preserve a peaceful resting place for a "warrior of the Wilderness," but he also wants the land itself to remain free from the "improvements" of white society. Despite the narrator's demonstrated investment in Euro-American culture—as evidenced by his ignorance of the burial site and his reliance on the aesthetic of the vanishing Indian—his vow to preserve the land reveals a sincere desire to remain connected to his Native heritage.

Early poems such as "Far in a lonely wood" and "The Stolen White Girl" represent an apprenticeship phase of Ridge's poetic career as he attempted to think through the challenges involved in mediating between whites and Native Americans. The mature poetry of Ridge's later years, all of which he wrote in California, draws on a much more sophisticated set of images to depict the possibilities of cultural and racial amalgamation. In California, as the following section explains in greater detail, Ridge would be given a number of opportunities to read his poems in public and to assume the office of the bard. During the late 1850s and early 1860s, Ridge was often sought after to compose and recite poems for high-profile public celebrations, such as the Fourth of July, the anniversary of California's statehood, and the 1858

laying of the Atlantic telegraph cable.[48] The lyric voice of inward contempla-
tion that predominates in Ridge's early poetry is replaced in his later poetry
by the authoritative, even proscriptive, voice of the bard. One of the reasons
why Ridge was solicited to deliver his poems on commemorative occasions
was because, as an Anglo-Cherokee author and journalist who had presumably renounced savagery for civilization, he was viewed as an embodiment
of the success of the American mission, as Manifest Destiny in the flesh.
(Ridge's public persona as an Indian poet was well known, leading a fellow newspaper editor to refer to him—with more scorn than praise—as the
"poet laureate of the Cherokee Nation.")[49] Ridge often consented to play
the role of the civilized Indian for such public events, but there were also
occasions when he used the bully pulpit of commemorative poetry to challenge his audience's preconceived notions about Native Americans and to
encourage them to rethink the place of indigenous peoples within a collective national identity. The role that Ridge preferred to play on such occasions
was that of the harbinger of radical cultural amalgamation; the immigrant
culture of California provided him with the ideal setting for performing that
role.

WHEN RIDGE LEFT for California in 1850, he was hoping to make a quick
fortune and return as soon as possible to his family in the Cherokee Nation.
As did many of the would-be fortune-seekers who traveled to California in
the early 1850s, however, Ridge had limited success as a gold miner and was
soon forced to rethink his dream of easy money and a speedy return home.
Some of the Cherokees who had accompanied Ridge to California decided
to cut their losses and return to the Indian Territory as soon as they had
gathered the means to do so. After publishing his firsthand account of the
gold rush in the *New Orleans True Delta*, however, Ridge began to seriously
consider a literary career.[50] Ridge's career took off, and he was soon being
published alongside Bret Harte, Joaquin Miller, and Mark Twain in some
of the most respected periodicals of the region. By 1853 Ridge had found
enough success as both a journalist and a poet that he put his dream of returning to the Cherokee Nation on hold and sent for his wife and daughter
to join him.[51] In 1856 Ridge was hailed by a fellow newspaper editor as "one
of California's most popular writers," and according to one obituary published at the time of his death in 1866, "As a writer probably no man in California had a wider and better reputation than John R. Ridge."[52]

While Ridge is largely remembered today as the author of *The Adventures of Joaquin Murieta*, a sensational novel about Mexican American resistance to white settlers in gold-rush California, he was known to his contemporaries first and foremost as a poet. Horace Greeley, the influential editor of the *New York Tribune*, called him "quite a poet," and a newspaper editor in northern California referred to him as "a poet of no mean pretensions" whose works "may be justly classified among the brilliant gems of the more celebrated of American poets."[53] Much of the attention that Ridge received can be attributed to the fact that many of his published poems were local color pieces about the landscape of northern California and the people who inhabited it. (Not everyone in California, it bears noting, received Ridge so warmly: A group of newspaper editors in the 1860s challenged Ridge's citizenship and questioned his right to vote because of his Cherokee ancestry.)[54] Antebellum Californians were anxiously awaiting a body of literature that would aid in the development of a distinctive regional identity, and Ridge's work was a welcome contribution to this effort. Indeed, when Ridge was asked to reprint one of his California poems in a newspaper that he was editing during the late 1850s, he prefaced the poem with a self-effacing disclaimer that privileged local color over poetic craft, writing that the poem has "the merit of being Californian, if nothing else."[55] Even *Joaquin Murieta*, which he confessed to having written solely for the money—he wrote in a letter to his cousin, "I expected to have made a great deal of money off of my book, my life of Joaquin Murieta"—has been credited with creating one of California's earliest and most enduring myths.[56]

Around the same time that Ridge's literary career was taking off, an 1855 article in the *San Francisco Golden Era* said that California literature would form an integral, if not essential, part of a larger national literary tradition. Arguing that East Coast writers "have exhausted their fount of nationality" and that the "rising, meritorious poets" of California should take their place, the article makes one of the boldest claims for the importance of a California literary tradition: "American literature languishes in its old haunts," the article states. "Let the literati of California look to it."[57] That California writers could see themselves as the vanguards of a new regional tradition as well as a reinvigorated national tradition forms part of what historian Michael Kowaleski refers to as the belief that nineteenth-century California "embodied America's new sense of itself."[58] When the *Overland Monthly* boasted in 1883 that California was "America, only more so," it reinforced the idea that the Golden State had provided the United States with an image of itself that virtually no other state or region could match.[59]

In far-off New York City, Walt Whitman was similarly aware of the iconographic status that California had achieved as a representative national space, and this awareness worked its way into a number of his poems. Whitman treated California as he would any other state, that is, as merely one more piece to be aggregated into the larger national whole. In an 1860 poem, for example, he included California alongside a half-dozen or more other states that make up "America always!": "Always Florida's green peninsula! Always the priceless delta of Louisiana! Always the cotton-fields of Alabama and Texas! / Always California's golden hills and hollows—and the silver mountains of New Mexico!" (*LG60* 159). In a number of other poems, however, Whitman identified California not merely as one more region to be incorporated into his poetic union, but as an emblem of the entire nation.

In "A Promise to California," for example, Whitman calls out to a group of states from across the Great Plains and declares his intention to visit them as their representative bard. "Sojourning east a while longer, soon I travel to you," he promises. "For These States tend inland, and toward the Western sea—and I will also" (*LG60* 371). Even though the first published version of the poem begins with the lines "A promise and gift to California, / Also to the great Pastoral Plains, and for Oregon" (*LG60* 371), the original manuscript of the poem does not mention California at all but begins, instead, with a much longer list of states: "A promise to Indiana, Nebraska, Kansas, Iowa, Minnesota, and others."[60] In replacing this catalog of states with the single, iconic California, Whitman drew on a cultural shorthand for describing the vision the United States had of itself as a continental empire that was inevitably moving toward "the Western sea" (*LG60* 371). California, Whitman knew, represented the expansive nature of "These States" in a way that virtually no other state—or list of states—could. Even "A Promise to Oregon" would have lacked the iconographic stature that California had achieved by the middle of the century as evidence of the U.S. success in expanding from coast to coast. Similarly, in the 1873 poem "Song of the Redwood-Tree"—which he referred to as "A California song"—Whitman called California "the true America, heir of the past so grand, / To build a grander future," and said that the "Pacific half of America" was the nation's "better half" (*LG* 165, 169).[61]

Ridge also considered California to be, in many ways, a representative American space. In one newspaper article he described California as fulfilling the democratic charter of the national mission of the United States. "California still goes ahead, reversing the old order of things," he wrote. "The beggar of today is the prince of tomorrow, and the aristocracy of wealth smells of every trade and calling from a butcher to a perfumer." Ridge also wrote that, because the state's climate allowed farmers to grow the same crops as are "grown anywhere on the Atlantic side between Maine and the Gulf of Mexico," California could be considered a synecdoche of the entire nation.[62] Yet even though Ridge saw in California's agricultural climate a representative image of the larger nation, there were also ways that he viewed California as a space outside the nation itself. A half-century before Theodore Roosevelt would say "When I am in California, I am not west, I am west of the west," Ridge could talk of California as a separate and distinct region that was only connected to the United States by virtue of a common residence in North America.[63]

As a correspondent for the *New Orleans True Delta* in 1850, for example, Ridge described his arrival in California as if he were entering a separate nation entirely. When he wrote of crossing through "the desolate region which lies between 'the States' and this land of Pilgrim's hope," Ridge pictured California as geographically isolated from the United States. In the same correspondence, he described this gulf between the United States and California as more than just a factor of geography, writing that in California there was no sense of the national unity that Whitman celebrated in "A Promise to California." Instead, California was a place of isolated individuals who lacked the fraternal bonds that would connect them to one another and to a larger polity: "I was a stranger in a strange land," he wrote. "I knew no one, and looking at the multitude that thronged the streets, and passed each other without a friendly sign, or a look of recognition even, I began to think I was in a new world, where all were strangers."[64] There was something about the experience of being lost in a sea of strangers that Ridge found appropriate to his own circumstances: He used the phrase "stranger in a strange land" again in an autobiographical poem about a lonesome poet sitting on the banks of "Sacramento's stream" as he laments his "exile doom" (*Ridge* 51–52).

When Ridge left for California in 1850, he considered himself an exile of two nations. He felt that the Ridge family and those who had supported the removal treaty were exiles of the Cherokee Nation, or, as he put it, "a suffering minority, standing isolated from the general mass [of the Cherokee], marked for destruction, hated and oppressed." At the same time, Ridge considered himself and all other Native Americans, regardless of their politics, as exiles of the United States. He blamed the United States for the factionalism plaguing the Cherokee and for violations against Native Americans in general, writing that "it was the policy of the U.S. Gov., which removed not only [the Cherokee], but the numerous other Indian tribes, west of the Mississippi; and it was owing to the oppressions, practised [*sic*] upon them by the State of Georgia, and those who followed her example, that parties arose amongst [the Cherokee], producing confusion and bloodshed."[65] As a land of strangers and a home to exiles, California could be a place both geographically and ideologically outside the United States, a place not unlike "the depths of the forest" that Ridge depicted in "The Stolen White Girl," where "a wild half-breed" could go to imagine a different kind of life.

California's immigrant population similarly reinforced for Ridge that California was a different kind of American space, a pressure point on the national form as much as a representative of national ideals. With midcentury immigrants coming from such places as Chile, Hawaii, Australia, Malaysia, China, Italy, Ireland, and France, historian Kevin Starr has noted that "the Gold Rush, in its first phases at least, was an intrinsically international—rather than American—event."[66] Louisa Clappe, whose observations on the gold rush were widely circulated under the penname "Dame Shirley," commented that so many "wanderers from the whole broad earth" had descended on the Golden State that there were "as many foreigners as Americans" in California. She wrote of immigrants who had come to California from all over the world:

> From those palm-girdled isles of the Pacific, which Melville's gifted pen has consecrated to such beautiful romances; from Indies, blazing through the dim past with funeral pyres, upon whose perfumed pyres, ascended to God the chaste souls of her devoted wives; from the grand old woods of classic Greece, haunted by nymph and satyr, naiad and grace, grape-crowned Bacchus and beauty-zoned Venus; from the polished heart of artificial Europe, from the breezy backwoods of young America, from the tropical languor of Asian Savannah; from *every* spot.[67]

Not everyone, however, shared Dame Shirley's enthusiasm for this influx of immigrants. Many Americans worried that the increasingly international character of California was a threat to the health and well-being of the nation as a whole. One of Ridge's contemporaries contended that these immigrants, whom he characterized as "the dissolute and dishonest from all countries," had no love for the United States, but that they had come, in his words, "without feeling any sympathy for our institutions, and contributing nothing for the support of our government."[68] Dame Shirley herself commented on "a gradually increasing state of bad feelings exhibited by our countrymen . . . towards foreigners" that resulted in the state of California issuing a heavy taxation upon the profits of non-American miners. Indeed, in poem titled "A Fourth of July Welcome to the Miners" included in her letters, the only foreign miners who are warmly welcomed to the Golden State are those from France, England, and Spain.[69]

Ridge's initial vision of the international society that was emerging in California was similarly negative. In *The Adventures of Joaquin Murieta*, Ridge's depiction of white settlers hunting Mexican outlaws who, in turn, remorselessly massacred Chinese immigrants painted a picture of a violent and fractured society born of a confluence of disparate nations. In some of his later poems, however, Ridge began to imagine California as uniquely suited to receive the peoples of the world. Some of Ridge's poems display an awareness of how intimately California was connected to networks of travel and trade that extended far beyond national boundaries. He wrote in one poem that the state's economic reputation is known "the world around," and he praised California for welcoming "the nations [that] visit thee from far":

> And, while the messengers of commerce wait,
> She opens wide and free her Golden Gate.
> From far to her the nations laden come
> With silks and wares and precious stones and gum,
> And of the spoils she every land beguiles
> And ocean yields them from his thousand isles. (*Ridge* 92, 89)

As these lines indicate, Ridge could regard California as a node in a network of international trade. (He wrote in one newspaper article that "the products of [California's] mines add largely and constantly to the circulating wealth of the world.")[70] He could also consider it a point of convergence for people from across the globe, a place where races and nationalities could blend and mingle to an unprecedented degree. "California is indeed a singular country," he wrote in one newspaper article. "Or rather the people in it are strange compounds."[71]

The "strange compounds" of California provided Ridge with an image of what a "universal amalgamation of the races" would someday be, an image that he incorporated into some of his most successful late-career poems. All of Ridge's later poems were public verses that he was commissioned to write and recite at large public gatherings. Ridge often took the opportunity that these public settings provided him to get across a message of racial and international unity, as he did when, in a poem written to celebrate the laying of the Atlantic telegraph cable in 1858, he wrote of how "Nation unto Nation soon shall be / Together brought in knitted unity" (*Ridge* 21). The festivity surrounding the Atlantic telegraph lent itself to pronouncements of international unity, as did a number of the other occasions for which Ridge's services as a poet were in demand. For example, at an 1861 event where Ridge had been asked to present a poem, the speaker who shared the podium with him described California's population as consisting of "a greater variety of nationalities than were ever before united to form a State." The speaker at a similar event said, mere moments from when Ridge took the stage, that California had been "liberally sprinkled with elements from every quarter of the globe, presenting . . . a heterogeneous compound of opposites."[72] But there were also events where Ridge was the poet of the day that required him to actively work against the racist assumptions of his audience in order to present California as a space where disparate cultures, and in particular, the cultures of Euro-Americans and Native Americans, could harmonize into a unified whole.

For example, when Ridge was approached by the College of California to recite a poem celebrating the sixth anniversary of the fledgling institution, his belief that California was home to the "strange compounds" of people from across the world came into conflict with the narrative that the college presented of California as a representative example of the Anglo-Saxon civilization that had conquered North America. As the plenary speaker said within moments of Ridge reciting his poem, the College of California was considered to be "the vanguard of the army of pacific conquest, the conquest of mind over matter, of intellect over brute force, of liberal, of Christian culture, over practical heathenism."[73] Within this context, College of California administrators no doubt saw in Ridge—with his Cherokee origins and his Western education—a model for the "conquest" of the "intellect" over "heathenism" that paralleled the establishment of an institution of higher education on the westernmost edge of the U.S. frontier. Reminiscent of Whitman's statement that American poets are more convincing in their physical presence than they are in their written words—"I and mine do not convince by arguments, similes, rhymes, / We convince by our presence" (LG 126)—it appears that, in addition to being asked to write a poem, Ridge himself was put on display as a representative embodiment of the civilizing mission that the college was promoting. Just as a Cherokee could be civilized and educated, the regents of the college suggested by their choice of poet, so too has the wilderness of California been tamed by the forces of American culture.

Ridge might have been willing to participate in such a display to a certain degree, but there was also much about the situation that would have disturbed him. The regents of the college apparently wanted Ridge to write a poem emphasizing how the establishment of higher education in California connected America's West Coast to the rest of Western civilization, and Ridge was willing to comply: "Science," he wrote in the poem he composed for the occasion, has taken her dominion over the Golden State just "As was her wont when Greece was blest, / In Academic groves" (*Ridge* 83). The college's decidedly racialized perspective on California's educational achievements, however, required that Ridge play a role in the day's events that he had not necessarily agreed to. For example, when the plenary speaker told the same audience addressed by Yellow Bird the Indian poet that "an Anglo-Saxon origin lies at the root of American progress," and when he illustrated that point by recalling the period in early American history when "a race of aboriginal occupants of the soil, crafty and enduring, [had] to be driven back, in accordance with those relentless laws of progress under which the inferior race has to yield to the superior," Ridge must certainly have bristled.[74] Not only did this comment about Anglo-Saxon racial superiority contradict his belief that human progress tended toward "a universal amalgamation of the races," but Ridge himself had been co-opted into endorsing this position—as is often the case for a public bard—merely by virtue of his presence at the event.

Something similar happened in 1860 when Ridge was invited to compose and recite a poem for the Agricultural, Horticultural, and Mechanics' Society of the Northern District of California. A scarcity of extant documents makes it difficult to ascertain why the members of this agrarian society invited Ridge to present a poem at their annual fair, but the Cherokees' reputation as one of the few tribes to have embraced American farming practices (including African American slavery) might have led them to see in Ridge an apt representative of what they considered to be Native Americans' successful integration into white society.[75] Just as the regents of the College of California wanted an educated Indian poet to testify to the triumph of civilization over savagery, the Agricultural, Horticultural, and Mechanics' Society no doubt wanted an Anglo-Cherokee poet to confirm the widely held assumption that the benighted peoples of the Americas could be civilized if they adopted European farming practices. While there is no record of how Ridge responded to the racism of the College of California, in the poem he wrote for the Agricultural, Horticultural, and Mechanics' Society he explicitly confronted his audience's racist attitudes toward Native Americans, often by sternly rebuking them in ways that reminded his readers that, as their representative public bard, one of his responsibilities was to aid in identifying the cultural values that defined them as a community.

In this poem, an untitled work that begins with the invocation "Hail to the Plow!," Ridge asserts that the indigenous peoples of the Americas had learned more about the proper use of agriculture than had either Europeans or Euro-Americans, and therefore Native Americans were in a position to teach rather than be taught about how to create the prosperous agricultural society that would serve as the foundation of a successful nation. As Ridge assumes the duty of the bard in this poem, he is careful to remind his readers that the very facet of his identity that would threaten to disqualify him from serving as a representative national figure—specifically, that his lineage includes "a race of aboriginal occupants of the soil, crafty and enduring"—is actually what qualifies him to speak to and even for the nation. Additionally, in a spectacular moment at the end of "Hail to the Plow!" Ridge presents a vision of a millennial California society that has successfully blended its Native legacy with the dreams of its European settlers, thus creating a world civilization commensurate with his vision of a "universal amalgamation of the races." At this moment in the poem, Ridge conceives of California as more than merely a representative American space; he looks beyond the nation-state entirely as he praises California both for its distinctiveness as a local culture and for its network of connections with the larger globe.

"HAIL TO THE PLOW!" begins with an encomium of the farmer's plow as "the first, great civilizer" of humanity and then proceeds to say that it is "to Agriculture" that "we trace / The first faint gleam of progress in the race" (*Ridge* 114–15). By praising agriculture in the persona of Yellow Bird the Indian poet (and by doing so in heroic couplets), Ridge appears to confirm the Jeffersonian doctrine that Native Americans would be civilized if they were taught to farm.[76] The members of the Agricultural, Horticultural, and Mechanics' Society must have been surprised, then, when Ridge's poem claimed that Native Americans had made greater advances in the fields of agriculture and social engineering than Europeans and Euro-Americans ever did. Indians, the poem contends, are more likely to provide a pattern for making a better America than white Americans are to provide a pattern for making better Indians. Ridge's poem is based on the following assumption: While the civilizations of the Old World all descended into fruitless warfare after achieving a certain degree of competence with agriculture, the indigenous cultures of the Americas would have continued peacefully in unabated progress had it not been for European intervention in the New World. Admittedly, this approach requires Ridge to take a number of liberties with historical fact, but in so doing, he is able to suggest an alternative history of the Americas that foregrounds the accomplishments of Native peoples.

Ridge's poem depicts Old World civilizations as having gradually progressed through a series of increasingly complex stages of human development: An initial "hunter state" where humans lived off wild game was followed by "pastoral days" when humans cultivated pastures and tended flocks, after which arose a "third and better state" based on advances in agriculture, law, and commerce (*Ridge* 115–17). Ridge says that all of the Old World cultures that followed this pattern of development fell from this "third and better state" because "They loved the bannered pomp of conquering war" more than they cared about cultivating their fields (*Ridge* 118). As these societies descended into constant warfare, their attention to agriculture waned and their civilizations perished: "While fought the soldier at a despot's will, / The rusting plow within the field stood still" (*Ridge* 118). Ridge's narrative of the rise and fall of civilization would have been very familiar to his antebellum audience. In the five paintings of Thomas Cole's "The Course of Empire" (1834–36), for example, human society is depicted as progressing through "savage" and pastoral stages before becoming fully developed, after which it faces the inevitable destruction and desolation that accompany the decline of civilization.[77]

A number of late-eighteenth- and early-nineteenth-century white Americans believed that the only way for the United States to avoid this seemingly inevitable decline into warfare and devastation was to ensure that the nation remain in a permanent pastoral state. Believing that the increased complexity of a society would be the cause of its eventual downfall, adherents to this romantic agrarianism argued that a simple rural lifestyle was preferable to the hazards of further social growth. Ridge says that the Inca and Aztec civilizations of pre-Columbian America, however, contrary to the pattern that existed in the Old World, were able to achieve lasting peace without compromising social complexity. Citing these indigenous civilizations as precedent that another American culture can potentially develop into a complex and enduring society, Ridge says later in the poem that California stands poised to fulfill the potential for greatness that European settlers denied the indigenous inhabitants of the Americas when imperialism, and not internal warfare, led to their decline (*Ridge* 119). The implication is that California agrarians should be taught by, rather than presume to teach, Native Americans, and that the presumed liability of being a "savage" Indian in "civilized" America is actually a tremendous asset.

Trained not in the arts of war but in the "arts of peace," he says (idealistically, if not naively), the Inca and the Aztec flourished where the cultures of the Old World perished (*Ridge* 119). These indigenous peoples were able to do what the cultures of the Old World never could, namely, develop progressive, agriculture-based societies that never degenerated into self-destructive war. In contrast to the Jeffersonian vision of a simple agricultural republic, the Inca of Ridge's poem are said to have lived in a highly complex society wherein all citizens "labored duly for the State" according to a regimented social organization "which gave with equal hand / To each his due proportion of the land" (*Ridge* 121). In this workers' paradise, an intricate social organization oversaw an ideal society the likes of which, according to Ridge, never existed in the Eastern Hemisphere and did not yet exist in the United States: "No happier lot the poet's dream can find," he writes, neither in "all the Old World's civilization vast, / Nor yet our own, the grandest and the last" (*Ridge* 121). In identifying the Aztec and the Inca as the only civilizations in the history of the world to have lived peacefully with the full blessings of agriculture, Ridge makes indigenous American cultures the model for his audience's hope that California would escape the rise-and-fall pattern of the Old World.

In asserting the competency of America's indigenous civilizations and critiquing the idea that progress is the unique province of whites, Ridge directly addresses the racism of his audience in a series of pointed rhetorical questions designed to refute the assumption that Europeans brought civilization to a savage America:

> Was art, that built those cities vast, less art,
> Because of Aztec genius 'twas a part?
> Was patient toil, that led thro' channels deep,
> And aqueducts, and 'long the rocky steep,
> The streams a thousand fertile fields supplied,
> Less toil, because no white man's arm was tried?
> Were peace and plenty but the Spaniard's right?
> The Aztec *barbarous* because not *white*?
> (*Ridge* 119, emphasis in original)

The italicization of the terms "barbarous" and "white" in the printed version of the poem is the only remaining trace of the verbal invective that Ridge leveled against the members of the Agricultural, Horticultural, and Mechanics' Society of the Northern District of California. It is worth pausing here to consider how these lines would have been received by Ridge's audience. Antebellum public speaking, according to James Perrin Warren, created a space where citizens could feel that they were part of "a society formed by a unison of minds, hearts, and souls."[78] Just as an audience could be held in collective rapture by the words of a powerful poet or orator, so, too, could an otherwise fractured nation feel unified, if only for a moment, when listening together in public. More often than not, Ridge was willing to use his poetry to build community consensus on such occasions, as he did in the public poems he wrote for the Fourth of July and the anniversary of California's statehood. As a public poet expected to reinforce community values rather than antagonize his audience, however, Ridge was momentarily remiss in his duties when he read the section of "Hail to the Plow!" that explicitly rejected the notion that whites were superior to the indigenous peoples of the Americas.

Nevertheless, there are ways in which even this overt critique of his audience's racism could be seen within the larger context of Ridge's project to serve as a mediator between whites and Natives. In focusing his defense of Native American accomplishments on the fallen cultures of Central and South America rather than on the Native North American tribes facing extinction in the nineteenth century, Ridge appealed to a romantic connection with the Aztec and the Inca that white Americans did not feel for other indigenous peoples.[79] Antebellum literary tastemaker Rufus Griswold, for example, wrote in the introduction to his influential *Poets and Poetry of America* (1842) that a great American poem could be written about the vanished civilizations of the Southern Hemisphere: "A true creator," he wrote, "with a genius great as John Milton's, might invent an epic equal to 'Paradise Lost', by restoring Palenque and Copan to their meridian splendour."[80] In addition, influential ethnological texts such as William Robertson's *History of America* (1777) deemed the Aztec and the Inca to be the only Native American civilizations that did not merit the distinction of "savage."[81] By using the Aztec and the Inca as his representatives of Native American achievements, Ridge was able to critique the racist beliefs his audience held about Indians without entirely alienating himself from many of their preconceived notions.

Another example of Ridge's desire to confront racism while still aligning himself with white Americans occurs earlier in the poem when he describes the "hunter state" of early human society and, predicting a sneer of superiority from his white audience, writes, "Smile not—such were our own rude ancestry!" (*Ridge* 116). It is not difficult to extrapolate from Ridge's stern language an implied connection between the primitivism of the "hunter state" and the indigenous peoples currently living in what white Americans considered to be a similarly primitive manner. In this direct confrontation of his white audience's sense of superiority over indigenous peoples, Ridge reveals how acutely aware he was of his position as a mixed-race bard expected to broker between disparate cultures. When he reprimands his white audience, he does so by saying that the "hunter state" is a remnant of "*our* own rude ancestry," implying that he, too, has moved beyond this primitive condition. (In *Joaquin Murieta* there is a similar moment when Ridge the author steps from behind the voice of the narrator to comment on a particularly horrific scene of violence, saying, "Bah! It is a sight that I never like to see, although I have been civilized for a good many years.")[82]

It is tempting to accuse Ridge of exploiting the posture of the white aboriginal by assuming the moral authority of the Indian while still holding on to the privilege of his whiteness. There is, to be sure, a mercenary quality in Ridge's desire to have it both ways. At the same time, in wanting to find a common ground between whites and Natives, Ridge puts himself in a position to present the image of an emerging American culture that partakes equally of Euro-American and Native American influences. As he concludes the poem, he presents an image of California as an island paradise that unites European myths about the fabulous islands of the New World with Native American island legends. He writes in an apostrophe to the Golden State,

> Oh Land of Beauty! why the theme prolong?
> Like that delicious isle of Indian song,
> Which, o'er the waters gliding, fled pursuit,
> Thou hast all gems, all wealth, all golden fruit,
> And, far more blest than Indian dreamers were,
> We lose thee not, a vision of the air! (*Ridge* 127)

That the sources of Ridge's image of a "delicious isle of Indian song" are both European and Native American is consistent with his larger effort to amalgamate white and Native traditions. The island of California is a consummate hybrid space: It is both the "El Dorado dream" of European explorers and the "delicious isle of Indian song" that Native American bards from numerous traditions had sung about for years (*Ridge* 123). Myths about islands of great wealth and beauty appear in many different Native American traditions. In the version of the Cherokee creation story that Ridge would have been most familiar with, the earth is depicted as an island tethered to the heavens by cords that will break at the end of the world, leaving Cherokee society to vanish like "a vision of the air." In another version, the Cherokee are said to have come to the mainland of North America after being forced by some geological cataclysm from their original island home.[83]

Just as important as Native American legends are to this image of California as an elusive—though now captured—island paradise are European myths about the island of California. Beginning in the sixteenth century and continuing until as late as the eighteenth century, European explorers to the New World frequently referred to California as an island. Explorers who wrote about island paradises that were always just beyond their reach began to attach their hopes and dreams to the island of California, a place that, according to Dora Beale Polk, embodied "the single, simple, common ideal of a dream island" impelling European explorers in the New World.[84] California received its name from one such account: Garci Rodríguez de Montalvo's sixteenth-century Spanish epic *Las Sergas de Esplandián*, a fanciful tale of exploration in the New World involving a gold-filled island populated by a group of Amazonians led by California's namesake, a warrior woman named Calafía. In addition to the island of Calafía, *Esplandián* also tells of a mysterious magician who inhabits an island that he can make disappear at will, which could be the basis of Ridge's "isle of Indian song" that "fled pursuit."[85] If Ridge were aware of *Esplandián*, he might have attributed Montalvo's tale to an indigenous legend, making the Spanish epic into an "Indian song."

Whether or not he had read *Esplandián*, Ridge was aware that California was believed to have been an island. A brief article titled "The Island of California" that he ran in the *Marysville Weekly California Express* two years before he wrote "Hail to the Plow!" says the following:

> We lately came across an old book, says an exchange, entitled "Geography Anatomyzed," published in London in 1728. . . . Feeling a slight curiosity to see how our State figured in the geographies of olden time, we searched the book and found the following: "California. This island was formerly esteemed a Peninsular, but now found to be entirely surrounded with Water. . . . The inland parts thereof were afterwards searched into, but being found to be only a dry, barren, cold country, Europeans were discouraged from sending Colonies to the the [*sic*] same, so that it still remains in the Hands of the Natives; and there being nothing remarkable either in them or in it."[86]

Coming as it does from the eighteenth century, this British text deflates the myth of a paradisiacal California while still retaining the island geography. And while this text saw "nothing remarkable" in either California or its indigenous inhabitants, Ridge believed that California was a space that could unite the aspirations of European explorers with the frustrated potential of the indigenous peoples of the Americas.

It should be noted here that by making the Aztec and the Inca the symbolic ancestors of nineteenth-century California, Ridge elides the existence of Native Californians who have a more direct claim to the aboriginal heritage of the state than do the Inca, the Aztec, or even a well-meaning Cherokee poet. Ridge's inability to include Native Californians in the vision of a millennial California that he records in "Hail to the Plow!" stems from a hierarchical ranking of Native peoples that he adhered to throughout his life. Ridge once questioned whether the Cherokee and the indigenous peoples of California even "belong at all to the same stock," since in his opinion, the Cherokee had "abandoned their savage customs and habits for the condition of civilized life" while Native Californians remained "a poor, humble, degraded, and cowardly race."[87] (Whitman similarly wrote, "Are not the Rocky

Mountain and California aborigines quite as bestial a type of humanity as any?" [*NUPM* 4:1976].) Despite the negative comments he made about California's Native population, Ridge was also an outspoken advocate against atrocities such as murder, rape, and slavery that "white savages" inflicted upon Native Californians, and he used the bully pulpit of the press to question why "these poor and imbecile people cannot better be protected than they are by the General Government." In response to the suggestion that Native Californians be placed on reservations, removed from the state, or even exterminated, Ridge proposed interracial marriage as a more humane alternative.[88]

While Native Californians are noticeably absent from "Hail to the Plow!," the same faith in amalgamation that Ridge thought would resolve the conflict with California Indians lies at the heart of his poem. In a lengthy digression that precedes the concluding image of the island of California (itself an amalgam of white and Native myths), Ridge draws an analogy between the amalgamation of plant species in agricultural practice and the potential for human amalgamation. Agricultural hybridity, as this digression suggests, provides Ridge with a language for conceptualizing hybridity of other kinds:

> For while the genius of the plow and spade
> Improvement still on willing nature made —
> The cultured flower expanding into size
> Unknown before and tinct with richer dyes,
> New forms assuming from the fecund dust
> Not left to chance and to the zephyr's trust,
> But, like with unlike pollen mixed, till strange
> Creations bloomed and wonder marked the change;
> The human soul, the Man, expanded too,
> And found in realms of thought the strange and new. (*Ridge* 122)

Rather than praise agriculture for making "Improvement . . . on willing nature," Ridge writes that "the genius of the plow" is the ability to mix "like with unlike" and create "New forms" that had never before existed. "Improvement" was a loaded concept in the debates that surrounded Indian Removal because it suggested that land belongs to whoever would appropriately cultivate it (i.e., white American settlers) regardless of who currently inhabited it (i.e., Native Americans).[89] Because the idea of "Improvement" potentially eliminates Native populations from consideration whereas amalgamation does not, the hero of Ridge's poem is not the farmer who tills the field but the botanist who creates hybrid plants.

Ridge minimizes the importance of "improving" the land through farming and suggests instead that the true wonder of agriculture is its ability to produce "strange / Creations" by combining familiar strains in unfamiliar ways. The agricultural "wonder" of combining "like with unlike" finds an obvious parallel in Ridge's belief that a "universal amalgamation of the races" was not only imminent but essential. In the same way that agricultural hybridity transforms and reshapes the natural world (e.g., "The cultured flower expanding into size / Unknown before and tinct with richer dyes"), there are accompanying transformations experienced by "The human soul, the Man" as human beings become "strange and new" through a comparable mixing of different strains. As a mixed-race Indian living among the "strange compounds" of California, Ridge considered people like himself and places like California to have undergone a hybridization analogous to that achieved through the transformative powers of agriculture.

Accordingly, "Hail to the Plow!" presents California's landscape as a hybridization of various world climates. Even though he calls California the fulfillment of "the El Dorado dream," Ridge says that what makes the state so spectacular is not that its mines hold the wealth of a fabled El Dorado ("California's glory is not told," he writes, "By wealth of resource like to this—her gold"), but that its landscape has been made to replicate every climate from across the globe. California, he says, has a "Prolific soil" that "within itself it yields / Of every clime the fruits." He initially attempts to construct a catalog of the world geographies that have been replicated in California's "clime / Of wonder"—including "the hills of Greece," the "woods that skirt the Arabian sea," and "Italia's purpled vales"—but, realizing that such an exercise would prove exhausting, is satisfied to say that California duplicates the geography of "All climes and lands" (*Ridge* 123–25). While the "third and better state" of civilization in the Old World was marked by international commerce (he writes that during this era "What lacked one clime another clime possest"), Ridge suggests that California has achieved an unprecedented fourth stage of civilization that lacks nothing but is, in effect, a self-contained world in miniature (*Ridge* 117).

The program for agricultural and social engineering that Ridge lays out in "Hail to the Plow!" differs from that of the antebellum agrarianists who wanted to freeze the United States in a pastoral state. Indeed, Ridge's desire to create a self-contained global society within the metaphorical geography of the island of California is even more ambitious than anything accomplished by the Inca and Aztec civilizations he claims as his predecessors. It is as if Ridge wants California's landscape to reflect the homelands of the immigrants who have given rise to the "strange compounds" of the state's international population. Ridge wrote in the *San Francisco Herald*, "There is nothing to deter the immigrant from our shores; but, on the contrary, everything to invite and encourage him to make his home [here]."[90] California, Ridge suggests in "Hail to the Plow!," can welcome immigrants from across the globe because its geography already duplicates the lands of their origin. Glenna Matthews has argued that "northern California was 'born cosmopolitan' to an unprecedented extent."[91] Ridge hoped to ease these birth pains with a poem describing the global landscape that mirrored the state's increasingly international inhabitants. Ridge often expressed a fierce devotion to his adopted home in California. (He was even accused by fellow newspaper editors of urging Californians to secede from the Union.)[92] Ridge's devotion to the Golden State as a local culture existing separately and distinctly from the larger nation is intimately connected to his image of California as a node in a network of global forces. At once local and global, the California of Ridge's imagination offered him a compelling alternative to the American nation.

One of the reasons why California—or at least the idealized California of such poems as "Hail to the Plow!"—offered Ridge such comfort is because it appeared to have rejected the conclusion that Native Americans were destined to be eliminated either through physical violence or cultural assimilation. As one New York newspaper put it in 1844, "There are but three hundred thousand Indians in our territories, and they are rapidly diminishing by the two causes of annihilation and intermixture. The Caucasian flood must soon overwhelm them all."[93] That Ridge found such solace in California is ironic, given that the Golden State should have, by rights, been the place where the threats of "annihilation and intermixture" were at their greatest: In the imagery of the period, the westernmost edge of the frontier was where Indians were supposed to vanish into oblivion. (Indeed, an 1830 poem titled "The Hymn of the Cherokee Indian," by a white poet, published on the eve of the Cherokee Trail of Tears, grimly commands, "Indian people, flee / To the farthest western sea.")[94] Just as Whitman would consider that being "one of the roughs" was a qualification to claim the title of American bard rather than an insult to his social standing, Ridge would turn the liability of being a "half-breed" Indian on the western frontier into the vantage point from which he could lead both the nation and the world into a promising future.

If "Song of the Redwood-Tree" is any indication, Whitman would not have been easily convinced that Native Americans had a place in California's future, let alone that of the nation or the world. "Song of the Redwood-Tree" is, on the surface, an elegy to the trees that were cleared from the California landscape to make room for "the New arriving" white settlers (*LG* 168). Throughout the poem, as a number of scholars have recently shown, Whitman draws an implicit comparison between redwood trees and Native Americans, both of whom, the poem suggests, have no place in the California of the future.[95] In the poem, Whitman purports to hear the songs of "a mighty dying tree in the redwood forest dense," songs that he reproduces (in italicized text) as if they were the final words of a dying Indian. "*Farewell my brethren,*" laments the tree in language that echoes Hiawatha's valedictory address. "*Farewell O earth and sky, farewell ye neighboring waters, | My time has ended, my term has come*" (*LG* 165–66). Because Whitman never personally witnessed the deforestation of the Pacific Coast, he drew upon cultural material that he was more familiar with—namely, the demise of Native Americans—to provide a voice for what he considered to be the inevitable passing of the old that was necessary to make way for the new. Like the noble Indians of popular literature who dutifully acknowledge that a new era had dawned on the American continent, the redwood trees in Whitman's poem similarly admit that they must yield to the encroachment of white settlers: "*We welcome what we wrought for through the past, | And leave the field for them*" (*LG* 166). The trees in Whitman's poem concede that this "*superber race*" will establish an "*empire new*" once the state's former inhabitants have been completely eliminated (*LG* 167).

Similar to what Ridge proposes in "Hail to the Plow!" the "new empire" that Whitman says will arise in California is depicted in "Song of the Redwood-Tree" as a hub of global exchange: "Ships coming in from the whole round world, and going out to the whole world, / To India and China and Australia and the thousand island paradises of the Pacific" (*LG* 168). But whereas Ridge contends in "Hail to the Plow!" that an amalgamation of white and Native elements is a necessary prerequisite to California's becoming a model for both the nation and the world, in "Song of the Redwood-Tree," California can only become a "true America" with links to the larger world

once its indigenous inhabitants recede before the "swarming and busy race
. . . taking possession" of the land (*LG* 168). Despite the radically different
conclusions that they come to, both poems share an interest in putting California's status as a representative national space in tension with a smaller-
than-national indigenous presence and a larger-than-national population of
immigrants and merchants. Whitman's poem ultimately resolves this tension
by eliminating Native Americans from the equation altogether, resulting in
a largely nationalistic celebration of how California has confirmed the U.S.
position on the world stage. In "Hail to the Plow!" however, Ridge sought to
create an image of California as a space that preserved this tension between
the indigenous past and an emerging international future.

Even though Whitman assents to the inevitable extermination of indigenous peoples in "Song of the Redwood-Tree," this poem is neither his
final nor his only thought on the matter. There are moments when Whitman suggests, as does Ridge in "Hail to the Plow!," that by embracing its
Native populations, the United States will be transformed into something
closer to a multinational gathering of peoples than to an Anglo-Saxon ethnic
state. In 1883, Whitman explicitly linked the continuing presence of Native
Americans with the prospect that U.S. national identity would be radically
altered by what he referred to as "the contributions of foreign lands." Saying
that it is "a very great mistake" to "abandon ourselves to the notion that our
United States have been fashion'd from the British Islands only, and essentially form a second England only," Whitman spoke idealistically of a "composite American identity of the future" reminiscent of Ridge's belief that the
blending of Europeans and Native Americans was an overture to the time
when "the present identity of nations and tribes will some day be entirely
lost."[96] Whitman wrote,

> As to our aboriginal or Indian population—the Aztec in the South, and
> many a tribe in the North and West—I know it seems to be agreed that
> they must gradually dwindle as time rolls on, and in a few generations
> more leave only a reminiscence, a blank. But I am not at all clear about
> that. As America, from its many far-back sources and current supplies,
> develops, adapts, entwines, faithfully identifies its own—are we to see it
> cheerfully accepting and using all the contributions of foreign lands from
> the whole outside globe—and then rejecting the only one distinctively its
> own—the autochthonic ones?[97]

Whitman foresaw a time when immigration would create conditions that would require the nation to "entwine" its present population with people from the "whole outside globe," and he connected that vision of a "composite" (or "amalgamated," as Ridge would have it) national identity with the persistence of "our aboriginal or Indian population." Just as Ridge did, Whitman could imagine that Native Americans would be an essential part of a heterogeneous "race of races"—as he referred to the increasingly diverse immigrant population of the United States in the 1855 preface to *Leaves of Grass*—that would someday revolutionize U.S. national identity (*LG55* xi).

Also similar to Ridge's depiction of California as an island whose blending of white and Native elements heralded a new internationalism was Whitman's treatment of Manhattan as a global city that had remained faithful to its indigenous heritage. In "Mannahatta," one of his many love poems to New York City, Whitman searches for a gift to give his city appropriate to its character as a bustling metropolis of workers and immigrants: "I was asking for something specific and perfect for my city," he muses. "Whereupon, lo! upsprang the aboriginal name" (*LG* 360). Whitman wrote elsewhere of his dislike for the name "New York," arguing that it should be abandoned because it recalled the European past, whereas "Mannahatta," the name by which the island of Manhattan had been known to its indigenous inhabitants, was "a fitter name" for his city (*NUPM* 1:407–8, 3:1010). As was Ridge's California, Whitman's Manhattan was a space where the fusion of white and Native influences opened the city to the larger world. In "Mannahatta" Whitman writes of "Immigrants arriving, fifteen or twenty thousand in a week," just as in a similar poem he calls Manhattan a "City of the world! (for all races are here, / All the lands of the earth make contributions here)" (*LG* 361, 231). Island geographies, whether real or imagined, allowed both poets to imagine a place where national identity would be diffused first by a union of white and Native elements and then by the world at large. On opposite sides of the continent and from opposite sides of the color line, both poets imagined an alternative path for their nation in an era when it was a foregone conclusion that indigenous peoples would vanish from the earth and the United States would single-handedly dominate the globe.

Ridge would never live to see the day when racial and cultural amalgamation transformed the face of both the nation and the world. This was not, unfortunately, the only frustrated ambition of his life. He would never live to see honor returned to his family name among the Cherokee—some would argue that this, too, has yet to happen—nor would he ever even set foot in the Cherokee Nation. Within a year of returning to California from his failed 1866 trip to the Bureau of Indian Affairs in Washington, D.C., Ridge took ill and died, believing that he had left behind an incomplete, if not entirely thwarted, legacy. In 1933, however, the Native Sons of the Golden West replaced Ridge's nineteenth-century tombstone with one that honored him with the title of "California Poet."[98] It is beyond ironic that the Native Sons of the Golden West—a nativist group comprised of the descendants of white pioneers—would choose to so recognize Ridge, given their belief that "California was given by God to white people, and with God's strength we want to keep it as He gave it to us."[99] Nevertheless, it is an irony that Ridge may have taken as further proof that he was helping to usher in the inevitable amalgamation of races and cultures that would redefine both the nation and the world.

chapter FOUR

AN AMERICAN, ONE OF THE ROUGHS, A KOSMOS

Five years ago a new poet appeared, styling himself the representative of
America, the mouthpiece of free institutions, the personification of all that
men had waited for. . . . He regards himself as the fertilizing agent of American
Poetry; perhaps all the better for fertilizing purposes that the rains and snows of
a rough life have caused it to fester in a premature and unwholesome decay.

— *"The New Poets,"* New York Times, *19 May 1860*

In the early fall of 1855, Walt Whitman wrote and published three anonymous reviews of the first edition of *Leaves of Grass*, a bold and audacious move intended not only to generate publicity for his book but also to instruct critics and potential readers on how they were to receive it. By far the boldest and most audacious moment in all three of these reviews occurs when Whitman refers to himself as "the true American poet," proclaiming that he is "an American bard at last!"[1] For years scholars have commented on how Whitman used this review to introduce himself as the poet that antebellum literary nationalists had anxiously been awaiting: the poet who spoke to and for the nation as its representative bard. Curiously absent from this scholarly commentary, however, is a consideration of *how*, precisely, Whitman fulfilled the duties of the American bard in the years immediately following his self-appointment to that role. The prevailing assumption has been that, prior to the Civil War, Whitman viewed the office of national bard rather narrowly, believing that his sole responsibility was to write lyric poems about the distinctive features of the United States.

It would take the Civil War and the death of Abraham Lincoln, scholars have held, for Whitman to expand his bardic duties to include commemorative poems about events of national importance in addition to lyric poems about national traits and characteristics. As such, it has been widely assumed that not until the crisis of the Union did Whitman step up to write the kind of commemorative verses that have

Walt Whitman

historically been the duty of poets laureate and national bards to compose. But there is more to the story of Whitman's career as an American bard than has been acknowledged by this narrative of a ten-year gap between the moment in 1855 when Whitman christened himself the representative poet of the United States and the 1865 publication of *Drum-Taps*, his volume of poems about the Civil War. The missing chapter in the story of Whitman's antebellum claim to the title of national bard centers around the publication of "A Broadway Pageant," a poem Whitman wrote in the summer of 1860 to commemorate the visit of a delegation of Japanese ambassadors who had come to the United States to ratify Townsend Harris's 1854 treaty granting America exclusive trading rights with Japan.

Published less than a year before the outbreak of the Civil War, "A Broadway Pageant" has been lost in the shuffle between the release of the third edition of *Leaves of Grass* in May 1860 and Whitman's decision to dedicate both his poetry and his personal life to mending the wounds of the war. The visit of the Japanese ambassadors itself has been overshadowed by the Civil War as a major moment in nineteenth-century U.S. history, even though most newspapers at the time agreed with the assessment of the *New York Illustrated News* that the U.S. diplomatic coup over Europe in securing trade rights with the isolationist government of Japan was a "great national event," and that the Japanese ambassadors were themselves, as Whitman later put it, "celebrities of the time."[2] Despite this conspicuous neglect, both the text of "A Broadway Pageant" and the context surrounding its publication tell a rich and involved story about how Whitman defined the office of American bard at a crucial moment of his career. While Donald Pease has commented that "Whitman's poetry seems to take place against the backdrop of a national celebration," "A Broadway Pageant" is the only poem Whitman wrote after publishing the 1855 *Leaves of Grass* and before adopting the post–Civil War persona of America's "Good Gray Poet" that *literally* takes place amid a national celebration—the only antebellum poem, that is, in which Whitman takes upon himself the duty of the bard to publicly commemorate an event of national importance.[3]

The first section of this chapter situates "A Broadway Pageant" within Whitman's antebellum career, focusing in particular on how he developed the persona of the national outsider-*cum*-national bard. On a number of occasions between 1855 and 1860, Whitman very publicly reminded readers of his association with New York City's working-class "roughs," implying that, contrary to what one might think, his connection to this oft-maligned population made him more rather than less likely to serve as the nation's representative poetic voice. Scholars have commented on Whitman's movement between the margin and the center of national life as both American poet and "one of the roughs," but the spatial metaphors of margin and center do not fully account for how he assumed the role of bard either in "A Broadway Pageant" or in other antebellum poems (such as *Calamus*) where he adopts a similar posture.[4] As explained in previous chapters, James M. Whitfield, Eliza R. Snow, and John Rollin Ridge similarly leveraged their social liabilities into assets as they each claimed to be the nation's poetic representative. But in attempting to speak for the nation from the margins of national culture, these poets came to experience their relationship with the United States less as an outsider's longing for acceptance and more as a complex set of affiliations that put national allegiance into tension with deeply felt loyalties both to subcultures within the United States and to communities beyond national borders. The same dynamic, it turns out, is true of the antebellum Whitman.

The argument of the second section of this chapter is that when Whitman decided to commemorate the 16 June 1860 parade for the Japanese embassy in his first official act as an American bard, he chose a moment that offered him as great an opportunity to celebrate his affinity for working-class New Yorkers and his faith in global unity as it did his nationalist fervor. Whitman's antebellum career has often been characterized as part of what Malcolm Cowley calls the "bumptious American nationalism" that dominated the literary discourse of the period.[5] But the same poet who so aggressively presented himself as a literary nationalist was also deeply invested in writing poetry for a smaller-than-national community of urban laborers and a larger-than-national community of people from across the globe. Whitman said that one of his primary goals with *Leaves of Grass* was to create a space for working Americans in national life and literature: "I resolved at the start to diagnose, recognize, state, the case of the mechanics, laborers, artisans, of America—to get into the stream with them—to give them a voice in literature" (*WWC* 2:142–43). By the same token, he insisted that his poetry had an explicitly cosmopolitan design: "I had more than my own native land in view when I was composing Leaves of Grass," he wrote. "I wished to take the first step toward calling into existence a cycle of international poems."[6] This network of loyalties to a local working-class culture, the global community, and the nation itself is present throughout *Leaves of Grass*, but it is most keenly articulated in "A Broadway Pageant," due, in no small part, to its being Whitman's first attempt since 1855 to define the office of national bard.

Whatever desire Whitman may have had to praise the United States for its diplomatic savvy in "A Broadway Pageant" was matched, if not exceeded, by his eagerness to record the spectacle of New York City's working-class population filling the streets of Manhattan to greet a group of people bearing tidings from the rest of the world. This is not to say that Whitman put his nationalism on hold in "A Broadway Pageant"—indeed, there are portions of the poem that are as nationalistic as anything he ever wrote—but, rather, that as he lauded U.S. diplomatic success, he did so as someone who felt his connection to a mass of working-class New Yorkers as strongly as he felt his communion with the world. In "A Broadway Pageant," Whitman found a venue for articulating his antebellum identity as "Walt Whitman, an American, one of the roughs, a kosmos," an identity, that is, that tempered his national loyalties as "an American" with his working-class affiliations as "one of the roughs" and his cosmopolitan desire to transcend national boundaries as "a kosmos" (*LG55* 29). Wai Chee Dimock has recently made a case for situating American literature within a "layered ontology of the world, sustaining an associative network sometimes above the nation and sometimes below it."[7] The template that Whitfield, Snow, and Ridge present for rereading Whitman's career as a national bard does precisely this: It points to those moments where his otherwise nationalist poetry was fraught with global and local tensions from both "above the nation and . . . below it." The final section of this chapter reflects on the implications of these poets' "layered ontology of the world," not only for Whitman studies, but for the enduring legacy of multiculturalism, whose encouragement to reexamine canonical figures like Whitman in light of poets from the margins of society must adopt a more sophisticated sense of the "associative network[s]" shaping U.S. literary culture than the metaphors of margin and center often allow.

THE STORY OF WHITMAN's antebellum career has been told many times. The highlight reel goes something like the following: After a hit-and-miss career as a journalist, the thirty-six-year-old author of a handful of poems and short stories self-publishes a volume of poetry that (in his mind) will revolutionize American literature and launch him to international stardom. The first edition of *Leaves of Grass* does not sell very well, but it gets a fair amount of attention in both the American and the British presses, and none other than Ralph Waldo Emerson sends Whitman a personal letter expressing his admiration for the book. Emboldened by this praise, Whitman publishes a second, more expanded edition of *Leaves of Grass* in 1856, but the book is, again, a commercial flop. Whitman largely retreats from the public eye for the next four years, and in his time off from writing new poems and revising the old ones he can be found licking his wounds at Pfaff's bar in lower Manhattan, surrounded by friends and lovers. In late 1859 and into 1860, a core group of Whitman's supporters rally around him to get a third edition of his book into print and to raise his visibility in the popular press. It works. The 1860 *Leaves of Grass* is a legitimate success, both commercially and critically. Whitman is vindicated, ready to take on the literary world anew. Then fighting breaks out at Fort Sumter in 1861, and everything changes.[8]

It is a commonplace of American cultural history to say that the Civil War changed the entire landscape of literary production in the United States, but in Whitman's case there is as much truth to this statement as hyperbole. Following the Civil War, Whitman completely overhauled his public persona as a working-class outsider and began depicting himself as the nation's grandfatherly "Good Gray Poet." Beginning with the 1867 edition of *Leaves of Grass*, Whitman removed the phrase "one of the roughs" from the line in "Song of Myself" where, in every antebellum version of the poem, he identifies himself as "Walt Whitman, an American, one of the roughs, a kosmos."[9] Between 1855 and 1860, however, Whitman went to great lengths to present an image of himself as one of the "toughs" and "rowdies" from the lower strata of New York society. The frontispiece of the first edition of *Leaves of Grass*, for example, included an engraving of Whitman dressed as a city laborer, staring down his readers with what one reviewer referred to as "a dammee-sir air" and bearing an appearance that another reviewer noted "would answer equally well . . . as the true likeness of half a dozen celebrated criminals." "Walt Whitman," this latter review continues, "is evidently the 'representative-man' of the 'roughs.'"[10] Whitman, who referred to this frontispiece image as "the street figure" (*WWC* 2:412), believed that an urban ne'er-do-well from the streets of New York was particularly suited to be America's representative bard, despite the fact that many of his contemporaries shared the opinion of a nineteenth-century New York City guidebook that "the metropolitan rough is . . . a social hyena, a rational jackal, utterly devoid of reverence or respect, whom education does not reach, and society cannot tame."[11]

Whitman was not content to let the occasional reference to working-class outlaws in his poetry serve as the only reminder that the author of *Leaves of Grass* felt entirely at home among the criminal classes of New York. Throughout the antebellum era, Whitman developed an aggressive marketing campaign designed, as Kenneth Price has argued, "to frame key interpretive questions" about his poetic persona.[12] One of the anonymous self-reviews Whitman published for the first edition of *Leaves of Grass*, to recall, laid the groundwork for the persona of the national outsider as national bard by calling Whitman "the true American poet" in one breath and then questioning the audacity of so "rough and unbidden" a figure in another.[13] Similarly, in an appendix for the second edition of *Leaves of Grass* in 1856, Whitman included a handful of reviews of his work—some of which were negative to the point of viciousness—as a way to remind readers that their national bard was unwanted by the national mainstream.[14] As part of the publicity for the third edition of his book in 1860, Whitman collected even more reviews into *Leaves of Grass Imprints*, a pamphlet of related documents that framed his persona in the same manner as did both the 1855 self-reviews and the 1856 appendix to *Leaves of Grass*. A number of the reviews included in both the 1860 pamphlet and the 1856 appendix specifically latch on to the phrase "Walt Whitman, an American, one of the roughs." One reviewer noted, "That he was an American, we knew before, for, aside from America, there is no quarter of the universe where such a production could have had a genesis. That he was one of the roughs was also tolerably plain," while a British reviewer similarly commented, "The words 'an American' are a surplusage, 'one of the roughs' too painfully apparent."[15] Such reviews played right into Whitman's narrative of the national outsider who is unmistakably representative of the nation as a whole.

Whitman also included in *Leaves of Grass Imprints* a poem by the editor of the *New York Illustrated News* that applauded him for "seizing the rough words, / Such as he finds them spoken by brother and sister Manhattans." Explicitly connecting Whitman with Manhattan's "roughs," the poem goes on to say that Whitman's affiliation with the working classes qualified rather than disqualified him to be a representative national poet. Whitman, the poem continues, "Is not ashamed of mechanics as friends of his and companions. / This is the new Yankee poet, this is the man for my money!"[16] Whitman reinforced the notion that he had "mechanics as friends" by including in *Leaves of Grass Imprints* a pair of newspaper articles concerning the rumor that he had been recently employed as an omnibus driver: "It is very likely," one of these article states, "that the poet Walt Whitman, as is reported, now drives a Broadway omnibus."[17] Even with such documents framing his public persona, however, Whitman did not leave it to chance that his image as a working-class outsider would follow the 1860 *Leaves of Grass*.

Whitman called upon his friend Henry Clapp Jr., the editor of a new but influential literary weekly called the *New York Saturday Press*, to keep this narrative before the reading public. Between December 1859 and December 1860, Clapp published more than forty items in the *Saturday Press* that were either by or about Whitman, including original contributions to the *Saturday Press* as well as reprintings from newspapers across the country.[18] Clapp actively promoted the idea that Whitman was the representative poet of the United States, referring to him in the pages of the *Saturday Press* as "the Poet of the American Republic in the Present Age."[19] He also followed the pattern that Whitman had established of coupling praise for Whitman's uniquely American character with harsh critiques of his lower-class sensibilities. Clapp reprinted one review, for example, that called Whitman "an unredeemed New York rowdy of the lowest stamp" and wondered "by what extraordinary hallucination as to the character of poetry Americans have been led to regard Mr. Whitman as a poet."[20] He also picked up a review written by a young William Dean Howells that neatly summarized the persona that Whitman had worked for a half-decade to create: "If he is indeed 'the distinctive poet of America,'" Howells wrote, "then the office of poet is one which must be left hereafter to the shameless and the friendless, for WALT WHITMAN is not a man whom you would like to know."[21] Such comments pushed readers toward the conclusion that the poet referred to in the pages of the *Saturday Press* as "the most American of Americans" had no intention of finding his way into the good graces of his fellow citizens.[22]

Although Whitman actively promoted his image as a social outcast, there are only a few moments in the poetry of *Leaves of Grass* itself where he explicitly signals his exclusion from the national community. The poems that are the most instructive about Whitman's sense of what it meant to assume the office of national bard from the lower levels of society are to be found in *Calamus*, a cluster of forty-five poems about homosocial comradeship and homosexual love that first appeared in the 1860 *Leaves of Grass*. A number of scholars have noted that, in the *Calamus* poems, Whitman recasts the social liability of his "deviant" sexuality as his principal asset by presenting the homoeroticism of male comradeship as a pattern for the affectional bonds of American democracy.[23] (Malcolm Cowley memorably referred to this as Whitman's "very strange amalgam . . . between democracy and cocksucking.")[24] Whitman's *Calamus* lovers are depicted in one poem, for example, as "swarthy and unrefined" working-class outsiders who turn their backs on social convention—"the timid models of the rest, the majority"—in exchange for the manly love of urban comrades, a love that Whitman conspicuously defines as quintessentially American:

> Yet comes one a Manhattanese and ever at parting kisses me lightly on
>   the lips with robust love,
> And I on the crossing of the street or on the ship's deck give a kiss in
>   return;
> We observe that salute of American comrades, land and sea. (*LG*60 364)

Robert K. Martin writes that, in the *Calamus* poems, "Whitman is constructing himself as the outsider, the outlaw, the blackguard, at the very same moment that he is asserting his assumption of that role as fundamentally American."[25] Whitman himself wrote that "the special meaning of the 'Calamus' cluster of *Leaves of Grass* . . . mainly resides in its political significance," insisting that "the beautiful and sane affection of man for man" that he celebrates in the poems would be the means by which the citizens of the United States could be "most effectually welded together, intercalated, anneal'd into a living union" (*PW* 2:471).

Throughout the *Calamus* poems, Whitman leverages the liability of his nonnormative sexuality as an asset by offering homoerotic comradeship as the key to a prosperous democracy. "The dependence of Liberty shall be lovers, / The continuance of Equality shall be comrades," he writes in one poem, specifying that these comrade-lovers embrace liberty and equality as passionately as they embrace one another: "It shall be customary in all directions, in the houses and streets, to see manly affection, / The departing brother or friend shall salute the remaining brother or friend with a kiss" (*LG*60 351). He goes on to prophesy that this erotic comradeship will spread across the continental nation: "There shall be countless linked hands— namely, the Northeasterner's and the Northwesterner's, and the Southwesterner's, and those of the interior, and all their brood" (*LG*60 350). Many of the *Calamus* poems envision a nation of fraternal harmony as loving comradeship unites men across the vast geographic expanse of the nation. In "Calamus 5" (the poems were numbered rather than titled when they originally appeared in the 1860 edition), Whitman speaks of "a new friendship" between men that "shall circulate through The States, indifferent of place":

> One from Massachusetts shall be comrade to a Missourian,
> One from Maine or Vermont, and a Carolinian and an Oregonese, shall
>   be friends triune, more precious to each other than all the riches of
>   the earth.
>
> . . . .
>
> There shall be countless linked hands—namely, the Northeasterner's,
>   and the Northwesterner's, and the Southwesterner's, and those of the
>   interior, and all their brood. (*LG*60 349–50)

Identifying the cardinal points of national territory through representative locations—Massachusetts, Maine, and Vermont in the Northeast; the Carolinas in the Southeast; Missouri in the Southwest; and Oregon in the Northwest—this poem conjures a national community figured as a homosocial and, as other poems make more explicit, homoerotic "new friendship." Listing these disparate regions together allows Whitman to map out a national community that, despite the geographical distances that separate its members, can still feel as connected as intimate comrades holding hands. Regardless of the fact that these comrade-lovers hide their affection from mainstream national culture—Whitman says that they communicate by "secret and divine signs" (*LG*60 376)—Whitman uses their loving embrace as a metaphor for the interlinked geographic regions of the nation. Elsewhere, Whitman described his vision of a quintessentially "National Poem" in precisely this manner, saying that national poetry should provide "a comprehensive collection of touches, localés, incidents, idiomatic scenes, from every section, South, West, North, East, Kanada, Texas, Maine, Virginia, the Mississippi Valley, &c. &c. &c."[26] The *Calamus* poems fulfill this nationalist vision by making the love of comrades the mechanism by which the continent's various regions will be "fused," as he wrote, "into the compact organism of a Nation" (*LG* 269).

The interpretations of *Calamus* that argue that Whitman turns the social stigma of his homosexuality into a template for national unity offer a compelling account of how Whitman created a simultaneously public and private persona that inhabits both the margin and the center of national culture. Because these readings employ a critical vocabulary based on the spatial metaphors of public/private and margin/center, however, they do not fully account for the local and global spaces that put pressure on Whitman's efforts to be the American bard. Betsy Erkkila, for example, astutely observes, "The *Calamus* poems . . . [express] a separatist impulse toward a private homosexual order at the same time that they invoke a national and global community of democratic brotherhood."[27] But as Erkkila conflates Whitman's national and global affiliations into a single public sphere that contrasts with his "private homosexual order," she potentially collapses a much more dynamic set of local, global, and national coordinates into the binaries of public/private and margin/center.

Whitman's negotiation of a private sphere of stigmatized sexuality and a public sphere of national political influence in *Calamus* is articulated between two competing spaces: the geopolitical space of the continental nation, and a conceptual space that is alternately smaller than national and larger than national in scope. There are moments in *Calamus* when the homosocial bonds between men forge a national community across the geographically vast continent. But Whitman also imagines that his poems will either be read by a group of people too small to be called a nation or be circulated so widely that they will spill over national borders. As Tenney Nathanson says, Whitman's poems "conjure a 'you' simultaneously intimate and universal: as unique as the single addressee the intimate tone implies, yet as numerous as the audience reached by his text."[28] Nathanson accurately identifies the language Whitman uses to address his imagined readership, but he falls short of pursuing the implications of this "simultaneously intimate and universal" audience in the context of the national geography of the *Calamus* poems. That is to say, the physical terrain of *Calamus* may provide images of representative national scenes, but Whitman uses an entirely different model to identify the poems' readership, and it is a model that highlights the local and global framework within which his otherwise nationalist poetics operates.

At numerous moments throughout *Calamus*, Whitman asks, "Who is now reading this?" implying that his text can potentially escape the national boundaries depicted by the comrade-lovers whose "countless linked hands" define the geopolitical nation (*LG*60 361, 350). While defining a national community seems an easy task to a poet who considers a list of representative places enough to re-create the nation, such addresses to an unknown reader imply that Whitman cannot be confident that the national citizens he hails at moments in *Calamus* will be the exclusive audience of his poems. This address to an anonymous reader is sometimes the poet's projection of a future audience, but it also expresses a geographically vast audience living in the present moment. In "Calamus 23," the central poem of the forty-five-poem cluster, Whitman embraces the possibility that the readership of his poems could potentially expand across the globe:

> This moment as I sit alone, yearning and thoughtful, it seems to me
>   there are other men in other lands, yearning and thoughtful;
> It seems to me I can look over and behold them, in Germany, Italy,
>   France, Spain—Or far, far away, in China, or in Russia, or India—
>   talking other dialects;
> And it seems to me if I could know those men better, I should become
>   attached to them, as I do to men in my own lands,
> It seems to me they are as wise, beautiful, benevolent, as any in my own
>   lands;
> O I know we should be brethren and lovers,
> I know I should be happy with them. (*LG*60 367)

The comradeship that elsewhere in *Calamus* unites men into a nation here spills over national boundaries as Whitman recognizes that there are "men in other lands" with whom he feels a profound sense of attachment. The catalog of international locations in this poem—"Germany, Italy, France, Spain . . . China, or in Russia, or India"—directly rewrites the descriptions of the national landscape in *Calamus*. The contiguity of political geography that otherwise unites men in *Calamus* is replaced here by a "yearning and thoughtful" disposition that is felt throughout the world regardless of national political borders. Whitman imagined that such global solidarity would result in "a vaster, saner, more surrounding Comradeship . . . uniting all nations and all humanity, every nation, each after its distinctive kind . . . the fraternity over the whole globe—that dazzling, pensive dream of ages."[29] *Calamus*, then, can expand the boundaries of an otherwise national fraternity to an international scale. It can also, as other poems in the cluster show, follow the same pattern to contract those boundaries down to a space much smaller than the nation.

"Calamus 3," where Whitman imagines himself to be embodied as his book, begins with a similar sense of a vast and potentially global reader-ship as the poet addresses his reader as "Whoever you are holding me now in hand." This address to an unknown reader, however, soon becomes an at-tempt to define the reader on an intimate and local scale that turns the act of reading into a sexual encounter. In one of the most commented-upon images of the *Calamus* poems, Whitman speaks to his reader-lover as if he were "thrusting me beneath your clothing" as he would a small book of poems:

> Where I may feel the throbs of your heart, or rest upon your hip,
> Carry me when you go forth over land or sea;
> For thus, merely touching you, is enough—is best,
> And thus, touching you, would I silently sleep and be carried eternally.
> (*LG*60 346)

This description of an intimate audience with whom the poet consummates a sexual relationship is the obverse of the poem's initial recognition that the poem could be read by the uncontainable and unknown audience of "Who-ever you are." The image of a readership defined by sexual contact reappears throughout *Calamus* as Whitman takes the leaves of the phallic-shaped cala-mus root and instructs young men to "Interchange it, youths, with each other," thereby conflating the calamus plant with the *Calamus* poems in a symbolic act of sexual intercourse that mimics the pattern by which *Leaves of Grass* is passed from one reader to the next (*LG*60 342, 348). Modeling the distribution of his book after the exchange of sexual energy between men allows Whitman to depict an esoteric community of male lovers who know one another on an intimate level while at the same time feeling connected to a community of comrade-lovers that spreads, potentially, across the globe.

Superimposed on the images of the national landscape that recur throughout *Calamus*, then, is a model for a social order other than that of the nation-state. Rather than inhabit a geographically delimited national space, this community of comrades and lovers can alternately expand to fill the en-tire world or contract to a space populated by as few as two people. The two distinct social spaces in *Calamus* can be thought of as the axes of a Cartesian plane: The x-axis is a flattened and horizontal topography of national space, whereas the y-axis is a continuum that begins with a small number of reader-lovers and grows into an expanding community of international comrades.

Whitman may have intended to give *Calamus* a "political significance" that would forge the nation's citizens "into a living union," but he also proposes in these poems that the political geography of the nation is not the only way to structure social relations (*PW* 2:471). And while he offers only the roughest outline of an alternative model that weds the global with the local, what Whitman succeeds in presenting is a space of possibility, a pressure point on the national form comparable to Snow's "City of the Saints," Ridge's California, and Whitfield's sense of African Americans as both a "nation within a nation" and citizens of the world.

Just as *Calamus* presents two different configurations of social space, the voice behind the poems similarly alternates between two separate modes of address: the lyric and the bardic. In some of the poems, Whitman addresses himself directly to the nation, assuming the position of the bard who instructs, counsels, and challenges the people, while in others he is a reclusive lyric poet who expresses his interior thoughts in solitude. One example of the bardic mode is in "Calamus 5," the entire first line of which is a one-word address to the nation, followed by a summons to remember the true meaning of national unity and an invitation to receive the offerings of the national poet:

> States!
> Were you looking to be held together by the lawyers?
> By an agreement on a paper? Or by arms?
>
> Away!
> I arrive, bringing these, beyond all the forces of courts and arms,
> These! to hold you together as firmly as the earth itself is held together.
> (*LG*60 349)

In contrast to this moment in "Calamus 5" when Whitman directly addresses a national readership and physically hands them the poems that will bind them together as a community, "Calamus 1" establishes a setting where Whitman can adopt the pose of a lyric poet who revels in solitary introspection: "Here, by myself, away from the clank of the world," he writes from an isolated woodland scene, "No longer abashed—for in this secluded spot I can respond as I would not dare elsewhere" (*LG*60 341). But there is something disingenuous about the lyric pose here. The isolated scene of this confessional moment takes on the character of a public commemorative poem when Whitman names both the moment that the poem commemorates and the audience toward whom the poem is directed:

> Afternoon, this delicious Ninth Month, in my forty-first year,
> I proceed, for all who are, or have been, young men,
> To tell the secret of my nights and days,
> To celebrate the need of comrades. (*LG*60 342)

He identifies the day in September 1859 when he wrote the poem ("Afternoon, this delicious Ninth Month, in my forty-first year"), the community who share with him a sense of the importance of the moment ("I proceed, for all who are, or have been, young men"), and the reason for the celebration ("To celebrate the need of comrades"). Structurally, this could be a Fourth of July poem, a poem on the anniversary of a famous battle, or any number of other commemorative verses that position the bard as the representative speaking voice of a community that has gathered on a specific occasion to reinforce the values that define it.

"Calamus 1" is, in many ways, a lyric poem that wants to be a commemorative poem; it is the utterance of a lyric poet who aspires to be a bard. But as eager as the would-be bard of *Calamus* is to directly address a specific audience, he is adamant about setting the terms by which he will fulfill his duties. The same poet who speaks directly to the United States with lessons of national unity is quick to note that he has allegiances elsewhere than the nation. In one such poem, Whitman insinuates that the title of poet laureate has already been conferred upon him in the national capitol, only to turn around and decline this coveted appointment because it interferes with the loyalty he owes to a comrade-lover. He writes that, even though his "name had been received with plaudits in the capitol," he rejects that recognition so that he might commune with a male lover. The fete at the capitol "was not a happy night for me," he writes, finding happiness instead while secluded with the beloved: "the one I love most lay sleeping by me under the same cover in the cool night, / . . . / And his arm lay lightly around my breast— And that night I was happy" (*LG*60 357–58). In a similar poem Whitman recalls the moment when he was called to be America's poet—"it came to me to strike up the songs of the New World, / And then I believed my life must be spent in singing"—but then rejects that calling to be with his comrade-lover. "I can be your singer of songs no longer," he says to the nation. "The grandeur of The States," he writes, compels him "no more, / I am indifferent to my own songs—I will go with him I love" (LG60 354-55).

In "Calamus 32," Whitman lays out the terms under which he will execute the duties of the bard. The poem puts him on a crowded pier near the harbor where a military vessel sails by, leading him to ask what a bardic poet would be obliged to commemorate on such an occasion: "What think you I take my pen in hand to record? / The battle-ship, perfect-model'd, majestic, that I saw pass the offing to-day under full sail?" (LG60 372). But rather than praise the nation responsible for this "majestic" craft, he rejects the impulse to celebrate so trite an occasion and instead turns his gaze from the boat in the harbor to the crowd of spectators on the pier, focusing in particular on a pair of comrade-lovers like those elsewhere in *Calamus*. He writes,

> But I record of two simple men I saw to-day, on the pier, in the midst of
>   the crowd, parting the parting of dear friends,
> The one to remain hung on the other's neck, and passionately kissed
>   him,
> While the one to depart, tightly prest the one to remain in his arms.
>   (LG60 372-73)

Rather than celebrate the battleship that has drawn a crowd to the harbor, Whitman chooses instead to celebrate the men in the crowd. In "Calamus 1" Whitman announces that his goal is "To celebrate the need of comrades," and he remains true to that commitment in "Calamus 32," despite the expectation that he do otherwise (LG60 342).

In *Calamus* Whitman vowed to be a different kind of American bard, and when he took it upon himself to do the work of the bard in "A Broadway Pageant" (which he did only a few weeks after publishing the *Calamus* poems in the 1860 *Leaves of Grass*), he made good on this promise. The press coverage of the parade for the Japanese ambassadors that Whitman commemorated in "A Broadway Pageant" was critical of the unruly behavior of the working-class "roughs"—and journalists used the term explicitly—that filled the parade route. Just as he did in "Calamus 32," in "A Broadway Pageant" Whitman turned from the spectacle of the event and focused instead on the people in the crowd. Faced with the opportunity of commemorating an event of national importance, Whitman remained loyal to the population with whom he had identified for years. While the working-class men in the asexual crowd of "A Broadway Pageant" demonstrate none of the passionate affection of their brethren in *Calamus*, what remains consistent between the poems is Whitman's commitment to fill the office of bard on his own terms, even if doing so made it more difficult for him to be recognized as a representative national figure.[30] Whitman's decision to confront his audience over how a bard should commemorate an important event is reminiscent of Whitfield's insistence that the August First celebration of the end of the Atlantic slave trade was as important as the July Fourth celebration of American independence, of Snow's use of a public event like the Fourth of July to question how national outcasts can participate in national culture, and of Ridge's refusal to play the role of the civilized Indian for a group who had gathered to celebrate the triumph of Manifest Destiny. Similar to the work of these poets as well is that both *Calamus* and "A Broadway Pageant" begin with an attempt to access the center of national culture from the margins of society and end with a much more complex sense of the relationship between the nation, its subnational populations, and people from across the globe.

AS THE SUMMER OF 1860 BEGAN, Whitman's primary concern was with generating publicity for the newly released edition of *Leaves of Grass*. The visit of the Japanese ambassadors, which the editors of *Harper's Weekly* referred to as "a matter of the highest national and commercial importance" and the *New York Times* called "the most magnificent display our city has ever seen," dominated newspaper headlines during the same months when Whitman was doing everything in his power to keep his name in the popular press.[31] If Whitman was to maintain his visibility, he had to find a way to capitalize on the visit of the Japanese embassy rather than compete with it.[32] "A Broadway Pageant" provided Whitman with the attention he desired: In the space of four months it was published in the *New York Times*, reprinted in the *Saturday Press*, parodied twice in *Vanity Fair*, and discussed in the pages of *Harper's Monthly*, the *Milwaukee Daily Sentinel*, and the *Portland Transcript* in Maine.[33] But the poem was more than just a public relations stunt. Whitman intuited that writing a poem to commemorate an event such as the visit of foreign ambassadors was precisely the sort of thing that an American bard should do. And by the summer of 1860, Whitman felt closer than ever to claiming the title of national poet.

A few days before the Japanese embassy arrived in New York City, Whitman learned that the initial printing of the third edition of *Leaves of Grass* had almost sold out and that his publishers were preparing a second run for distribution.[34] The *New York Illustrated News* had recently called *Leaves of Grass* an "immense success" and Whitman himself "the new American poet."[35] In contrast to the commercial flops that were the previous two editions of *Leaves of Grass*, this publishing success must have seemed to Whitman a significant step toward being recognized as the nation's representative poet, a recognition that he capitalized on by commemorating in verse an event that dominated the front pages of U.S. newspapers as readers from across the nation celebrated the country's diplomatic prowess in securing a trade agreement with Japan. The timing, it appears, was perfect: Whitman was presented with evidence that his public acceptance was growing just as the nation needed a bard to commemorate what was widely regarded as a commercial and political cultural triumph for the United States. But the same poet who so aggressively presented himself as the nation's representative bard was also deeply invested in speaking for a smaller-than-national community of urban laborers and a larger-than-national community of people from across the globe.

The parade for the Japanese ambassadors gave Whitman the opportunity to highlight the allegiance to the working-classes he expressed in poems such as "Poem of The Daily Work of The Workmen and Workwomen of These States" as well as the cosmopolitan sentiment of poems such as "Salut au Monde!" Even though Whitman felt that he was positioned to claim the title of national bard in the summer of 1860, "A Broadway Pageant" is not a transparently nationalistic poem. It does, indeed, have its nationalistic moments—as when Whitman refers to the United States as "the new empire, grander than any before" and "a greater supremacy" than the world has ever seen—but overall it is not a naked hymn to U.S. power. Many readers would have preferred it that way. *Harper's Monthly*, along with many other contemporary sources, presented the celebration for the Japanese ambassadors as an exclusively nationalist occasion, writing that "to America belongs the honor of again opening communication with this interesting people, so long shut out from the rest of the world."[36] Nevertheless, "A Broadway Pageant" gives a more-than-sympathetic portrait of the working-class New Yorkers who gathered on crowded city streets to witness the procession, despite the fact that the same newspaper that published Whitman's poem characterized "the roughs" as an unrepresentative national population. When Whitman published "A Broadway Pageant" in the *New York Times* on 27 June, the paper had already run a number of articles saying that the crowd of working-class "roughs" that attended the parade for the Japanese ambassadors was a disruptive force that prevented New York City from coming across as a stellar representative of American culture. The visit of the Japanese embassy also gave Whitman the opportunity to emphasize his cosmopolitan affinity for cultures beyond national borders at a time when many of his contemporaries were asking whether open trade with Japan was an indication of emerging international unity or of U.S. national might. The poet who asked, "Are all nations communing? is there going to be but one heart to the globe? / Is humanity forming en-masse?" took the 1860 visit of the Japanese ambassadors as an answer in the affirmative (*LG* 371).

If newspaper estimates are to be trusted, 500,000 people — or almost half of the population of New York City at midcentury — turned out to welcome the delegates of the Japanese embassy in what New Yorkers were confident was the most impressive public display the ambassadors would see on their visit to the United States. American and Japanese flags hung from windows and across city streets, military guns fired salutes, and steam jets wrote "Welcome" in huge, ephemeral letters.[37] If anything could have put a damper on the occasion, local papers reported, it was the working-class crowds that packed the parade route on Broadway and the Bowery from Battery Park to Union Square. Concerned with putting forward the best possible face for both the city and the nation, New York journalists dedicated a significant number of column inches to identifying the ways that "the roughs" among the city's working classes potentially jeopardized Manhattan's status as a representative American space. The *New York Times* wrote, "The 'roughs' of all orders and degrees had the occasion in their hands, to deal with it as a day of enlightened curiosity and good-humored welcome, or to make it a boisterous, vulgar, and scandalous riot. Those who have known our City and its Government only in their ordinary conditions, no doubt expected that the latter alternative would be chosen."[38] The inherent mistrust of New York City's working classes expressed here — it was "expected" that they would turn the day into "a boisterous, vulgar, and scandalous riot" — is presented alongside an offhand comment about the democratic character of "the roughs" as the city's "Government."[39] Such representations of urban workers were common fare as negative depictions of the "dangerous classes" accompanied what Sean Wilentz calls a "republicanism of the streets."[40] Despite this off-hand reference as New York's "Government," however, the working classes in the *Times* report did not make the city a representative national space.

Similarly, a poem written about the visit of the Japanese ambassadors that appeared in several different newspapers opined that the city's unsavory characters would ruin the event not only for "respectable" New Yorkers but for the entire United States. Referring to New York City's lower classes as Swiftian "Ya Hoos"—a term that by 1861 was used as an antonym for "gentlemen"—the poem worries that misbehavior by the ungentlemanly population of the city will force the Japanese to reconsider their decision to trade with the United States.[41] "Let us hope the New York Ya Hoos, to a man," the poem states,

Will receive their namesakes from Old Japan
As befits their birth and station;
That they will not insist on twitching their queues,
Or on pulling off their embroidered shoes,
Or on spitting into their lacquered hats,
Or on wiping their shoes on their sitting-mats.

The poem concludes with a warning that if the city's "Ya Hoos" treat the ambassadors from Japan as roughly as is their wont, it will reflect negatively on the entire nation. "Because, if they do," the poem concludes, "Japanese ports will close with a snap, / Never to be opened again mayhap, / To the courteous Yankee nation."[42] It is worth noting in this context that in 1860 two separate newspapers—one in Ohio, the other in New Orleans—referred to Whitman himself as the "Yahoo of American literature."[43]

Fears that the city's roughs and yahoos would give the Japanese ambassadors a poor impression of the United States were unfounded, however. As the *New York Times* wrote in its account of the parade,

Yet never was New-York more free from everything like riot, more good-humored, more considerate, more fit to be held up as a model and example to the great nation of which the common consent of the world agrees with the Japanese in regarding her as the representative.... They [the roughs] sunk away out of sight and left the City to the overwhelming majorities of well-conducted, civil and quick-witted citizens who compose the real strength of the population of New-York.[44]

Despite the good behavior of the working classes, according to the *Times* the "real" population of the city that deserved to be regarded as "the representative" of "the great nation" being celebrated for its diplomatic acumen in securing a coveted trade agreement with Japan are the city's "well-conducted, civil and quick-witted" citizens, and not "the roughs." Here and elsewhere, the *Times* presents New York as a divided city: One section represents the United States, and another section—despite being the city's democratic "Government"—has to sink "away out of sight" for the city to represent the nation. As M. Wynn Thomas writes, "Mid-nineteenth-century New York was a city divided several ways along new lines both of economic interest and of social class."⁴⁵ Nowhere was the economic division that split New York society more vividly illustrated than in the sections of lower Manhattan that formed the core of the parade route: the working-class Bowery and mercantile Broadway, or as the *Times* had it, "the warlike Bowery" and "polite Broadway."⁴⁶

The *New York Herald*'s report of the parade similarly called the Bowery "one of the most celebrated representative spots of the city," but it also said that for the city to represent the nation on the day of the parade, the Bowery had to alter its fundamental character. The *Herald* said that on the day of the procession, "The democratic element was in its glory. The 'governing classes' . . . owing to a high patriotic sense of the occasion, or to some other equally potent motive, . . . comported themselves in a manner really deserving of the adjective decent. How much violence to their feelings this effort caused the writer sayeth not, merely mentioning it as a praiseworthy incident."⁴⁷ While the *Herald* follows the *Times* in referring to the denizens of the Bowery as the "democratic element" and "governing classes" of the city, their "high patriotic sense" was probably not what kept them from disrupting the procession. Rather, it was "some other equally potent motive," which is no doubt a reference to the significant police presence on the Bowery during the day's festivities.⁴⁸ Based on sentiments that he expressed elsewhere, Whitman would have taken umbrage at such statements. Whitman considered working-class men and women to be a representative national subpopulation. In an unpublished political tract from the period, he wrote that the "real America" consisted of "the laboring persons, ploughmen . . . carpenters, masons, machinists, drivers of horses, [and] workmen in factories."⁴⁹

By publishing "A Broadway Pageant" alongside these reports of the roughs' questionable status as city and national representatives, Whitman intervenes in a debate over what "the crowd" meant not only to New York City but to American democracy as well. These newspaper reports partake of two prevailing notions about "the crowd" as a social form: The crowd's blending of individuals into a mass is, in many ways, an illustration of democratic unity, but crowds were also associated with anarchy and poverty in ways that many Americans would not have recognized as representative of their nation.[50] Whitman praised the United States in the 1855 preface to *Leaves of Grass* for "the tremendous audacity of its crowds" (*LG55* iii) and wrote in an 1868 letter to Peter Doyle that "I always enjoy seeing the city let loose, and on the rampage."[51] Not all Americans, however, shared his enthusiasm. Ralph Waldo Emerson, for one, wrote, "Masses are rude, lame, unmade, pernicious in their demands and influence, and need not to be flattered but to be schooled."[52]

In an effort to depict the crowd as the embodiment of American democracy rather than as a threat to social order, Whitman spends the lengthy first section of "A Broadway Pageant" placing himself within the crowd scene. And since "A Broadway Pageant" follows the conventions of the Pindaric ode form that was often employed by poets on public occasions, by making the first section of the poem an invocation of an urban muse, Whitman grants the crowd a poetic status that supersedes the negative reports given in the press.[53] Contra Emerson, he "flatters" the crowd by giving it the power to summon a muse that will make the occasion worthy of public praise:

> When million-footed Manhattan, unpent, descends to its pavements,
> . . . .
> When pennants trail, and festoons hang from the windows,
> When Broadway is entirely given up to foot-passengers and foot-
>   standers—When the mass is densest,
> When the façades of the houses are alive with people—When eyes gaze,
>   riveted, tens of thousands at a time,
> When the guests, Asiatic, from the islands, advance—When the pageant
>   moves forward visible,
> When the summons is made—When the answer that waited thousands
>   of years, answers,
> I too arising, answering, descend to the pavements, merge with the
>   crowd, and gaze with them.[54]

In many ways this catalog is typical of Whitman, with the repeated word "When" used to preface a list of raw sensations that the poet hopes will have the cumulative effect of translating the scene into words. But as part of a public poem following the pattern of a Pindaric ode, this catalog is designed not only to convey the presence of the scene but also to summon the presence of the muse.

Conflating poet and muse in a gesture that is similar to the invocation of "I sing myself" in "Song of Myself," Whitman says that the poet/muse will answer the call and descend to the scene when the urban crowd is fully realized. Repeating "When" before every image suggests that these urban sights are preconditions that must be met before the bard will emerge and commemorate the occasion: When "the mass is densest," when the buildings come alive with faces in the windows, and when the eyes of "tens of thousands" of New Yorkers "gaze, riveted" on a single common focus, only then will the poet answer the summons that he immortalize the occasion in verse. In describing the crowd of 500,000 New Yorkers as "million-footed Manhattan," Whitman presents this group of Manhattanites as an individual entity describable with the singular pronoun "its," as when he writes that the crowd "unpent, descends to its pavements." This is, again, a typically Whitmanian image depicting the merge of the many into one that defines democratic unity. At the same time, however, the grotesque image of a million-footed creature that is "unpent" onto city streets recalls fears about the group mentality of the crowd, particularly the unruly crowds depicted in New York papers. As the *New York Herald* reported, "The crowd was so great at one time that it was impossible for anyone to attempt locomotion on his own part, but he had to permit himself to be carried along with the crowd."[55]

Containing both the promise of democracy and the perils of anarchy, the crowd is "the rough" writ large. Thus the parallel language that Whitman uses in the opening and closing lines of this catalog—"Manhattan . . . descends to its pavements" and "I too . . . descend to the pavements"—reinforces his affiliation with the crowd. Whitman could have placed himself somewhere else along the parade route in the poem. He could have been in a storefront window with merchants, in a ship on the harbor, in one of the military formations that saluted the ambassadors, or even in the procession itself, but he chose instead to identify with the very crowd that had been so harshly criticized in the popular press. A number of contemporary readers of "A Broadway Pageant" noted specifically that Whitman's attention in the poem was focused on the working-class crowds.

The editor of *Harper's Monthly*, for one, commented that Whitman was less interested in the prominent city figures who attended the parade than in the crowd itself. "So, when the Japanese Princes arrive," *Harper's* writes, Whitman "does not see the Seventh Regiment, apparently, nor Alderman Boole, nor Bagley, nor Balteel [*sic*]."[56] The energy of the crowd better held Whitman's attention, according to *Harper's*, than did either the military processional or the array of city dignitaries that included Aldermen Francis Boole and James Bagley and Councilman William Bulteel. Similarly, the *Portland Transcript* ran a commentary on "A Broadway Pageant" titled, conspicuously, "Rough Poetry" that explicitly connected Whitman with the working-class roughs who had attended the parade: "Walt Whitman is one of the roughs, a filibuster on Parnassus," the article states. "He thinks himself the American poet, when he is only a sort of inspired rowdy."[57]

Along the same lines, *Vanity Fair* published a parody of "A Broadway Pageant" that satirized Whitman's affinity for the crowd. One section of the poem in particular, which mimics the style of Whitman's summons to the crowd, follows contemporary newspaper accounts in depicting the crowd as coarse and unrefined:

> When, terrible in the midnight, begins the wild roar of cannon;
> When the ear-cracking cracker awakes me with its continual cracks;
> When punch and confusion are in the house and the "morning call" is
>   brought to me in a tumbler;
> When the stars and stripes hang round in a very miscellaneous manner;
> When Broadway is entirely given up to the patriotic youth—when
>   Young America bristles;
> . . . .
>
> I descend to the pavement, I merge with the crowd, I roar exultant, I am
>   an American citizen, I feel that every man I meet owes me twenty-
>   five cents.[58]

Not only does the parody poem echo the language Whitman uses to express his desire to "merge with the crowd," but it also identifies the tension at the heart of "A Broadway Pageant" over whether a crowd of working-class New Yorkers could be considered representative of the nation as a whole. The poem identifies Whitman as "an American citizen" and places him among the "patriotic youth" of "Young America," but it is also careful to note that this patriotism is half-hearted at best and disrespectful at worst: An American flag hangs "in a very miscellaneous manner" while Whitman himself, depicted as a drunken freeloader walking the streets with a tumbler in hand, shamelessly confesses from the depths of his poverty, "I feel that every man I meet owes me twenty-five cents."

Whitman did not agree with the consensus of newspapers such as the *New York Times* that the "well-conducted, civil and quick-witted" citizens of New York—and not the working-class crowds—best represented the United States to the Japanese embassy. When Whitman announced in "A Broadway Pageant" that he would "descend to the pavements" and "merge with the crowd," he was implicitly responding to the prejudice against the working-class crowds that had been expressed only days earlier in the same newspaper that published his poem. Similarly, Whitman's direct address to the audience in "A Broadway Pageant" identifies two distinct populations, the residents of "Superb-faced Manhattan" and a national community of "Comrade Americanos":

> Superb-faced Manhattan,
> Comrade Americanos—to us, then, at last, the orient comes.
> To us, my city.[59]

And given that, for Whitman, the city *is* the working-class crowd (as in "million-footed Manhattan"), his address to two different audiences contrasts a maligned urban subculture with the nation as a whole. The same poet who casually referred to himself in "Song of Myself" as both "an American" and "one of the roughs" found in "A Broadway Pageant" the opportunity to articulate the very real tension between those competing loyalties.

The circumstances surrounding the composition of "A Broadway Pageant" also allowed Whitman to think about what he meant in "Song of Myself" when he stated his cosmopolitan allegiance to the world at large by referring to himself as "a kosmos." Whether or not Whitman knew that "cosmopolitan" was based on the Greek root *kosmos*—or even that the use of "cosmopolitan" to mean "citizen of the world" was undergoing a revival in the mid-nineteenth century—his use of the term expressed a similar desire to broaden one's affections beyond the limits of the nation.[60] For Whitman, "A Broadway Pageant" was not only a celebration of the men and women who had gathered en masse on the city streets; it was also as a celebration of an international unity of the type that threatened to render national loyalty irrelevant. At moments in "A Broadway Pageant" he addresses "Young Libertad," referring to the idea that his young nation was the standard-bearer of liberty. But he also addresses a more ambiguously figured "Libertad of the world," which potentially collapses the United States into a larger community of nations that together would bring freedom to the world.[61] The same features of commemorative verse that allowed Whitman to rethink his nationalism as "one of the roughs" in "A Broadway Pageant" also opened up the possibility for a cosmopolitan mindset as "a kosmos."[62]

Just as the working-class crowds along the parade route highlighted the tension between the nation and one of its national subcultures, so too did the arrival of the Japanese embassy give Whitman a sense of how New Yorkers could think of themselves not just as national citizens but also as citizens of the world. As did many of his contemporaries, Whitman believed that the visit of the Japanese ambassadors was proof of the growing power of the United States. The *New York Illustrated News*, for instance, stated that "it is no slight national honor that the first accredited political embassy which has left [Japanese] shores, has been sent to the capital of this great Republic."[63] At the same time, Whitman and others believed that trade between the United States and Japan heralded the emergence of an era when nation-states would cede some of their authority to a larger international order. *Frank Leslie's Paper*, for one, commented that the visit of the Japanese ambassadors was "a step towards mutual understanding, an aid towards cosmopolitanism."[64] The parade route itself testified to this dual message. While marching bands played "Hail Columbia" in celebration of U.S. diplomatic prowess, the streets were also lined with banners proclaiming such messages of global unity as "Gates of All Nations this Day Open," "One Blood, All Nations," and "All Nations, Union Forever," suggesting that another cause for celebration was the withering of national boundaries in an era of international unity.[65]

By 1860, New Yorkers had grown accustomed to thinking that their city had as many connections to the outside world as it had to its home nation. As one city official said in a public statement directed to the Japanese ambassadors, "Our city is bound by ties of interest to every nation on the face of the globe, and to none more warmly than Japan."[66] But antebellum New Yorkers were not unified in saying that trade with Japan heralded the dawn of a global era; rather, many believed that New York's role in securing this U.S.-

Japanese alliance signaled the rise of the United States to national prominence. The *Times* commented,

> New York represents the full grandeur of that mighty American com-
> merce which has won from the hitherto impregnable East a recognition
> denied to the arms of more exacting and more arrogant powers. The
> selection of America as their point of destination by the envoys of Japan
> has inflicted a flash of light upon the political optics of Great Britain. . . .
> The age of [British] commercial preponderance in the world is past, and
> that the maritime enterprise of the Republic whose shores touch either
> ocean [i.e., the United States] has become a fact of the first magnitude
> in contemporaneous history. Of that enterprise New York is the unques-
> tioned capital and heart.[67]

Just as "the roughs" were seen both as the city's democratic "Government"
and as a population that threatened to make the city an unrepresentative
national space, so too did the arrival of the Japanese embassy suggest that
New York City was both the vanguard of American political power and the
site of an emerging cosmopolitanism. This conflict would have struck a particular chord with Whitman, who allowed to his confidant Horace Traubel
later in life, "There is a sense in which I want to be cosmopolitan: then again
a sense in which I make much of patriotism—of our native stock, the American stock" (*WWC* 3:132).

Accordingly, "A Broadway Pageant" addresses whether New York's status
as an international trading hub makes it the "capital and heart" of the nation (as the *Times* has it) or a node in a much larger network of global inter-
actions. At moments, Whitman turns "A Broadway Pageant" into a hymn to
American nationalism, calling the United States "the new empire, grander
than any before" and "a greater supremacy" than the world has ever seen.
But at other points in the poem he counsels the United States to humbly
accept its place in the world, urging it to "Bend your proud neck" both to
Japan and to other nations that are "now sending messages over the archi-
pelagoes to you."[68] Whitman negotiates this conflict between national pride
and international unity by describing New York City as having been transformed into a cosmopolitan space where global influences compete with
and eventually overwhelm the otherwise American character of the city.

As he does in "Crossing Brooklyn Ferry" when he turns an urban spectacle into a visionary experience, in "A Broadway Pageant" Whitman pur-

ports to see the entire continent of Asia accompanying the Japanese ambassadors on their way through downtown New York. "I do not know whether others behold what I behold," Whitman writes early in the poem, "But I will sing you a song of what I behold." He then chronicles his vision of the Asian continent manifesting itself along Broadway and the Bowery: "the whole continent itself appears—the past, the dead, / . . . / Vast desolated cities—the gliding Present—All of these, and more, are in the pageant-procession." Whitman then extends the boundaries of his visionary processional to include not only Asia but the entire world, writing that "Geography, the world, is in it."[69] Following the convention of the Pindaric ode that the second section of a public occasional poem be formally parallel to the first, Whitman depicts a global crowd in the parade procession similar to the city crowd of parade-goers he describes earlier in the poem:

> The countries there, with their populations—the millions en masse—
>   are curiously here,
> The multitudes are all here—they show visibly enough to my eyes,
> The swarming market-places—the temples, with idols ranged along
>   the sides, or at the end—bonze, brahmin, and llama, also,
> The mandarin, farmer, merchant, mechanic, and fisherman, also,
> The singing-girl and the dancing-girl—the ecstatic person, absorbed,
> The interminable unpitted hordes of toilsome persons—the divine
>   Buddha,
> The secluded Emperors—Confucius himself—the great poets and
>   heroes—the warriors, the castes, all.[70]

The "When" that precedes every line of the earlier catalog describing the denizens of New York is replaced here with the definite article as Whitman introduces a parallel crowd scene of "millions" of people from across the world flooding into lower Manhattan. While the Asiatic images in the catalog might lack the authenticity of Whitman's firsthand experience with the New York City crowd—indeed, many of these images sound as if their origin is Barnum's Chinese Museum rather than an inspired vision—the idea of "interminable unpitted hordes" from throughout the world descending upon the city is intended to have the same impact on the urban space as do the crowds of "roughs" from earlier in the poem. That these are "hordes of *toilsome* persons," that is, crowds of working men and women, reinforces Gay Wilson Allen's contention that Whitman figured his internationalism as part of a world proletarian movement that united America's working class with laborers from across the globe.[71]

Whitman was not the only New Yorker to draw a connection between the crowds attending the parade and the city's cosmopolitan character. The *New York Herald* said that the crowds surrounding the Japanese procession offered proof that the world had already arrived in Manhattan: "There were Dutch and Irish, French and English, Spanish, Italian, and even Chinese people crowding the road and sidewalks . . . and from the unintelligible jabbering of tongues one might almost suppose oneself at the Tower of Babel."[72] Lower Manhattan already had an established reputation as a cosmopolitan space. A midcentury observer noted, "A walk through Broadway is like a voyage round the Globe," while Whitman himself referred elsewhere to Broadway as a "thoroughfare of the world" and New York City as a "City of the world."[73] Another contemporary account claimed that by standing near Manhattan's bays "one feels in communication with the rest of the World" as the city is "touched by ships from every clime."[74] The events surrounding the visit of the Japanese embassy further intensified what was already a strong sense of New York City's intimate connection to the rest of the world. As the *Times* wrote, "This crowded, nay, cosmopolitan life of ours was never so crowded, or so cosmopolitan, as it promises to be in the summer months of 1860."[75]

Just as the working-class inhabitants of the city preclude New York from taking on a purely national character, so too do Manhattan's global ties prevent the city from being bound exclusively to any single nation-state. As such, in "A Broadway Pageant" Whitman depicts New York City as an erstwhile American space that is transformed by its communion with the globe. In Whitman's poem, the Japanese ambassadors are said to have brought with them an amorphous sense of primitive maternal energy that is "Florid with blood, pensive, rapt with musings, hot with passion, / Sultry with perfume, with ample and flowing garments." In contrast with the masculine technology that created the "iron beauties" of the modern city, Asia is spiritual ("rapt with musings"), sexual ("hot with passion"), sensuous ("Sultry with perfume"), and even menstrual ("Florid with blood").[76] As "the Originatress" of human civilization, the Asia of Whitman's vision is everything the United States is not: old rather than new, feminine rather than masculine, and primitive rather than modern. Whitman's vision of Asian exoticism must have been motivated in part by what the *New York Times* described as "a general disappointment in [the Japanese ambassadors'] personal appearance, and the absence of rich and gorgeous dresses, with which most of the Eastern nations are usually associated."[77]

While "A Broadway Pageant" seems at first to provide New Yorkers with the fantasy of Asian exoticism that the realities of the event denied them, there is more than mere Orientalism to Whitman's descriptions. While Rob Wilson says that Whitman's poem "helped to idealize imperial Western designs" in Asia, "A Broadway Pageant" allows for a more supple interaction between American and world cultures than such hard critiques afford.[78] By the same token, Guiyou Huang's assessment that "the poet's embrace of Asia [in 'A Broadway Pageant'] seems complete and unconditional" is perhaps too generous.[79] The most significant feature of Whitman's depiction of the Japanese ambassadors in "A Broadway Pageant," rather, is how Whitman transforms New York City into a cosmopolitan space that partakes equally of Western and Eastern influences. As often as Whitman projects a gauzy exoticism onto the Japanese ambassadors, he also paints Manhattan in a similarly exotic light. In "A Broadway Pageant," the technology of Whitman's modern city—not the Japanese ambassadors themselves—creates the exoticized and premodern ambience that transforms lower Manhattan into a cosmopolitan space where East and West unite:

> When the thunder cracking guns arouse me with the proud roar I love,
> When the round-mouth'd guns, out of the smoke and smell I love, spit
>   their salutes,
> When the fire-flashing guns have fully alerted me—When heaven-
>   clouds canopy my city with a delicate thin haze,
> When, gorgeous, the countless straight stems, the forests at the wharves,
>   thicken with colors,
> When every ship richly drest carries her flag at the peak.[80]

The phallic and technological images of guns and ship masts in this passage contrast a sense of masculine American modernity with the Asian primitivism depicted as feminine and organic in the figure of "the Originatress" elsewhere in the poem. At the same time, however, these supposedly modern images are what enable Whitman's numinous vision of the ancient East.

As opposed to the "ample and flowing" garments of the Japanese ambassadors, the image of "the forests at the wharves" used to describe the ships in the harbor stands as a monument to the artificiality of modern technology.

In a later essay, however, Whitman says that ship masts invest Manhattan with a premodern and Asian air as the city is seen "rising out of the midst, tall-topt, ship-hemm'd, modern, American, yet strangely oriental."[81] Just as the forest of ship masts gives a "strangely oriental" feel to a "modern, American" city, the gunfire that Whitman focuses on for three lines in the above passage produces a "delicate thin haze" of canopied "heaven-clouds" reminiscent of Orientalist depictions of harems and opium dens. Critiques levied against exotic images of Asia in "A Broadway Pageant" appropriately identify Whitman's dependence on Orientalist imagery, but they fail to account for the way that he uses these images to depict Manhattan's transformation into an Asian space as the city opens its doors to visitors from abroad.

When "A Broadway Pageant" is read alongside other poems from the period about the visit of the Japanese ambassadors, Whitman's willingness to embrace the globe in ways that many of his contemporaries were not becomes even clearer. In marked contrast to Whitman's work, these poems are all characterized by an inordinate fixation on racial difference. One poem that refers to the ambassadors as "copper-faced types of the race of man, / Who dwell in the islands of Japan" goes so far as to dehumanize the Japanese, comparing them to "beasts in a caravan" and describing their features as piglike: "Gorgeous to see are their tunics fine, / Funnily twinkle their eyes porcine."[82] Another poem, which similarly describes the Japanese as a "copper race, with cues and curls," ridicules the ambassadors' ignorance of American culture:

> And, strange to say, they cannot tell
> New-Jersey Col's from New-York Belles,
> But drink Champagne and oyster-messes,
> And dislike hoop-bound ladies' dresses.[83]

For most of the poets who commemorated the 16 June parade, the Japanese ambassadors were a reminder of American racial and cultural supremacy; for Whitman, the ambassadors were the bearers of cosmopolitan tidings. That Whitman would so warmly welcome visitors from the other side of the world would have come as no surprise to his most attentive readers, who, by the summer of 1860, had already prepared themselves to see in his poetry an equal regard for the nation and the globe.

Only a few weeks before Whitman would use the visit of the Japanese ambassadors as an occasion to express his affinity for world culture, the editor of the *New York Illustrated News* praised Whitman for his "orientalism of vision," characterizing him as "the most oriental and the most American of Americans."[84] (Later that summer, a British reviewer would similarly describe Whitman's poetry as "somewhat Oriental in appearance.")[85] Even though the editor for the *Illustrated News* went on to say that Whitman was a "devout and prophetic son of America" who possessed a "voice which speaks for America," he also wrote that Whitman "represents the 'Cosmos', and all nature and humanity." While Whitman focused much of his attention on people and places within the United States, he also hoped that his poetry would form part of an emerging global culture, promising that he would "make joyous hymns for the whole earth" and "acknowledge contemporary lands" as he traversed "the whole geography of the globe" (*LG* 311, 105, 21). In poems such as "Salut au Monde!" Whitman celebrates the entire globe as "a great round wonder rolling through space" and claims to feel as connected to the other nations of the earth as he does to his own nation: "I see distant lands, as real and near to the inhabitants of them as my land is to me" (*LG* 113–14). Indeed, he once claimed that the audience for his poetry was equally national and international: "For America—for all the earth, all nations, the common people, / (Not of one nation only—not America only)."[86]

Whitman often tried to resolve the tension between his patriotism and his cosmopolitanism by insisting that the United States itself was a cosmopolitan nation, as when he said that "the best of America is the best cosmopolitanism."[87] Claiming that the United States "cheerfully welcomed immigrants from Europe, Asia, Africa," Whitman called his country a "nation of nations" and said that his countrymen and countrywomen were a "race of races" (*LG56* 346; *LG55* iv). Whitman felt a constant tug between his loyalty to the nation and his loyalty to the world at large. Whether or not he ever fully resolved his cosmopolitanism with his nationalism is an open question, as is whether he ever reconciled his affinity for the working classes with his desire to speak for the national mainstream. What remains clear is that Whitman's early career is better characterized as a set of tensions between global, local, and national influences than as any sort of straightforward or unproblematic nationalism. "A Broadway Pageant," more so than any other antebellum document, foregrounds these tensions at a moment when Whitman self-consciously assumed the role of American bard.

IN THE WANING YEARS of his life, Whitman was taken to task by one of his friends for aligning himself with the fringe elements of society. "Walt," his friend said, "you seem determined to be in the minority." Whitman responded, apparently in earnest, "Yes, I do: that's the only safe place for me" (*WWC* 4:321). Similarly, twenty years after he had traded the persona of "one of the roughs" for that of the "Good Gray Poet," Whitman continued to insist that *Leaves of Grass* was "a book for the criminal classes" and that he himself was "in the criminal class" (*WWC* 1:375). Such comments reveal as much as they conceal about Whitman's persona as a national outsider, offering as many questions as answers about whether being "one of the roughs" was an integral facet of Whitman's life or merely an imaginative pose. A persistent undercurrent of Whitman scholarship has argued that it was entirely Whitman's choice "to be in the minority," and that his affiliation with the working classes was imaginative at best and exploitative at worst.[88] Other scholars, however, have made a compelling case for how deeply embedded Whitman was in his working-class environment, arguing that "the only safe place" for Whitman was among the lower strata of American life.[89] A related school of thought has similarly contended that, given the nineteenth century's lack of a clearly articulated identity for gay men, the homosocial camaraderie of working-class men provided Whitman with a "safe place" for the most important intimate relationships of his life.[90]

It remains the task of the biographer to judge whether Whitman was actually of "the criminal class" or whether such posturing merely fed into a persona that was, either wholly or in part, a work of fiction. Nevertheless, in light of the outsider personae similarly deployed by James M. Whitfield, Eliza R. Snow, and John Rollin Ridge, it is worth considering whether or not, to put it bluntly, all outsiders are created equal.[91] The lived experiences of an African American who felt compelled to leave the United States, a Mormon woman who was driven from her home by mob violence, and an exile of the Cherokee nation who spent most of his life separated from the source of his cultural heritage are radically different from those of a man who registered little, if any, distress for having affiliated himself with the working class. It also bears noting that there are as many (if not more) differences in life experience among these poets as there are in their points of contrast with Whitman. Snow, for example, may have felt her exclusion from the national community acutely, but she retained the privilege of her whiteness in ways that Whitfield and, to a lesser degree, Ridge did not. Conversely, Whitfield was arguably at the greatest risk of all these poets because of his race, but he also benefited from the position of his gender in ways that he failed to register: He made no mention, for example, of the voting rights of women in the poem he wrote to celebrate the ratification of the Fifteenth Amendment to the Constitution.[92] By the same token, Ridge abhorred the treatment of Native peoples by the U.S. government, but he expressed no remorse for the fact that his family, like a number of other wealthy Cherokees at the time, owned African American slaves.

While these poets experienced their lives as national outsiders in ways that Whitman never did, this alone should not excuse them from undergoing a scrutiny similar to that which Whitman himself has been subjected for failing to live up to the democratic ideals espoused in his poetry. Whitfield, for example, may have had a sophisticated understanding of race relations in the United States, but he fully embraced the ideology of Manifest Destiny when he claimed the right to colonize the land in Central and South America already held by indigenous peoples. Similarly, Snow may have deftly negotiated the limitations set on Mormon women in her patriarchal culture, but not only did she publicly defend the practice of polygamy; she also went so far as to actively recruit young women into polygamous marriages.[93] Ridge, for his part, did not hesitate to distinguish between the "good" and "bad" tribes of Native Americans, concluding, in effect, that the only good Indian was a civilized Indian. It would be unethical to praise these poets for complicating the Whitmanian posture of the national outsider-*cum*-national bard without calling attention to such shortcomings, but it is also problematic to reduce literary scholarship to a pass-or-fail test on issues of social responsibility. This is a complicated matter, to be sure, as is any effort that seeks to chart the space where literary production and social justice meet. Instructive on this point is Timothy Powell's notion of "historical multiculturalism," which he characterizes as a self-reflexive posture toward negotiating the troubling aspects of an author's politics with attempts to establish him or her as a multicultural icon.[94]

In the interest of self-reflexivity, allow me to underscore that my tendency has been to alternate between emphasizing the social realities of the mid-nineteenth century and explicating the imaginative uses to which each of these poets put the persona of the outsider bard. I have wanted Whitfield's involvement in the antebellum emigration movement, for example, to cast a harsh light on the ways in which Whitman's treatment of race often elides the social reality of the period. At the same time, however, I have granted full flight to the imaginative leap that, say, Ridge made when he described California as an island empire that replicates the globe in minia-ture. My goal has been to carve out a space where "imaginative" is not the antitheses of "social reality" but functions instead as a complimentary term. Poetry is both the domain of the imagination and an entrée for analyzing social concerns—poems, as Marianne Moore memorably put it, are "imagi-nary gardens with real toads in them."[95] For this reason, among others, I have tempered the urge to claim that Whitfield, Snow, and Ridge are more "authentic" national outsiders than Whitman by identifying instead those moments when the poems themselves complicate the metaphor of insider/ outsider. Rather than rank these poets on a sliding scale from most to least authentically marginalized, I have instead argued that all of these poets— Whitman included—can help us reevaluate the usefulness of central/mar-ginal and insider/outsider as analytic concepts.

Given that my methodology has involved comparing and contrasting the poet most central to American culture with poets from some of the nine-teenth century's most marginalized communities, I have, admittedly, run the risk of reinforcing rather than overturning the margin/center binary that has traditionally been at the heart of multicultural critique. Indeed, one of the most frequently challenged aspects of multicultural literary criti-cism has been precisely this inclination to posit that marginalized figures can serve as a corrective to the hegemonic force of the canon. Paul Giles, for example, has warned that when "marginal figures are incorporated into the ever-expanding circle of a national narrative," we end up with a "Whitman-ian gesture of enfolding oppressed or minority cultures in a Neoplatonic embrace [that] has the paradoxical effect of dislocating the established liter-ary canon while simultaneously validating the processes through which the canon was constructed."[96] Giles's warning is well taken, particularly given that I have used the "Whitmanian gesture of enfolding oppressed or mi-nority cultures" not merely as a metaphor, but as the methodology of this entire book: Insofar as Whitfield, Snow, and Ridge can serve as convenient foils to Whitman, I have argued, they deserve a closer look by the powers that be.

As much as statements such as those by Giles give me pause as I pon-der the outcome of the methodology I have employed, the approach I have taken in *American Bards* has led me to question the reliance that Giles and others place on the metaphor of "the canon" to describe the frequency with which certain authors are taught in university courses or discussed in academic scholarship. A canon, strictly speaking, is a group of sacred texts that the governing body of an ecclesiastical organization approves as doctrinally correct. Anything else, to follow the metaphor to its natural conclusion, is apocrypha. The metaphor of canon/apocrypha can be as limited in its usefulness as are the binary metaphors of margin/center or outsider/insider. A hard-edged critique of the canon, for example, might relegate Whitman to the realm of apocrypha with the other dead white males of the period, or, conversely, it could recuperate him into a new-and-improved canon, given that his class and sexual identity make him a different kind of dead white male than the rest. Neither argument is wholly satisfying, largely because neither captures the complexity surrounding the production and reception of Whitman's poetry.

Betsy Erkkila has proposed an alternative to such limiting binaries, and it is an alternative that resonates with the methodology I have followed in *American Bards*. In an essay regarding the usefulness of the vexed term "American Renaissance" to describe the literature of the antebellum period, Erkkila argues that there is no need to replace "American Renaissance"— which, in F. O. Matthiessen's 1941 book of the same name, originally covered only Whitman, Emerson, Hawthorne, Melville, and Thoreau—because, as she writes, "the term has, in accord with Bakhtin's notion of the dialogism of language, already been 'populated—overpopulated—with the *intentions of others*' through the revisionary scholarship of the past two decades."[97] Erkkila's Bakhtinian take on the scholarship of the mid-nineteenth century could be called an abundance model for literary history: Rather than a canonical center and an apocryphal margin in American literature, we have a proliferation of texts and authors as succeeding generations of scholars and teachers redefine literary history with an expanding corpus of texts. Authors are not banished from the canon like poets from Plato's republic, but they remain like layers of sediment or the traces of a palimpsest, complexly striated and historically textured, offering a picture of the period and its scholarship that the metaphors of margin/center or canon/apocrypha would otherwise struggle to present.

My goal with *American Bards* has been similar. Rather than argue that Whitman's spot in the canon be replaced by Whitfield, Snow, and Ridge— or, conversely, that these poets be folded into the canon by way of Whitman's all-encompassing embrace—I have instead attempted to "overpopulate" Whitman with the lives, careers, and poetry of others. My goal has been to entangle Snow's poetic reimaginings of Mormon doctrine with Whitman's proclamation to be the poet of a new American religion, to summon Ridge's vision of a radically hybridized world whenever Whitman sounds forth as "the first white aboriginal," and to evoke Whitfield's poeticized national text alongside Whitman's insistence that "the United States are essentially the greatest poem." More broadly, I hope that by offering Whitfield, Snow, and Ridge as counterpoints to Whitman, I have raised the specter of even more poets from the period who are waiting to be rediscovered or introduced to the discussion anew.

American Bards has also attempted to "overpopulate" a restrictive notion of national identity with the complex nexus of forces that connect smaller-than-national communities with larger-than-national locales. The mid-nineteenth-century United States that I have presented in these pages is populated with sites like Snow's "City of the Saints," which connects a group of national exiles to streams of immigrant converts from across the world; with a space like Ridge's California, which contracts the globe down to a metaphoric island that hybridizes race, culture, and nationality before sending that amalgamated identity back out to the world; with a transatlantic network such as that which Whitfield describes as connecting African Americans to populations in both Africa and Europe; and with Whitman's New York, where urban laborers reach out and touch the world. Similarly, I have proposed that the settings where commemorative poetry takes place are more densely populated than the posture of lyric solitude would suggest, and that whenever bards approach their audiences on public occasions, they engage in a debate over meaning-making and identity formation where audiences attempt to populate poets with their desires and intentions while poets themselves try to populate the audience with intentions of their own. This sense of literary history as overpopulated and overabundant—the sense, that is, that there is more going on than we might appreciate—is fundamentally an attempt to open up further sites of possibility. We students of American poetry would do ourselves a disservice—and let's give the final word to Emily Dickinson on the matter—not to "dwell in Possibility—," which we all know to be "A fairer House than Prose."[98]

Preface

1. Quoted in Lippy, *Faith in America*, 149.
2. [Anonymous], "[Review of *Leaves of* Grass (1855)]," *The Critic*.

Introduction

1. Rossetti, "Prefatory Notice," 26.
2. Whitman, *Uncollected Poetry and Prose*, 2:91. Gay Wilson Allen used the phrase "solitary singer" for his influential biography, *The Solitary Singer: A Critical Biography of Walt Whitman*.
3. Greenfeld, *Nationalism*, 11.
4. [Whitman], "Walt Whitman and His Poems."
5. Ibid.
6. Browne, *Great Metropolis*, 66. Whitman identifies himself as "one of the roughs" in all three antebellum editions of *Leaves of Grass* (*LG55* 29; *LG56* 41; *LG60* 54). Whitman's postbellum attempt to reinvent himself as the "Good Gray Poet" involved removing the phrase "one of the roughs" from *Leaves of Grass* and then overseeing a biography of the same name designed to mainstream his image, O'Connor's *Good Gray Poet*.
7. Erkkila, *Whitman the Political Poet*, 3, 102. For an additional perspective on how Whitman's lower-middle-class background allowed him access to both bourgeoisie culture and the street life of city workers, see Lawson, *Walt Whitman and the Class Struggle*.
8. While dominant, this narrative has not remained unchallenged. Lawrence Buell, for one, has argued against the tendency to "enshrine Whitman, the most iconoclastic and charismatic of national bards, as the 'archetypal American poet'" (Buell, *New England Literary Culture*, 106). Similarly, Sacvan Bercovitch calls attention to the irony that "the canon that substituted *Song of Myself* for *The Song of Hiawatha* . . . also sanctified Whitman as outsider and nonconformist" (Bercovitch afterword, 428). See also the discussion of Whitman in Golding, *From Outlaw to Classic*.
9. See Cherkovski, *Whitman's Wild Children*; Gardner, *Discovering Ourselves in Whitman*; Miller, *American Quest for a Supreme Fiction*; Walker, *Bardic Ethos and the American Long Poem*; and Perlman, Folsom, and Campion, *Walt Whitman*.
10. Berlant, "On the Case," 665. Other attempts to situate Whitman with respect to less-well-known poets from the period include a comparison between Whitman and Latin American poet Rafael Pombo, in Gruesz, *Ambassadors of Culture*, and a comparison between Whitman and African American poet Frances Ellen Watkins Harper, in Bennett, "Frances Ellen Watkins Sings the Body Electric."
11. Similar parallels between Whitman and issues surrounding African Americans, American religion, and Native Americans are treated in, respectively, Klammer, *Whitman, Slavery, and the Emergence of* Leaves of Grass; Kuebrich, *Minor Prophecy*; and Folsom, *Whitman's Native Representations*.

12. Robert Levine's introduction to his online edition of *America and Other Poems* (⟨http://www.classroomelectric.org/volume1/levine/⟩), in which he foregrounds the similarities between Whitman and Whitfield's respective projects for American poetry, is the genesis for this point of comparison and, in many ways, provides the methodology behind all three comparative analyses in *American Bards*.

13. The cosmopolitan and transnational aspects of Whitfield's life and work are also discussed in Wilson, *Specters of Democracy*.

14. Whitman, *Notes and Fragments*, 55.

15. See Beecher, "Priestess among the Patriarchs."

16. Lawrence, *Studies in Classic American Literature*, 185–86.

17. See Rohrbach, "'Blast That Whirls the Dust,'" and in particular her comment that "as radically as critical views of Dickinson and Whitman have been revised over the last five years, their contemporaries have been viewed through a glass darkly, if at all" (3).

18. Folsom, "Talking Back to Walt Whitman," 37.

19. Morris, *Becoming Canonical in American Poetry*, xv.

20. [Whitman], "Walt Whitman and His Poems," 13.

21. Rossetti, "Prefatory Notice," 26.

22. Stalin, "The Nation," 20.

23. Delany, *Condition*, 42–43.

24. Edward Tullidge quoted in Hansen, *Quest for Empire*, 182. The *Latter-day Saints' Millennial Star* of 10 May 1856 reprinted a comment from the *Manchester Guardian* that similarly noted that the Mormons were "bent on constituting an *imperium in imperio*" in the United States.

25. Quoted in Kinshasa, *Emigration vs. Assimilation*, 89.

26. Snow, *Personal Writings*, 69.

27. *Sacramento Daily Bee*, 26 Feb., 24 July 1857.

28. Kadir, "Introduction," 21.

29. Wolosky, "Poetry and Public Discourse," 362.

30. Matthiessen, *American Renaissance*. The complementary posture of the Romantic outsider in British literature of the period is treated in Butler, *Romantics, Rebels, and Reactionaries*.

31. Bercovitch, *Rites of Assent*, 365, emphasis in original. For a retrospective on Bercovitch's influence on the field of American literary studies, see the essays in Alkana and Colatrella, *Cohesion and Dissent*.

32. Pease, "New Americanists," 29. For a survey of the impact on the field of American literary studies that the postnationalist approach Pease advocates has effected, see Kramer, "Imagining Authorship in America."

33. Soja, *Postmodern Geographies*, 189. See Buell, "Are We Post-American Studies?"; Rowe, "Nineteenth-Century United States Literary Culture"; Giroux, "National Identity"; and Giles, "Transnationalism and Classic American Literature."

34. Curiel et al. introduction, 2.

35. Bercovitch, *Rites of Assent*, 62.

36. Pease, "New Americanists," 29.

37. Cmiel, "Fate of the Nation," 189. Wai Chee Dimock has articulated the question that drives much of the scholarly work in this vein: "What would the world look like if

the nation were seen as no more than this: not foundational, not the seat of causation, but a 'ground' that is itself quite shaky, in need of heuristic supplement, and in need of analytic unbundling?" (Dimock, "Afterword," 226–27).

38. Whitman scholars have discussed the conflicts Whitman encountered as he attempted to reconcile his nationalism with his internationalism, his working-class consciousness, and his proscribed sexuality in a variety of ways. Whitman's internationalism is discussed in Gohdes, "Nationalism and Cosmopolitanism," and Asselineau, "Nationalism vs. Internationalism." A preliminary survey of scholarship on Whitman and sexuality includes Martin, *Homosexual Tradition*; Moon, *Disseminating Whitman*; and Maslan, *Whitman Possessed*. An introduction to Whitman and labor can be found in Thomas, *Lunar Light*; Trachtenberg, "Politics of Labor"; and Lawson, *Walt Whitman and the Class Struggle*.

39. Ted Genoways suggests that Whitman wrote and published "A Broadway Pageant" in the summer of 1860 in an effort to divert attention away from a spate of (mostly negative) reviews in the periodical press that had recently emphasized the sexually explicit nature of the poetry in the 1860 *Leaves of Grass*. See Genoways, *Walt Whitman and the Civil War*, 44–59.

40. Brogan, Preminger, and Warnke, "Poet Laureate," 924–25. There would be no formal mechanism for acknowledging anything resembling a national poet until the late 1930s when the Library of Congress appointed a "Consultant" in poetry, whose title was changed to "Poet Laureate" in 1985. Official recognition was not given to *any* person of letters in the United States until William Dean Howells was made the first president of the American Academy of Arts and Letters in 1908. See Steinman, "Public Cultural Expression." My thanks to Lisa Steinman for her insights on this issue.

41. Waldstreicher, *In the Midst of Perpetual Fetes*, 225, emphasis in original.

42. Gruesz, *Ambassadors of Culture*, 15–16.

43. Blasing, *Lyric Poetry*, 4.

44. Vendler, *"Tintern Abbey,"* 179.

45. Mill, *Essays on Poetry*, 12, 36; Frye, *Anatomy of Criticism*, 249–50.

46. Kamholtz, "Ben Johnson's *Epigrammes*," 80.

47. Culler, "Why Lyric?," 204. Culler draws much of his model from Jeffrey Walker's discussion of classical poetics in Walker's *Rhetoric and Poetics in Antiquity*. See also Gourgouris, *"Poiein,"* especially the discussion of classical poetic modes "whose work derives its primary meaning from the public sphere" (225).

48. Jackson, "Who Reads Poetry?," 183.

49. Keith D. Leonard has recently written in a similar vein about the office of the bard and the nature of representative identity with respect to the African American poets he refers to as "fettered geniuses." He writes, "I call these fettered geniuses *bardic poets*, then, because even in their occasional resistance to political obligation, they functioned as spokespeople for the race that articulated its cultural self through their resistance to social exclusion and to aesthetic limitation" (Leonard, *Fettered Genius*, 12).

50. Wolosky, "Claims of Rhetoric," 14.

51. Rohrbach, "'Blast That Whirls the Dust,'" 2. See Wolosky, "Claims of Rhetoric," and Prins, "Historical Poetics."

52. Wolosky, "Claims of Rhetoric," 14.

Chapter 1

1. Whitman's concern, as he wrote in 1847, was that slave labor would lead to the "degradation of free labor and the stagnation of enterprise" (Whitman, *Gathering of the Forces*, 1:205–6). Whitman also wrote, "I would preserve for free white labor a fair country, a rich inheritance, where the sons of toil, of my own race and color, can live without the disgrace which association with negro slavery brings upon free labor" (qtd. in Klammer, *Whitman, Slavery, and the Emergence of* Leaves of Grass, 30–31).

2. Quoted in Holland, *Frederick Douglass*, 201.

3. According to the 24 Oct. 1850 issue of the *North Star*, Whitfield was part of a "Mass Meeting of the Colored Citizens of Buffalo." For a biography of Whitfield, see Sherman, *Invisible Poets*, 42–53.

4. The convention is discussed in the 4 and 21 Aug. 1848 issues. The 24 Aug. 1849 issue of the *North Star* acknowledges "James M. Whitfield, do 1.00" as a subscriber to the newspaper "from the date of last acknowledgment to August 22, 1849."

5. See Levine, *Martin Delany, Frederick Douglass, and the Politics of Representative Identity*, 47–51.

6. His first poem was published in the *North Star* one year later on 10 Aug. 1849. For a record of Whitfield's publications, see Sherman, *Invisible Poets*, 222–23.

7. Brown, *Black Man*, 152.

8. See Whitman, *Collected Writings*.

9. Whitman, *I Sit and Look Out*, 90.

10. Douglass, Holly, Watkins, and Whitfield, *Arguments*, 30, emphasis in original.

11. See Horton and Horton, *In Hope of Liberty*, 177–202; Miller, *Search for a Black Nationality*; and Bell, "Negro Emigration Movement."

12. Whitman, *I Sit and Look Out*, 90.

13. Douglass, Holly, Watkins, and Whitfield, *Arguments*, 10, 30.

14. Emerson, *Portable Emerson*, 262.

15. *Proceedings of the National Emigration Convention*, 25. Whitfield attended this convention and signed this statement. The *North Star* of 24 Oct. 1850 reports that Whitfield was also part of a "Mass Meeting of the Colored Citizens of Buffalo" and signed a resolution opposing the Fugitive Slave Law.

16. Delany, *Condition*, 170.

17. *Proceedings of the National Emigration Convention*, 25, emphasis in original.

18. *Frederick Douglass' Paper*, 15 July 1853.

19. The essays Whitfield wrote for *Frederick Douglass' Paper* were collected in Douglass, Holly, Watkins, and Whitfield, *Arguments*.

20. Miller, *Search for a Black Nationality*, 138. Following the passage of the Fugitive Slave Law in 1850, interest in emigration experienced a resurgence as free northern blacks like Whitfield became convinced that their options for citizenship in the United States were increasingly limited. See ibid., 119, and Kinshasa, *Emigration vs. Assimilation*, 63.

21. Delany, *Condition*, 185–88.

22. Ibid., 7–8, 9, emphasis in original.

23. *Frederick Douglass' Paper*, 18 Nov. 1853. Miller says that by 1853 "Whitfield became the major protagonist for the emigrationists" (*Search for a Black Nationality*, 138). Whit-

field soon became a target for criticism in the press. A letter to *Frederick Douglass' Paper* attacking Whitfield's advocacy of emigration claimed that Whitfield had given a speech in 1846 accusing those who "leave their native land" of "moral cowardice," to which Whitfield rebutted that he had been an emigrationist "from boyhood" when in 1838–39 he had proposed that African Americans emigrate to California, which was then outside U.S. boundaries (Douglass, Holly, Watkins, and Whitfield, *Arguments*, 16).

24. *America*, 29, and Delany, *Blake*, 308.

25. *Frederick Douglass' Paper*, 18 Aug. 1854.

26. Holly, Lambert, and Whitfield, "Report of the Establishment of a Periodical," 30–31. No copies of this proposed journal—slated to be called *The Afric-American Repository*—have survived, leading scholars to question whether it was ever published. See Sherman, *Invisible Poets*, 44–45.

27. Holly, Lambert, and Whitfield, "Report of the Establishment of a Periodical," 28.

28. Whitman's pre-*Leaves of Grass* poems inspired by the Fugitive Slave Law are "Blood Money," "The House of Friends," and "Song for Certain Congressmen." See Whitman, *Collected Writings*, 40–48.

29. Whitman, "American Workingmen, Versus Slavery," 2.

30. In addition, one of the few pre-1855 poems included in the first edition of *Leaves of Grass* similarly centers around the return of a fugitive slave. "A Boston Ballad," a poem based on Boston abolitionists' refusal to return runaway slave Anthony Burns to his master, was included in the 1855 *Leaves of Grass* (*LG55*, 89–90).

31. See Erkkila, *Whitman the Political Poet*, 44–67; Reynolds, *Walt Whitman's America*, 115–30; Klammer, *Whitman, Slavery, and the Emergence of* Leaves of Grass; Sánchez-Eppler, *Touching Liberty*, 50–77; Folsom, "Lucifer and Ethiopia"; Beach, *Politics of Distinction*, 55–101; and Peeples, "Paradox of the 'Good Gray Poet.'"

32. Reynolds (*Walt Whitman's America*, 602n), Klammer (*Whitman, Slavery, and the Emergence of* Leaves of Grass, 3–4), and Erkkila (*Whitman the Political Poet*, 50) all identify this manuscript as the moment when Whitman developed both his distinctive poetic voice and his philosophy of democratic embrace. Andrew Higgins has argued that this manuscript fragment be dated to 1854 rather than 1847, making it a capstone of Whitman's thinking about slavery in the pre-*Leaves of Grass* era and not the initiating spark that Reynolds, Klammer, and Erkkila identify it as. Whether it came at the beginning or toward the end of the process that resulted in the first edition of *Leaves of Grass*, the manuscript fragment points to the importance of slavery in Whitman's conceptualization of the social contradictions that he addressed as an American bard. See Higgins, "Wage Slavery and the Composition of *Leaves of Grass*."

33. Folsom, "Lucifer and Ethiopia," 50. See also Sánchez-Eppler, *Touching Liberty*, 50–51.

34. Klammer, in contrast, argues in "Slavery and Race" that Whitman's racist attitudes persisted long after the declarations of egalitarianism that characterize the 1855 *Leaves of Grass*.

35. Reynolds, *Walt Whitman's America*, 122.

36. It is a terrible irony that the artful structure Whitfield employed for *America and Other Poems* was almost lost due to printing errors—such as duplicate printings of the same page—that were a result of the small budget he had for publishing his book. Whit-

field paid for *America and Other Poems* to be published by a small printing company in Buffalo, New York, that printed texts of various genres, including historical sketches, maps, and scientific treatises (Virgil, letter to author).

37. Fraistat, *Poem and the Book*, 6, 17. See also Jack, "Choice of Orders"; Fraistat, *Poems in their Place*; and Phelps, "Edition as Art Form."

38. Hinds and Matterson, "Introduction," 9, 3–4.

39. Culler, "Why Lyric?," 204.

40. Gray characterizes true poetry as "Thoughts that breathe, and words that burn," in Gray, "Progress of Poesy."

41. Delany, *Condition*, 170.

42. Documentary evidence of Whitfield's connection to these churches has survived, even if records of his delivering these particular dedicatory poems have not. See mention of Whitfield's connection with these churches in *North Star*, 24 Oct. 1850, and *Frederick Douglass' Paper*, 3 Sept. 1852.

43. *North Star*, 10 Aug. 1849. In addition to delivering his poem at this event, Whitfield also offered the following toast: "Our distinguished guest C[harles] L[enox] Remond, from his powerful advocacy of freedom in both hemispheres, entitled to the lasting gratitude of every philanthropist." For more on antebellum festive culture and the celebration of both the Fourth of July and the First of August, see Dennis, *Red, White, and Blue Letter Days*, and Waldstreicher, *In the Midst of Perpetual Fetes*.

44. Loeffelholz, "Religion of Art," 213.

45. Loeffelholz, "Anthology Form," 217.

46. Ibid., 220. On the relationship between public poetry and the political claims of women and minorities, see also Bennett, *Poets in the Public Sphere*.

47. Golding, *From Outlaw to Classic*, 9.

48. Smith, *American Poems*, iv. See also Carey, *Columbian Muse*.

49. Keese, *Poets of America*, 9–10.

50. Kettell, *Specimens of American Poetry*, iii.

51. Ibid., vi, iv.

52. *Frederick Douglass' Paper*, 23 Sept. 1853.

53. Du Bois, *Souls of Black Folk*, 11.

54. Delany, *Condition*, 42; Douglass, Holly, Watkins, and Whitfield, *Arguments*, 26.

55. Delany, *Condition*, 189–92, 198, 195.

56. Whitfield, "Letter from J. M. Whitfield," 501.

57. Douglass, Holly, Watkins, and Whitfield, *Arguments*, 26, 9.

58. Miller, *Nature's Nation*, 11.

59. See, for example, Bak and Hölbling, *Nature's Nation Revisited*; Tichi, *Embodiment of a Nation*; and Shaffer, *America First*.

60. Brückner, *Geographic Revolution*, 6.

61. Delany, *Condition*, 42; Douglass, Holly, Watkins, and Whitfield, *Arguments*, 26.

62. Quoted in Kinshasa, *Emigration vs. Assimilation*, 89. Bibb made this remark in 1850, at the same time that Delany was working as his correspondent; see Ullman, *Martin R. Delany*, 131. Bibb also signed his name alongside Whitfield's and Delany's in the call for the first national emigration convention in 1854; see Douglass, Holly, Watkins, and Whitfield, *Arguments*, 7.

63. Delany, *Condition*, 215, 226. The position of white raciologists is explained in Frederickson, *Black Image*, 145–52.

64. Frederick Douglass shared a similar opinion with Delany: "The history of the Negro race proves them to be wonderfully adapted to all countries, all climates, and all conditions" (qtd. in Holland, *Frederick Douglass*, 241).

65. Delany, *Condition*, 89.

66. Marx, *Machine in the Garden*, 156.

67. Delany, *Condition*, 78–80.

68. See Branham, "'Of Thee I Sing.'" A contributor to *The Liberator* wrote what is probably the first antislavery parody of the song in 1839 ("My country! 'tis of thee, / Stronghold of Slavery— / Of thee I sing"), and William Wells Brown published what was probably the most widely disseminated parody in his 1848 collection, *The Anti-Slavery Harp; A Collection of Songs for Anti-Slavery Meetings* ("Spirit of Freemen, wake; / No truce with Slavery make, / Thy deadly foe"). Other notable parodies were written by Joshua McCarter Simpson, Harriet Beecher Stowe, and James Madison Bell (Branham, "'Of Thee I Sing,'" 633–36).

69. Branham, "'Of Thee I Sing,'" 630.

70. See also Brückner, *Geographic Revolution*, 51–97, and Jehlen, *American Incarnation*, 5.

71. Miller, *Raven and the Whale*, 96.

72. Dixon, *Ride out the Wilderness*, 2.

73. Holly, Lambert, and Whitfield, "Report of the Establishment of a Periodical," 28.

74. Douglass, Holly, Watkins, and Whitfield, *Arguments*, 3.

75. Henry Bibb quoted in Kinshasa, *Emigration vs. Assimilation*, 89. See n. 62 above.

76. Emerson, *Portable Emerson*, 262; Brückner, *Geographic Revolution*, 6.

77. Bercovitch, *Rites of Assent*, 29. See also Bercovitch, *Puritan Origins*.

78. Hughes, *Collected Poems*, 23.

79. Reynolds, *European Revolutions*, 12, 81.

80. Douglass, Holly, Watkins, and Whitfield, *Arguments*, 26, emphasis in original.

81. Delany, *Condition*, 42–43.

82. See, for example, Ullman, *Martin R. Delany*.

83. Scott, *Poetical Works*, 89. It bears noting that Whitman, too, would refer to Europe as "the lair of slaves" in one of his poems (*LG* 212).

84. Critics who have commented on this include Gay Wilson Allen and M. Wynn Thomas. See Allen, "Walt Whitman," and Thomas, *Lunar Light*.

85. Whitman, *Complete Poetry and Collected Prose*, 1324.

86. Ibid., 1313.

87. Ibid., 1324–25. In the same essay, however, Whitman says that white northerners are duty-bound to support the Fugitive Slave Law, writing, "Must runaway slaves be delivered back? They must. Many things may have the go-by, but good faith shall never have the go-by" (ibid., 1320).

88. *America and Other Poems* was positively reviewed in the 15 July 1854 issue of the *Provincial Freeman* as well as in the 15 July and 23 Sept. 1853 issues of *Frederick Douglass' Paper*. Douglass called Whitfield a "sable son of genius" (qtd. in Sherman, *Invisible Poets*, 42); Delany called him "one of the purest poets in America" (*Condition*, 132); and Brown said

that Whitfield's poetry displayed "good taste and excellent language" (*Black Man*, 152–53). Indeed, the praise for Whitfield's poetry was often ebullient, with *Frederick Douglass' Paper* saying in the 15 July 1853 issue that "Mr. Whitfield is a genius, and a genuine lover of the muses."

89. See Sherman, *Invisible Poets*, 43.

90. Quoted in Sherman, *Invisible Poets*, 42.

91. This biographical information is available in ibid., 42–46.

92. Whitfield, "Poem by J. M. Whitfield," 3.

93. Johnson and Whitfield, *Emancipation Oration*, 25.

94. Ibid., 2.

Chapter 2

1. Whitman's trip west is recorded in Eitner, *Walt Whitman's Western Jaunt*.

2. See Twain, *Roughing It*, chaps. 12–16; Burton, *City of the Saints*; and "Horace Greely Interviews Brigham Young." Eric A. Eliason writes that "personally looking into what the Mormons were up to became an important item on the agenda of many westerning tourists, scholars, and travel writers" (Eliason, "Curious Gentiles," 156). J. Valerie Fifer similarly writes that Salt Lake City became "the first and forever the most popular of all the side-trips on the original Union Pacific–Central Pacific Railroad" (Fifer, *American Progress*, 285).

3. Fanny Ward Stenhouse used this phrase to describe Snow in her book, *"Tell It All,"* 252. Snow was also referred to as "a sort of poet laureate" among the Mormons by Ambrose Bolivar Carlton in his *Wonderlands of the Wild West*, 152. Jill Mulvay Derr, in her article "Lion and the Lioness," 62–63, records that Young would give copies of Snow's poems to visitors.

4. *Brooklyn Daily Times*, 19 Nov. 1858. For more on the Book of Mormon, see Givens, *By the Hand of Mormon*.

5. Stenhouse, *"Tell It All,"* 252. Maureen Ursenbach Beecher records that Snow served as an unofficial counselor to Brigham Young; see Beecher, "Eliza Enigma." Ann Eliza Young wrote that "Brigham [Young] regards her [Snow] very highly, because she is of such inestimable service in the church. . . . She is the most intellectual of all the wives" (Young, *Wife No. 19*, 502).

6. Stenhouse, *"Tell It All,"* 252; Tullidge, *Women of Mormondom*, 194. Derr, in her "Significance of 'O My Father,'" 88, records Snow's calling as "Zion's Poetess." Derr also writes that Snow "wielded phenomenal religious power: charismatic power (as prophetess, she exercised the gift of tongues, prophecy, and healing); liturgical power (as priestess, she presided over women who ministered temple rites in the Endowment House); and ecclesiastical power (as presidentess, she directed the work of Latter-day Saint women within the Church organization)" (Derr, "Form and Feeling," 29). Snow also secured what Beecher calls "a degree of public influence unequaled by [other] women on the frontier" (Beecher, "Priestess among the Patriarchs," 153).

7. Emerson, *Essays and Lectures*, 726.

8. Stenhouse, *"Tell It All,"* 289; Tullidge, *Women of Mormondom*, 31. Emmeline B. Wells, a prominent Mormon woman of the early twentieth century, described Snow in a verse tribute as not only the "regnant-mother" of the Latter-day Saints, but a "Priestess, Prophet too" (Wells, *Musings and Memories*, 326).

9. Perry is quoted in Kuebrich, *Minor Prophecy*, 2; James, *Varieties of Religious Experience*, 87. For more information on the Whitman disciples at the turn of the century, see Robertson, *Worshipping Walt*, and Willard, *Whitman's American Fame*, 32–84.

10. Stevenson, "Gospel According to Walt Whitman," 462.

11. Ludlow, *Heart of the Continent*, 523, 524.

12. "Future Home of the Mormons." Thanks to Halli Goldman for locating this source.

13. Hale, *Ladies' Wreath*, 3–4.

14. Quoted in Bennett, *Nineteenth-Century American Women Poets*, 3; May, *American Female Poets*, vi.

15. The restrictions placed on Snow's ability to preach to promiscuous gatherings of male and female Latter-day Saints is discussed in Derr and Davidson, *Eliza R. Snow*, xxxiv.

16. Watts, *Poetry of American Women*, 6.

17. Whitman wrote in 1872, "When I commenced, years ago, elaborating the plan of my poems . . . one deep purpose underlay the others, and has underlain it and its execution ever since—and that has been the Religious purpose" (*PW* 2:461).

18. Robertson, *Worshipping Walt*, 18.

19. Harris comments on the biblical design of the 1860 edition, in "Whitman's *Leaves of Grass*," 184 n. 3. See also these essays about the biblical feel of Whitman's poetry: Levine, "'Song of Myself' as Whitman's American Bible"; Stefanelli, "'Chants' as 'Psalms for a New Bible'"; and Zitter, "Songs of the Canon." Other discussions of Whitman and religion include Chari, *Whitman in the Light of Vedantic Mysticism*; Hutchinson, *Ecstatic Whitman*; Kuebrich, *Minor Prophecy*; Sowder, "Walt Whitman, the Apostle"; and Warner, "Civil War Religion and Whitman's Drum-Taps."

20. Emerson, *Essays and Lectures*, 761. See also Smith, "Whitman's Poet-Prophet and Carlyle's Hero."

21. Buell, *New England Literary Culture*, 183. While Buell is dismissive of the religious context within which Whitman made his claim to write a new American bible, he has since gone on to advocate for more scholarly inquiry into the role of religion in antebellum culture: "I stress the importance of pursuing religion as a focus of inquiry because contemporary U.S. literary and cultural studies . . . generally fails to reckon with religion's force as a motivating concern either domestically or abroad" (Buell, "Introduction," 11).

22. A number of scholars have made brief mention of Mormonism in their discussions of Whitman and religion. See, for example, Kuebrich, *Minor Prophecy*, 25; Killingsworth, *Whitman's Poetry of the Body*, 44; Harris, "Whitman's *Leaves of Grass*," 184 n. 5; Reynolds, *Walt Whitman's America*, 368; and Robertson, *Worshipping Walt*, 16. Genoways mentions an 1860 reviewer of *Leaves of Grass* who "warned his readers that the [sexual] naturalism advocated by Whitman would lead to polygamy of the sort embraced by the Mormons" (Genoways, *Walt Whitman and the Civil War*, 51).

23. Chapman, "Walt Whitman," 103–4.

24. [Anonymous], "Leaves of Grass"; [Lewes], "Transatlantic Latter-Day Poetry." Walter Parke's poem "St. Smith of Utah" similarly imitates Whitman's poetic style while parodying the Mormon prophet (261–62).

25. Gutjahr, "Sacred Texts," 377. See also Gutjahr, *American Bible*.

26. Buell, "Literature and Scripture," 1.

27. Burton, *City of the Saints*, 285.

28. Baym, *American Women Writers*, 48–49.

29. *Lantern*, 17 Jan. 1852, 15.

30. While the Mormons continued to revere the Bible as a sacred text, Joseph Smith said that "the Book of Mormon [is] the most correct of any book on earth . . . and that a man [will] get nearer to God by abiding by its precepts than by any other book," including, presumably, the Bible (qtd. in Roberts, *History of the Church of Jesus Christ of Latter-day Saints*, 4:461). For more on Mormonism and biblical Christianity, see Barlow, *Mormons and the Bible*.

31. Shipps, *Mormonism*, 52.

32. Lewis, *American Adam*, 44–45; Lawrence, *New Poems*, v; Matthiessen, *American Renaissance*, 651–52.

33. See Dimock, "Epic and Lyric"; Cutler, *Recovering the New*, 139–42, Friedl, "Making It Cohere"; Salska, "Growth of the Past"; Bové, *Destructive Poetics*, 131–80; and Steinbrink, "'To Span Vast Realms.'"

34. This is also recorded in Whitman, *Notes and Fragments*, 78.

35. Whitman, *Complete Writings*, 10:17.

36. For the story of Snow's conversion, see Davidson and Derr, "Wary Heart."

37. Smith, *Teachings of the Prophet Joseph Smith*, 172.

38. Bushman, *Joseph Smith*, 185. See also Shipps, "Reality of the Restoration," 191.

39. Hansen, *Mormonism and the American Experience*, 27.

40. Givens, *By the Hand of Mormon*, 50.

41. Ibid., 50; Tompkins, "Sentimental Power," 512–13. The difference between Tompkins's take on antebellum Christian sentimentalism and Givens's perspective on the Mormon restoration is admittedly a difference in degree rather than kind, but early Mormons would have been the first to argue that they were merely taking seriously the religious principles that, in their opinion, their countrymen only partially understood. See also Shipps's argument, in *Mormonism*, 52–87, that there was enough substantive difference between the Mormon experience and the American Christian origins of the religion to qualify it as a post-Christian religion that experienced a different kind of sacred time; see also Duffy, "'Religion by Revelation.'"

42. O'Sullivan, "Great Nation of Futurity," 426–30.

43. Snow, *Personal Writings*, 16. A theological impulse to restore ancient practices was not the only rationale given for polygamy, however. Other defenses of polygamy invoked the inherently promiscuous nature of male sexuality as well as women's punishment for Eve's having partaken of the forbidden fruit in the Garden of Eden. Hardy writes that "polygamy represented more to the Saints than only an opportunity to broaden their sexual experience. It was integral with their cosmology" (Hardy, *Solemn Covenant*, 10–11).

44. Stevenson, "Gospel According to Walt Whitman," 470.

45. Quoted in Winn, *Exiles in a Land of Liberty*, 229. Givens writes that "the pejorative nature of the comparison [of Mormonism] with Islam bespeaks a sense of outrage that what presents itself as 'us' (Mormonism is, after all, a religion laying claim to being quintessentially American and Christian) is, in reality, more like 'them', meaning Oriental in precisely those ways that are un-American and un-Christian" (Givens, *Viper on the Hearth*, 130).

46. *North American Review*, July 1862, 190. Allmendinger has similarly shown how nineteenth-century Americans compared Mormons with Native Americans, arguing that

"by defining Mormons as Indians, and polygamy as a refined form of savagery, the nation fashioned a political rhetoric that attempted to justify its intervention in Utah's affairs" (Allmendinger, *Ten Most Wanted*, 64).

47. Quoted in Bush, "Mormon 'Physiology,'" 225. Bartholow was quoted authoritatively in a wide variety of reputable sources, only one of which called the scientific nature of the report into question (ibid., 224–26). See also Givens, *Viper on the Hearth*, 121–52.

48. Ludlow, *Heart of the Continent*, 515; Hardy, *Solemn Covenant*, 41.

49. Dimock, "Deep Time," 760.

50. See Fabian, *Time and the Other*, and Kaplan, *Questions of Travel*.

51. *Frederick Douglass' Paper*, 18 Feb. 1853.

52. See Flanders, *Nauvoo*. The violent outbreaks between Mormons and Americans also grew out of fears that the Mormons' tendency toward block voting would jeopardize local elections and impatience at the Saints' bold territorial claims to lands that they said God had promised them. See Winn, *Exiles in a Land of Liberty*, 63–105; Arrington and Bitton, *Mormon Experience*, 44–82; and Furniss, *Mormon Conflict*.

53. Moore, *Religious Outsiders*, 27.

54. Arrington and Haupt, "Intolerable Zion," 253. In addition to novels, "by 1850, more than two hundred pamphlets, articles, and 'exposés' had been published" (Givens, *Viper on the Hearth*, 124). See also Cannon, "Awesome Power of Sex," 71.

55. Gordon, *Mormon Question*, 29. See also Handley, *Marriage, Violence, and the Nation*, 97–124.

56. Bentley, "Marriage as Treason," 343, 352. See also Hardy, *Solemn Covenant*, 42; Davis, "Themes of Counter Subversion," 67. Mormons were not the only group to experiment with alternatives to monogamy, but unlike the practices of the Shakers (who swore off sex entirely) or the Oneida Perfectionists (who promoted polyamorous relationships for both men and women), polygamy received the most attention and the most opprobrium. See Foster, *Religion and Sexuality*, and Kern, *Ordered Love*.

57. For discussions of the analogy equating slavery with polygamy, see Givens, "Caricature as Containment," and Allmendinger, *Ten Most Wanted*, 52.

58. *Times and Seasons*, 15 Apr. 1841, 383. Thanks to Jill Mulvay Derr for this citation.

59. Baym, *American Women Writers*, 56, 1.

60. Whitman, *Gathering of the Forces*, 1:28.

61. Snow's depiction of Time differs from that of her contemporaries, who personified Time as an old, silver-haired man with a grizzled beard wending a slow course through history. See Dunlap, "Ode to Time," and Morton, "Odes to Time."

62. See Johannsen, *Halls of the Montezumas*.

63. Wald, *Constituting Americans*, 16–17; Said, "Invention, Memory, and Place," 179.

64. Loeffelholz, "Anthology Form," 218, 220.

65. Snow, *Personal Writings*, 33.

66. Derr and Davidson, *Eliza R. Snow*, xii. Derr and Davidson further note, "From the 1840s to the 1880s, no public event in the Mormon community . . . was complete without a contribution from Zion's honored spokeswoman" (ibid., xxvii).

67. *Latter-day Saints' Millennial Star*, 16 Feb. 1856, 105.

68. See Travers, *Celebrating the Fourth*.

69. The 11 Apr. 1841 *Times and Seasons* records that the poem was published in broadside form the preceding week.

70. *Brooklyn Daily Times*, 14 June 1858. Whitman's other articles on Mormonism can be found in the following issues of the *Brooklyn Daily Times*: 9 and 10 July 1857, 19 Mar. 1858, and 14 June and 19 Nov. 1858.

71. Ludlow, *Heart of the Continent*, 278.

72. Ibid., 278–79.

73. Stenhouse, *"Tell It All,"* 171; O'Dea, "Mormonism and the Avoidance of Sectarian Stagnation," 287.

74. Snow, *Poems*, 2:39.

75. See Bigler, *Forgotten Kingdom*, 56.

76. Ludlow, *Heart of the Continent*, 524, 513.

77. Quoted in Tullidge, *Women of Mormondom*, 352.

78. *The Mormon*, 31 Mar. 1855.

79. Gordon, *Mormon Question*, 9.

80. Arrington, *Great Basin Kingdom*, 98, 139. By 1844, Mormon missionaries had been sent to Australia, India, South America, Germany, and Jamaica, and by the end of the Civil War, there were missionaries in Canada, the Hawaiian Islands, Tahiti, Chile, Scandinavia, England, Scotland, Ireland, Holland, France, Germany, Switzerland, Austria, Italy, Gibraltar, Palestine, South Africa, India, Ceylon, Burma, Siam, Hong Kong, Australia, Tasmania, New Zealand, Samoa, and Tonga. See Whittaker, "Missionary Journeys," 32–33.

81. Arrington and Bitton, *Mormon Experience*, 139.

82. Quoted in Nibley, *Brigham Young*, 128.

83. *The Mormon*, 17 Feb. 1855. Subsequent editions contain articles on Cuba (3 Mar. 1855), the Sandwich Islands (3 Mar. 1855), the Crimea (24 Mar. 1855), and China, as well as "Foreign News" announcements, such as one that includes news updates from Italy, France, Vienna, Russia, and Poland (24 Feb. 1855).

84. See Handley, *Marriage, Violence, and the Nation*, 110.

85. "The Mormons," from the *Manchester Guardian*, reprinted in *The Latter-day Saints' Millennial Star*, 10 May 1856.

86. *Holy Scriptures*, Book of Moses 7:62; Smith, *Personal Writings*, 229.

87. Snow, *Personal Writings*, 69.

88. Quoted in Hayden, *Seven American Utopias*, 114.

89. Bushman, *Making Space for Mormons*, 17, 6.

90. See Davis, "New England Origins," 27. The short-lived antebellum newspaper *The Mormon* ran an article that explicitly linked the Mormons to the Puritans: "Is there any resemblance, politically, between the position of the early Puritans toward their transatlantic sovereign and the Latter Day Saints toward their trans–rocky mountain parent? We think there is quite a resemblance. Did they leave their parent country on account of their religion? So did we. Did they leave their fathers, mothers, and nearest friends, to seek an asylum in a wild Indian country, far remote from their former homes? So did we" (Robbins, "Fourth of July Oration," 2).

91. Griswold, *Female Poets of America*, 8.

92. *Life and Labors*, 10.

93. [Griswold], "[Review of *Leaves of Grass* (1855)]."

94. Quoted in Derr, "Significance of 'O My Father,'" 85.

95. See Hicks, "'O My Father.'" For an account of public readings of "O My Father" in late-nineteenth-century Mormon women's clubs, see Gere, *Intimate Practices*, 232.

96. Wilford Woodruff quoted in Derr, "Significance of 'O My Father,'" 98. See also Wilcox, "Mormon Concept."

97. Snow, "Woman, Jan. 30, 1855," 2.

98. Ibid. Defining Snow's position with respect to the women's rights movement of the nineteenth century is a difficult task. Compton contends that "it would be naive to define her as feminist or anti-feminist by late-twentieth-century standards," given that her advocacy on behalf of women always came within the context of her devout faith in and support of the patriarchal male hierarchy of the Church of Jesus Christ of Latter-day Saints; see Compton, *In Sacred Loneliness*, 340. For an analysis of the ways in which Mormon women such as Snow work within a patriarchal society to find a place for women, see Derr and Derr, "Outside the Mormon Hierarchy," and Iversen, "Feminist Implications of Mormon Polygyny," 507, 519. Similarly, in a sociological analysis of the Mormon doctrine of the Mother in Heaven, John Hereen, Donald B. Lindsey, and Marylee Mason "arrive at the ironic conclusion that patriarchy and belief in a goddess go hand-in-hand in the Mormon case" ("Mormon Concept of a Mother in Heaven," 409).

99. Dixon, *New America*, 205. See also Foster, *Religion and Sexuality*, 198, for details on other such unconsummated polygamous marriages.

100. John W. Taylor quoted in *Life and Labors*, 24. Snow was thirty-eight when she married Joseph Smith and forty when she married Brigham Young, long past what would have been considered her childbearing years; this suggests that little if any stigma was ever attached to her childless status. My thanks to Jill Mulvay Derr for this observation.

101. Petrino, *Emily Dickinson and Her Contemporaries*, 14. Nina Baym expresses this worldview in a similar manner: "If worldly values could dominate the home, perhaps the direction of influence could be reversed so that home values dominated the world" (Baym, *Woman's Fiction*, 48–49).

102. See, for example, Heller, "Housebreaking History."

103. Erkkila, *Whitman the Political Poet*, 316–17. See also Ceniza, *Walt Whitman*, 35; Erkkila, "Federal Mother," 434; Wrobel, "'Noble American Motherhood,'" 7; Killingsworth, "Whitman and Motherhood"; and Jensen, *Leaving the M/other*.

104. Whitman, *Complete Writings*, 9:11.

105. Bitton and Bunker, *Mormon Graphic Image*, 57.

106. Tullidge, *Women of Mormondom*, 187–88.

107. Richardson, "Collaboration, Materialism, and Masochism," 173. See also Kete, *Sentimental Collaborations*.

108. Petrino, *Emily Dickinson and Her Contemporaries*, 34.

109. Snow, *Poems*, 2:1.

110. Hicks, "'O My Father,'" 33.

111. May, *American Female Poets*, vi. Walker has similarly written that "one of the defining features of sentimentalism is the reversal of the roles usually accorded to reason and emotion" such that emotion is privileged over reason; see Walker, "Nineteenth-Century American Women Poets Revisited," 235. For a discussion of one particular moment in Snow's life when Brigham Young demanded that she retract some of her thoughts on the theology of the resurrection that she had published, see Givens, *People of Paradox*, 177–78. Throughout his book Givens provides an insightful analysis of how Mormonism in general is shot through with paradoxes between authority and autonomy, reason and revelation, the individual and the community.

112. Derr, "Form and Feeling," 8.

113. Snow, *Personal Writings*, 64.

114. Dixon, *New America*, 205.

115. Dickinson, *Poems*, 434.

Chapter 3

1. Whitman, *Gathering of the Forces*, 2:136–47.

2. This story can be found in Wilkins, *Cherokee Tragedy*. See also McLoughlin, *After the Trail of Tears*, and Wardell, *Political History*.

3. Thobrun, "Cherokee Question," 238, quotes *The Official Records of the Union and Confederate Armies* as saying, "The full-blooded Indians are mostly adherents of Ross, and many of them—1,000 to 1,500 it is alleged—are on the side of the North, I think that number is exaggerated. The half-breeds or white Indians (as they call themselves) are to a man with us."

4. Lawrence, *Studies in Classic American Literature*, 186.

5. [Anonymous], "[Review of *Leaves of Grass* (1855)]," *The Critic*. See *LG56* 375.

6. Quoted in Rubin, *Historic Whitman*, 66, emphasis in original.

7. Rawson, "Bygone Bohemia," 105.

8. Quoted in Loving, *Walt Whitman*, 291.

9. Wahnenauhi, "Wahnenauhi Manuscript," 181–82.

10. Dale and Litton, *Cherokee Cavaliers*, 86–87.

11. Scholars are divided over whether Ridge turned his back on his Native heritage (as Ellis and Debo argue) or whether he maintained his commitment to Native American causes from within white society (as Owens argues). A number of other scholars (such as Powell) have instead focused on the desire of scholars to make of Ridge either a multicultural icon or a target of critique for essentialist racial politics. See Ellis, "'Our Ill Fated Relative'"; Debo, "John Rollin Ridge"; Owens, *Other Destinies*, 32, 40; and Powell, "Historical Multiculturalism."

12. Pearce, *Savages of America*, x. Pearce's insight that a dialectic between savagery and civilization forms the ideological foundation for much of U.S. culture has been extended in a number of more recent studies, including Drinnon, *Facing West*; Maddox, *Removals*; Scheckel, *Insistence of the Indian*; and Bellin, *Demon of the Continent*.

13. Longfellow, *Song of Hiawatha*, 134.

14. Folsom, *Whitman's Native Representations*, 65, 57. Folsom's work is indispensable for anyone seeking to understand Whitman's complex attitudes toward Native Americans. See also Nolan, *Poet-Chief*; Kenny, "Whitman's Indifference to Indians"; Clark, *Walt Whitman's Concept*; Soodik, "Tribe Called Text"; and Blakemore and Noble, "Whitman and 'The Indian Problem.'" The following works about Whitman's attitude toward U.S. expansionism and imperialism also provide a useful context for understanding the place that he made for Native Americans in his vision of American democracy: Erkkila, "Whitman and American Empire," and Grünzweig, "Noble Ethics and Loving Aggressiveness."

15. Whitman, *Gathering of the Forces*, 2:137.

16. Kirkland preface, viii. Susan Scheckel has summarized this line of thinking as follows: "By claiming Indians, with their long history and mysterious origins, as part of their own national story, nineteenth-century Americans found a way to ground national iden-

tity" in a continent to which they had no historic claim. See Scheckel, *Insistence of the Indian*, 8.

17. Longfellow, *Poems and Other Writings*, 794.

18. Whitman, *Notes and Fragments*, 40.

19. Kaup and Rosenthal introduction, xv.

20. Folsom, *Whitman's Native Representations*, 72.

21. Scheick, *Half-Blood*, 69. See also Deloria, *Playing Indian*, and Huhndorf, *Going Native*.

22. Cooper, *Leatherstocking Tales I*, 609.

23. While Ridge was able to move relatively freely through white society, he once had his right to vote called into question. See Parins, *John Rollin Ridge*, 202.

24. Porter, *Webster's Revised Unabridged Dictionary*, 45.

25. *Sacramento Daily Bee*, 25 Mar. 1857, 3.

26. Ibid., 7 Apr. 1857, emphasis in original.

27. Ridge, "Letter from John Rollin Ridge."

28. *Sacramento Daily Bee*, 24 July 1857.

29. Maddox, *Removals*, 24.

30. Dale and Litton, *Cherokee Cavaliers*, 83, 85–86, emphasis in original.

31. See the essays in Ridge, *Trumpet of Our Own*.

32. *Sacramento Daily Bee*, 6 May 1857.

33. Parins, *John Rollin Ridge*, 175.

34. *Sacramento Daily Bee*, 13 Apr. 1857.

35. Gordon, "Early California Journalism," 128.

36. Ridge, *Joaquin Murieta*, 2. His one published volume of poems similarly, albeit less dramatically, included a brief autobiographical statement providing "a knowledge of my parentage and how it happened that I am an Indian" (*Ridge* 5).

37. *Sacramento Daily Bee*, 4 Feb 1857.

38. *Marysville Express*, 7 Nov. 1857.

39. Parins similarly speculates that this poem was both loosely autobiographical and highly romanticized; see Parins, *John Rollin Ridge*, 78.

40. Whitman, *Half-Breed and Other Stories*, 24–25.

41. See Sturm, *Blood Politics*, 31–43, 56–57, 68; Perdue, *"Mixed Blood" Indians*; and Thornton, *Cherokees*, 52, 104.

42. Parins, *John Rollin Ridge*, 11. For a discussion of the debate in the popular press over the perceived evils of intermarriage between whites and Cherokees, see Coward, *Newspaper Indian*, 50–51.

43. *Maryland Gazette*, 26 Feb. 1824.

44. Ridge, "Far in a Lonely Wood." The poem is signed by "Yellow Bird" and dated "Osage, July 18, 1847." It was later reprinted in the *Arkansas Gazette*, 20 July 1941.

45. Quoted in Parins, *John Rollin Ridge*, 44.

46. See Maddox, *Removals*, 15–35, and Sweet, *American Georgics*, 97–152.

47. Emerson, *Political Emerson*, 29.

48. These poems can be found in Ridge's posthumous 1868 collection of poems under the following titles: "Poem," "California," "The Atlantic Cable." See *Ridge* 95–100, 87–92, 17–21.

49. Quoted in Parins, *John Rollin Ridge*, 201. Parins reports that the *Nevada Gazette* "published a satirical verse, 'A Noad to Ridge', on 24 Oct. 1864. It was signed 'Jaybird, first cousin to Yellowbird, poet laureate of the Cherokee Nation.'" The poem accused Ridge of opposing the U.S. government, saying "Against the Government you'll fight— / Your 'dander it has riz'—" and then claiming that the word "riz" was taken from the "Original Cherokee" (201–2).

50. See Evans, "Following the Rainbow," and Foreman, "Edward W. Bushyhead and Ridge." Ridge predicted that ultimately he would return from California "to my own people and to my own country. . . . I intend some day, sooner or later to plant my foot in the Cherokee Nation and stay there too, or die" (qtd. in Dale, "John Rollin Ridge," 317).

51. Parins, *John Rollin Ridge*, 73–76, 92.

52. Ranck, "John Rollin Ridge in California," 565; Parins, *John Rollin Ridge*, 137.

53. *Daily Alta California*, 27 May 1861, 2.

54. Parins writes that, during the mid-1860s, "the Nevada City Republican newspapers referred to Ridge as a 'half-breed Indian', and one of them even questioned his citizenship. The 17 and 18 Oct. issues of the *Nevada Daily Gazette* carried articles with identical headlines: 'Is John R. Ridge a Legal Voter?' The first piece cites section 1, article 2, of the California constitution, which limits suffrage to white males. . . . The second article asserts that the Cherokees are a separate nation and that Ridge should vote there instead of in California" (Parins, *John Rollin Ridge*, 201–2).

55. *Marysville Express*, 23 Jan. 1858. Ridge also had a poem published in Shuck, *California Scrapbook*, 480, under the heading "A sample of domestic manufacture."

56. Dale and Litton, *Cherokee Cavaliers*, 82.

57. *San Francisco Golden Era*, 21 Jan. 1855.

58. Kowaleski, "Romancing the Gold Rush," 206. See also Haslam, *Many Californias*, 17, and Hicks, Houston, Kingston, and Young, *Literature of California*, 3.

59. Quoted in Holliday, *Rush for Riches*, 332.

60. Whitman, "Promise to California."

61. Whitman, *Correspondence*, 2:282.

62. *San Francisco Herald*, 13 Sept. 1861; Ridge, *Trumpet of Our Own*, 23.

63. Quoted in Michaels, Reid, and Scherr, *West of the West*, xi.

64. Ridge, *Trumpet of Our Own*, 22.

65. Ibid., 51–52.

66. Starr, "Rooted in Barbarous Soil," 4.

67. Clappe, *Shirley Letters*, 124, 108, emphasis in original.

68. Delano, *On the Trail*, 359. See also Chan, "People of Exceptional Character"; Holliday, *World Rushed In*; and Johnson, *Roaring Camp*, for historical analyses of the social interaction between the diverse populations of antebellum California.

69. Clappe, *Shirley Letters*, 142, 140.

70. *San Francisco Herald*, 13 Sept. 1861.

71. *Sacramento Daily Bee*, 26 Feb. 1857.

72. Whitney, "Address," 48; Farwell, *Oration Delivered*, 13.

73. Whitney, "Address," 49.

74. Ibid., 31, 7.

75. Virtually no records have survived about the Agricultural, Horticultural, and Mechanics' Society of the Northern District of California. It was probably one of many such

short-lived farming organizations that eventually became part of the Grange. A single extant broadside from the society can be found at ⟨http://digitalassets.lib.berkeley.edu/ honeyman/ucb/images/HN001768aA.jpg⟩, accessed 4 Nov. 2009.

76. For a discussion of Thomas Jefferson's farming policies for Native Americans, see Sweet, *American Georgics*, 97–152, and Dippie, *Vanishing American*, 56.

77. Cole's paintings are titled *The Savage State, The Pastoral or Arcadian State, The Consummation of Empire, Destruction*, and *Desolation*. See Noble and Vesell, *Life and Works of Thomas Cole*, 13–17. For further discussion of such cyclical theories of history, see Maddox, *Removals*, 5–17, 29–38, and Carr, *Inventing the American Primitive*, 22–50, 60–68.

78. Warren, *Culture of Eloquence*, 25. See also Clark and Halloran, "Introduction."

79. See Wertheimer, *Imagined Empires*.

80. Griswold, *Poets and Poetry*, x.

81. Berkhoffer, *White Man's Indian*, 48.

82. Ridge, *Joaquin Murieta*, 138.

83. For various versions of the Native American legend about vanishing or wandering islands, see Thompson, *Tales of the Indians*, 275, and Mooney, *Myths of the Cherokee*, 239–40. Thanks to Suzanne Lundquist, Jane Hafen, Timothy Sweet, John Taylor, Denis Cutchins, and Daniel Justice for helping to locate possible sources of this island legend.

84. Polk, *Island of California*, 132.

85. Ibid. See also de Montalvo, *Labors of the Very Brave Knight Esplandián*.

86. *Marysville Weekly California Express*, 10 Apr. 1858.

87. Ridge, *Trumpet of Our Own*, 49, 62, 69.

88. *Sacramento Daily Bee*, 21 July, 7 Apr. 1857.

89. For a discussion of the way that "improvement" trumped literacy and Christianity as the primary criterion for civilization in the debates surrounding Indian Removal, see Sweet, *American Georgics*, 126.

90. *San Francisco Herald*, 10 Sept. 1861.

91. Matthews, "Forging a Cosmopolitan Civic Culture," 214.

92. Parins, *John Rollin Ridge*, 201–2.

93. Abbot, "Identity of the Different Races." Thanks to Katie Walker for identifying this source.

94. McLellan, "Hymn of the Cherokee Indian." Thanks to Laura Eull for identifying this source.

95. See Killingsworth, "Voluptuous Earth," 20, and Blakemore and Noble, "Whitman and 'The Indian Problem.'"

96. *Sacramento Daily Bee*, 24 July 1857.

97. Whitman, *Complete Poetry and Collected Prose*, 1146–47. Ed Folsom refers to Whitman's "dream of amalgamation, of melding, of absorption and open embrace" (Folsom, "Talking Back to Walt Whitman," 67).

98. Parins, *John Rollin Ridge*, 220; Foreman, "Edward W. Bushyhead and Ridge," 309.

99. Quoted in Wu, *Yellow*, 97.

Chapter 4

1. [Whitman], "Walt Whitman and His Poems."

2. "Arrival of the Japanese," 1; Whitman, *Specimen Days & Collect*, 17.

3. Pease, *Visionary Compacts*, 113. Whitman seized relatively few opportunities to play

the role of the public bard before 1855: in 1846 he wrote a Fourth of July ode that was published in the *Brooklyn Daily Eagle*, and after that he wrote a number of politically themed poems that addressed national issues (some of which later appeared in *Leaves of Grass* as "A Boston Ballad" and "Europe") with the authority of a bard. The Fourth of July poem appears in Whitman, *Collected Writings*, 34–35.

4. See, for example, Erkkila, *Whitman the Political Poet*, 3, 102.

5. Cowley introduction, xxvii.

6. Whitman, *Correspondence*, 3:369.

7. Dimock, "Afterword," 226.

8. For the most complete account of Whitman's life at this moment between the successful publication of the 1860 *Leaves of Grass* and the start of the Civil War, see Genoways, *Walt Whitman and the Civil War*.

9. Beginning with the 1867 edition of *Leaves of Grass* Whitman changed the phrase "Walt Whitman, an American, one of the roughs, a kosmos" to "Walt Whitman am I, of mighty Manhattan the son"; in subsequent editions he changed it again to variations on the phrase, "Walt Whitman, a kosmos, of Manhattan the son." See Whitman, *Leaves of Grass* (1867), 49; *Leaves of Grass* (1872), 54; *Leaves of Grass* (1881), 48; *Leaves of Grass* (1891–92), 48. The phrase "Good Gray Poet" comes from the title of an 1866 biography written by a friend to protest Whitman's dismissal from the Department of the Interior, William D. O'Connor's *The Good Gray Poet: A Vindication*.

10. [Anonymous], "[Review of *Leaves of Grass* (1855)]," *The Literary Examiner*, and "[Review of *Leaves of Grass* (1855)]," *Washington Daily National Intelligencer*.

11. Browne, *Great Metropolis*, 67.

12. Price introduction, xi, xiii.

13. [Whitman], "Walt Whitman and His Poems."

14. The narrative that Whitman creates out of the reviews in the 1856 appendix is described in Whitley, "Presenting Walt Whitman," and referred to in Grossman, *Reconstituting the American Renaissance*, in the chapter "Rereading Emerson/Whitman."

15. [Norton], "[Review of *Leaves of Grass* (1855)]"; [Anonymous], "[Review of Leaves of Grass (1855)]," *The Critic*.

16. Whitman, *Leaves of Grass Imprints*, 27–29. The poem, titled "A Letter Impromptu," is by January Searle, the penname of George S. Philips.

17. Ibid., 64.

18. See Gailey, "Walt Whitman and the King of Bohemia," and Genoways, *Walt Whitman and the Civil War*, 12–78.

19. [Clapp], "Walt Whitman," 2.

20. *New York Saturday Press*, 4 Aug. 1860, 3.

21. [Howells], "Hoosier's Opinion," 1.

22. [Philips], "Literature." This review was reprinted in the *Saturday Press* as an advertisement in the 30 June, 7 July, and 14 July 1860 issues.

23. This position has been argued to one degree or another in Cady, "'Not Happy at the Capitol'"; Greenspan, *Walt Whitman and the American Reader*, 195–97; Erkkila, "Public Love"; Larson, *Whitman's Drama of Consensus*, 153; Grossman, "'Evangel-Poem,'" 202; Reynolds, *Walt Whitman's America*, 384; Newfield, "Democracy and Homoeroticism"; and Maslan, *Whitman Possessed*, 175–200.

24. Quoted in Erkkila, "Whitman and the Homosexual Republic," 153.

25. Martin, "Whitman and the Politics of Identity," 177.

26. Whitman, *Correspondence*, 1:46.

27. Erkkila, *Whitman the Political Poet*, 179.

28. Nathanson, "Whitman's Addresses to His Audience," 137.

29. Whitman, *Complete Poetry and Collected Prose*, 297.

30. A number of scholars have called attention to the ways in which Whitman viewed his sexuality through class-inflected lenses, noting that his intimate comradeship was most often (if not entirely) with working-class men. See Sedgwick, "Whitman's Transatlantic Context," and Martin, "Walt Whitman."

31. "Japanese Ball," 4–5; *Harper's Weekly*, 26 May 1860.

32. Belasco also mentions the strategic timing of "A Broadway Pageant" in "From the Field," 256. The most comprehensive account of the newspaper coverage of the visit of the Japanese ambassadors can be found in Scott, "Diplomats and Poets." For further details about the 1860 visit of the Japanese embassy to the United States, see Shibama, *First Japanese Embassy*, and Miyoshi, *As We Saw Them*.

33. The poem appeared as "The Errand-Bearers" in the *New York Times*, 27 June 1860, and again in the *New York Saturday Press*, 30 June 1860. The *Vanity Fair* parody was reprinted in the *Saturday Press* as "The Torch-Bearers." The original poem was cited in *Harper's Monthly*, Sept. 1860, 555, and in the *Portland Transcript*, reprinted as "Rough Poetry" in the *New York Saturday Press* on 21 July 1860. I am indebted to Ted Genoways for calling my attention to two other appearances of "A Broadway Pageant" in the summer of 1860: a *Vanity Fair* parody titled "The Song of the Barbecue" and a reference to the poem in the *Milwaukee Daily Sentinel* on 30 June 1860. See Genoways, *Walt Whitman and the Civil War*, 56–69.

34. See the account in Reynolds, *Walt Whitman's America*, 387, and in Genoways, *Walt Whitman and the Civil War*, 61.

35. *New York Illustrated News*, 16, 2 June 1860.

36. "Editor's Easy Chair," *Harper's Monthly*, Aug. 1860, 411.

37. "Sensation Yesterday," 1–3; "Japanese Embassy," *New York Times*.

38. "Japanese in New-York."

39. See Gilje, *Road to Mobocracy*, 175–202.

40. Wilentz, *Chants Democratic*, 263.

41. "Yahoo, *n*."

42. Barber, "Japan-Ware."

43. The *New Orleans Sunday Delta* ran an article in June 1860 that includes the lines, "There is an unkempt, uncouth poet of New York, or rather of Brooklyn, whose name on earth, in common parlance, is Walt Whitman. The Cincinnati *Commercial* calls him the 'Yahoo of American literature'" ("Walt Whitman"). My thanks to Amanda Gailey for bringing this article to my attention.

44. "Japanese in New-York."

45. Thomas, "Whitman's Tale of Two Cities," 647.

46. "Japanese in New-York."

47. "Sensation Yesterday," 2.

48. The *New York Illustrated News* was more charitable, citing a nascent cosmopolitan sentiment among "the roughs" as the reason for their good behavior: "The Japanese themselves could not fail to be astonished and delighted by the grandeur and sublime

humanity of the scene; and we are proud to record that the hundred of thousands of people who thronged the streets for so many hours, conducted themselves with the greatest decorum, as if they were thoroughly penetrated with the great human idea upon which all this honor and ceremony are founded" ("Arrival of the Japanese," 1).

49. Whitman, *Complete Poetry and Collected Prose*, 1307, 1310.

50. See Mills, *Crowd in American Literature*, and Esteve, *Aesthetics and Politics*. Whitman himself wrote a few newspaper articles criticizing the unruly nature of the crowd that have puzzled scholars who see in his poetry an otherwise open embrace of the crowd. See Greenspan, *Walt Whitman and the American Reader*, 185, and Thomas, *Lunar Light*, 159.

51. Whitman, *Correspondence*, 2:55.

52. Emerson, *Essays and Lectures*, 1081.

53. While each stanza of the poem is individually numbered in the *New York Times*, in later editions of *Leaves of Grass* the poem is broken down into three numbered sections that correspond to the three sections of the Pindaric ode: invocation of the muse, recounting of heroic deeds, and vision of future greatness (*LG* 193–96).

54. Whitman, "Errand-Bearers."

55. "Sensation Yesterday," 2.

56. "Editor's Easy Chair," *Harper's Monthly*, Sept. 1860, 555.

57. "Rough Poetry."

58. "Torch-Bearers."

59. Whitman, "Errand-Bearers."

60. See Heater, *World Citizenship*, 7. Whitman wrote in the 1860 poem "Kosmos" that he used the word to mean, among other things, "the amplitude of the earth" and "the theory of the earth" (*LG* 303).

61. Whitman, "Errand-Bearers."

62. Whether Whitman's primary allegiances are national or international is a long-standing debate in Whitman studies. See Gohdes, "Nationalism and Cosmopolitanism"; Asselineau, "Nationalism vs. Internationalism"; and Qi, "Whitman's Poetry of Internationalism."

63. "Japanese Embassy," *New York Illustrated News*.

64. "Unity of Nations," 336.

65. "Sensation Yesterday," 3; "Japanese Embassy," *New York Times*.

66. "Sensation Yesterday," 1.

67. "Japanese in New-York."

68. Whitman, "Errand-Bearers."

69. By 1860, U.S. trade with the Pacific was shorthand for global trade in ways that Atlantic trade was not, which could account for why the October 1860 visit of England's Prince Albert did not inspire Whitman to write a companion piece to "A Broadway Pageant" about a vision of the hordes of Albion filling New York streets. See León, "Foundations," 29.

70. Whitman, "Errand-Bearers."

71. Allen, "Walt Whitman." I am indebted to Betsy Erkkila for this reference and for drawing my attention to Whitman's support of world proletarian struggle expressed by the line "unpitted hordes of toilsome persons."

72. "Sensation Yesterday," 2.

73. Browne, *Great Metropolis*, 339; [Whitman], "Walt Whitman, a Brooklyn Boy."

74. Browne, *Great Metropolis*, 59–60.

75. "Japanese in New-York."

76. Whitman, "Errand-Bearers."

77. "Japanese Embassy," *New York Times.*

78. Wilson, "Exporting Christian Transcendentalism," 540.

79. Huang, "Whitman on Asian Immigration," 161.

80. Whitman, "Errand-Bearers."

81. Whitman, *Complete Poetry and Collected Prose*, 823.

82. Barber, "Japan-Ware."

83. Roe, *Great Japanese Embassy*, 1.

84. [Philips], "Literature."

85. [Anonymous], "Walt Whitman and His Critics." See also McCormick, "Walt Whitman."

86. Whitman, *Complete Poetry and Collected Prose*, 1275.

87. Whitman, *Daybooks and Notebooks*, 3:729.

88. Esther Shephard, for example, in her *Walt Whitman's Pose*, attempts to expose Whitman for faking the pose of the working-class outsider, while Kenneth M. Price, in his *Whitman and Tradition*, considers how Whitman hid his erudition behind the screen of "one of the roughs." See also Lawson, *Walt Whitman and the Class Struggle*, for a consideration of how Whitman's lower-middle-class background put him in a position to move back and forth between working-class and middle-class spheres.

89. See, for example, Thomas, *Lunar Light*; Lawson, *Walt Whitman and the Class Struggle*; Grossman, *Reconstituting the American Renaissance*; and Erkkila, "Whitman, Marx, and the American 1848." See also the analysis of Whitman's complex relationship between the literary marketplace and his working-class loyalties, in Cohen, "'To reach the workmen direct.'"

90. See Sedgwick, "Whitman's Transatlantic Context," and Martin, "Walt Whitman."

91. I am indebted to Michael Borgstrom for the insights stemming from the useful statement, "Not all outsiders are created equal," which he wrote in an e-mail to me on 17 July 2006.

92. Whitfield, "Poem by J. M. Whitfield," 3.

93. Compton, *In Sacred Loneliness*, 332.

94. Powell, "Historical Multiculturalism."

95. Moore, *Complete Poems*, 267.

96. Giles, "Transnationalism and Classic American Literature," 63. See also Guillory, "Canonical and Non-Canonical."

97. Erkkila, "Revolution in the Renaissance," 17, emphasis in original.

98. Dickinson, *Poems*, 483.

BIBLIOGRAPHY

Abbot, John S. C. "Identity of the Different Races of Men." *New York Evangelist*, 25 July 1844. *American Periodical Series Online*, ⟨http://proquest.umi.com/⟩. 12 Apr. 2009.

Alkana, Joseph, and Carol Colatrella, eds. *Cohesion and Dissent in America*. New York: State University of New York Press, 1994.

Allen, Gay Wilson. *The Solitary Singer: A Critical Biography of Walt Whitman*. New York: Macmillan, 1955.

———. "Walt Whitman—Nationalist or Proletarian?" *English Journal* 26 (1937): 48–52.

Allmendinger, Blake. *Ten Most Wanted: The New Western Literature*. New York: Routledge, 1998.

[Anonymous]. "Leaves of Grass." *Spectator* 33 (14 July 1860): 669–70. *The Walt Whitman Archive*, edited by Ed Folsom and Kenneth M. Price, ⟨http://www.whitmanarchive.org⟩. 5 Nov. 2009.

———. "[Review of *Leaves of Grass* (1855)]." *The Critic* 15 (1 Apr. 1856): 170–71. *The Walt Whitman Archive*, edited by Ed Folsom and Kenneth M. Price, ⟨http://www.whitmanarchive.org⟩. 15 Nov. 2007.

———. "[Review of *Leaves of Grass* (1855)]." *Literary Examiner* 2512 (22 Mar. 1856): 180–81. *The Walt Whitman Archive*, edited by Ed Folsom and Kenneth M. Price, ⟨http://www.whitmanarchive.org/⟩. 5 Nov. 2009.

———. "[Review of *Leaves of Grass* (1855)]." *Washington Daily National Intelligencer*, 18 Feb. 1856, 180–81. *The Walt Whitman Archive*, edited by Ed Folsom and Kenneth M. Price, ⟨http://www.whitmanarchive.org/⟩. 5 Nov. 2009.

———. "Walt Whitman and His Critics." *Leader and Saturday Analyst* [London], 30 June 1860, 614–15. *The Walt Whitman Archive*, edited by Ed Folsom and Kenneth M. Price, ⟨http://www.whitmanarchive.org/⟩. 5 Nov. 2009.

Arrington, Leonard J. *Great Basin Kingdom: An Economic History of the Latter-day Saints, 1830–1900*. Cambridge, Mass.: Harvard University Press, 1958.

Arrington, Leonard J., and Davis Bitton. *The Mormon Experience: A History of the Latter-day Saints*. New York: Vintage, 1980.

Arrington, Leonard J., and Jon Haupt. "Intolerable Zion: The Image of Mormonism in Nineteenth Century American Literature." *Western Humanities Review* 22, no. 3 (1968): 243–60.

"Arrival of the Japanese." *New York Illustrated News*, 23 June 1860, 1.

Asselineau, Roger. "Nationalism vs. Internationalism in *Leaves of Grass*." In *Critical Essays on Walt Whitman*, edited by James Woodress, 320–29. Boston: G. K. Hall, 1983.

Bak, Hans, and Walter W. Hölbling, eds. *Nature's Nation Revisited: American Concepts of Nature from Wonder to Ecological Crisis*. Amsterdam: VU University Press, 2003.

Barber, Joseph. "Japan-Ware." *New York Saturday Press*, 26 May 1860, 4.

Barlow, Philp L. *Mormons and the Bible: The Place of the Latter-day Saints in American Religion*. New York: Oxford University Press, 1991.

Baym, Nina. *American Women Writers and the Work of History, 1790–1860*. New Brunswick, N.J.: Rutgers University Press, 1995.

———. *Woman's Fiction: A Guide to Novels by and about Women in America, 1820–1870*. 2nd ed. Urbana: University of Illinois Press, 1993.

Beach, Christopher. *The Politics of Distinction: Whitman and the Discourses of Nineteenth-Century America*. Athens: University of Georgia Press, 1996.

Beecher, Maureen Ursenbach. "The Eliza Enigma." *Dialogue* 11, no. 1 (Spring 1978): 40–43.

———. "Priestess among the Patriarchs: Eliza R. Snow and the Mormon Female Relief Society, 1842–1887." In *Religion and Society in the American West*, edited by Carl Guarneri and David Alvarez, 153–70. New York: University Press of America, 1987.

Belasco, Susan. "From the Field: Walt Whitman's Periodical Poetry." *American Periodicals* 14, no. 2 (2004): 247–59.

Bell, Howard H. "The Negro Emigration Movement, 1849–1854: A Phase of Negro Nationalism." *Phylon* 20 (1959): 132–42.

Bellin, Joshua David. *The Demon of the Continent: Indians and the Shaping of American Literature*. Philadelphia: University of Pennsylvania Press, 2001.

Bennett, Michael. "Frances Ellen Watkins Sings the Body Electric." In *Recovering the Black Female Body: Self-Representations by African American Women*, edited by Michael Bennett and Vanessa D. Dickerson, 19–40. New Brunswick, N.J.: Rutgers University Press, 2001.

Bennett, Paula. *Poets in the Public Sphere: The Emancipatory Project of American Women's Poetry, 1800–1900*. Princeton, N.J.: Princeton University Press, 2003.

Bennett, Paula Bernat, ed. *Nineteenth-Century American Women Poets: An Anthology*. London: Blackwell, 1998.

Bentley, Nancy. "Marriage as Treason: Polygamy, Nation, and the Novel." In *The Futures of American Studies*, edited by Donald E. Pease and Robyn Wiegman, 341–700. Durham: Duke University Press, 2002.

Bercovitch. Sacvan. Afterword to *Ideology and Classic American Literature*, edited by Sacvan Bercovitch and Myra Jehlen, 418–42. Cambridge: Cambridge University Press, 1986.

———. *The Puritan Origins of the American Self*. New Haven, Conn.: Yale University Press, 1975.

———. *The Rites of Assent: Transformations in the Symbolic Construction of America*. New York: Routledge, 1993.

Berkhoffer, Robert F., Jr. *The White Man's Indian: Images of the American Indian from Columbus to the Present*. New York: Knopf, 1978.

Berlant, Lauren. "On the Case." *Critical Inquiry* 33, no. 4 (Summer 2007): 663–72.

Bigler, David L. *Forgotten Kingdom: The Mormon Theocracy in the American West, 1847–1896*. Logan: Utah State University Press, 1998.

Bitton, Davis, and Gary L. Bunker. *The Mormon Graphic Image, 1834–1914: Cartoons, Caricatures, and Illustrations*. Salt Lake City: University of Utah Press, 1983.

Blakemore, Steven, and Jon Noble. "Whitman and 'The Indian Problem': The Texts and

Contexts of 'Song of the Redwood-Tree.'" *Walt Whitman Quarterly Review* 22, no. 2/3 (Fall 2004/Winter 2005): 108–25.

Blasing, Mutlu Konuk. *Lyric Poetry: The Pain and the Pleasure of Words*. Princeton, N.J.: Princeton University Press, 2007.

"Book Notices." *New York Illustrated News*, 16 June 1860.

Bové, Paul. *Destructive Poetics: Heidegger and Modern American Poetry*. New York: Columbia University Press, 1980.

Branham, Robert James. "'Of Thee I Sing': Contesting 'America.'" *American Quarterly* 48, no. 4 (1996): 623–50.

Brogan, Terry V. F., Alex Preminger, and Frank J. Warnke, eds. "Poet Laureate." In *The New Princeton Encyclopedia of Poetry and Poetics*, 924–25. Princeton, N.J.: Princeton University Press, 1993.

Brown, William Wells. *The Anti-Slavery Harp; A Collection of Songs for Anti-Slavery Meetings*. Boston: Bela Marsh, 1851.

———. *The Black Man, His Antecedents, His Genius, and His Achievements*. New York: Thomas Hamilton, 1863.

Browne, Junius Henri. *The Great Metropolis: A Mirror of New York*. Hartford, Conn.: American Publishing, 1869.

Brucke, Richard Maurice. *Cosmic Consciousness*. 1901. New York: Dutton, 1969.

Brückner, Martin. *The Geographic Revolution in Early America: Maps, Literacy, and National Identity*. Chapel Hill: University of North Carolina Press, 2006.

———. "Lessons in Geography: Maps, Spellers, and Other Grammars of Nationalism in the Early Republic." *American Quarterly* 51, no. 2 (June 1999): 311–42.

Buell, Lawrence. "Are We Post-American Studies?" In *Field Work: Sites in Literary and Cultural Studies*, edited by Marjorie Garber, Paul B. Franklin, and Rebecca L. Walkowitz, 87–93. New York: Routledge, 1996.

———. "Introduction: American Literary Globalism?" *ESQ* 50, no. 1–3 (2004): 1–22.

———. "Literature and Scripture in New England between the Revolution and the Civil War." *Religion and Literature* 15, no. 2 (Spring 1983): 1–29.

———. *New England Literary Culture: From Revolution through Renaissance*. New York: Cambridge University Press, 1986.

Burton, Richard F. *The City of the Saints*. Edited by Fawn M. Brodie. New York: Knopf, 1983.

Bush, Lester E., Jr. "Mormon 'Physiology,' 1850–1875." *Bulletin of the History of Medicine* 56 (1982): 218–37.

Bushman, Richard Lyman. *Joseph Smith and the Beginnings of Mormonism*. Urbana: University of Illinois Press, 1984.

———. *Making Space for the Mormons*. Logan: Utah State University Press, 1997.

Butler, Marilyn. *Romantics, Rebels, and Reactionaries: English Literature and Its Background, 1760–1830*. New York: Oxford University Press, 1982.

Cady, Joseph. "'Not Happy at the Capitol': Homosexuality and the 'Calamus' Poems." *American Studies* 19 (Fall 1978): 5–22.

Cannon, Charles A. "The Awesome Power of Sex: The Polemical Campaign against Mormon Polygamy." *Pacific Historical Review* 43 (1974): 71.

Carey, Matthew, ed. *The Columbian Muse: A Selection of American Poetry, from Various Authors of Established Reputation*. New York: J. Carey, 1794.

Carlton, Ambrose Bolivar. *The Wonderlands of the Wild West, with Sketches of the Mormons*. N.p., 1891.

Carr, Helen. *Inventing the American Primitive: Politics, Gender and the Representation of Native American Literary Traditions, 1789–1936*. New York: New York University Press, 1996.

Ceniza, Sherry. *Walt Whitman and 19th-Century Women Reformers*. Tuscaloosa: University of Alabama Press, 1998.

Chan, Sucheng. "A People of Exceptional Character: Ethnic Diversity, Nativism, and Racism in the California Gold Rush." In *Rooted in Barbarous Soil: People, Culture, and Community in Gold Rush California*, edited by Kevin Starr and Richard J. Orsi, 44–85. Berkeley: University of California Press, 2000.

Chapman, John Jay. "Walt Whitman." New York: Scribner's Sons, 1898. Rpt. in *A Century of Whitman Criticism*, edited by E. H. Miller, 103–4. Bloomington: Indiana University Press, 1969.

Chari, V. K. *Whitman in the Light of Vedantic Mysticism*. Lincoln: University of Nebraska Press, 1964.

Cherkovski, Neeli. *Whitman's Wild Children: Portraits of Twelve Poets*. South Royalton, Vt.: Steerforth Press, 1999.

[Clapp, Henry, Jr.] "Walt Whitman: *Leaves of Grass*." *New York Saturday Press*, 19 May 1860, 2.

Clappe, Louisa Amelia Knapp Smith. *The Shirley Letters: Being Letters Written in 1851–1852 from the California Mines*. Edited by Richard E. Oglesby. Santa Barbara: Peregrine, 1970.

Clark, Gregory, and S. Michael Halloran. "Introduction: Transformations of Public Discourse in Nineteenth-Century America." In *Oratorical Culture in Nineteenth-Century America*, edited by Gregory Clark and S. Michael Halloran, 1–28. Carbondale: Southern Illinois University Press, 1993.

Clark, Leadie M. *Walt Whitman's Concept of the American Common Man*. New York: Philosophical Library, 1955.

Cmiel, Kenneth. "The Fate of the Nation and the Withering of the State." *American Literary History* 8, no. 1 (1996): 184–201.

Cohen, Matt. "'To reach the workmen direct': Horace Traubel and the Work of the 1855 *Leaves of Grass*." In *Leaves of Grass: The Sesquicentennial Essays*, edited by Susan Belasco, Ed Folsom, and Kenneth M. Price, 299–320. Lincoln: University of Nebraska Press, 2007.

Compton, Todd. *In Sacred Loneliness: The Plural Wives of Joseph Smith*. Salt Lake City: Signature Books, 1997.

Cooper, James Fenimore. *The Leatherstocking Tales I: The Last of the Mohicans*. Edited by Blake Nevius. New York: Library of America, 1985.

Coward, John M. *The Newspaper Indian: Native American Identity in the Press, 1820–90*. Chicago: University of Illinois Press, 1999.

Cowley, Malcolm. Introduction to *Walt Whitman's Leaves of Grass: The First (1855) Edition*, edited by Malcolm Cowley, vii–xxxvi. New York: Viking, 1959.

Culler, Jonathan. "Why Lyric?" *PMLA* 123, no. 1 (2008): 201–6.

Curiel, Barbara Brinson, et al. Introduction to *Post-Nationalist American Studies*, edited by John Carlos Rowe, 1–21. Berkeley: University of California Press, 2000.

Cutler, Edward S. *Recovering the New: Transatlantic Roots of Modernism*. Hanover, N.H.: University Press of New England, 2003.

Dale, Edward Everett. "John Rollin Ridge." *Chronicles of Oklahoma* 4, no. 4 (Dec. 1926): 312–21.

Dale, Edward Everett, and Gaston Litton, eds. *Cherokee Cavaliers: Forty Years of Cherokee History as Told in the Correspondence of the Ridge-Watie-Boudinot Family*. Norman: University of Oklahoma Press, 1939.

Davidson, Karen Lynn, and Jill Mulvay Derr. "A Wary Heart: Eliza R. Snow's Conversion to Mormonism." *Journal of Mormon History* 30, no. 2 (Fall 2004): 98–128.

Davis, David Brion. "The New England Origins of Mormonism." In *Mormonism and American Culture*, edited by Marvin S. Hill and James B. Allen, 13–28. New York: Harper and Row, 1972.

———. "Some Themes of Counter Subversion: An Analysis of Anti-Masonic, Anti-Catholic, and Anti-Mormon Literature." In *Mormonism and American Culture*, edited by Marvin S. Hill and James B. Allen, 59–73. New York: Harper and Row, 1972.

de Montalvo, Garci Rodríguez. *The Labors of the Very Brave Knight Esplandián*. Translated by William Thomas Little. Binghamton, N.Y.: Medieval and Renaissance Texts and Studies, 1992.

Debo, Angie. "John Rollin Ridge." *Southwest Review* 17 (1932): 59–71.

Delano, Alonzo. *On the Trail to the California Gold Rush*. Edited by J. S. Holliday. Lincoln: University of Nebraska Press, 2005.

Delany, Martin R. *Blake, or the Huts of America*. 1859. Boston: Beacon, 1970.

———. *The Condition, Elevation, Emigration, and Destiny of the Colored People of the United States*. 1852. New York: Humanity Books, 2004.

Deloria, Philip J. *Playing Indian*. New Haven, Conn.: Yale University Press, 1999.

Dennis, Matthew. *Red, White, and Blue Letter Days: An American Calendar*. Ithaca: Cornell University Press, 2002.

Derr, C. Brooklyn, and Jill Mulvay Derr. "Outside the Mormon Hierarchy: Alternative Aspects of Institutional Power." *Dialogue* 15, no. 4 (Winter 1982): 21–43.

Derr, Jill Mulvay. "Form and Feeling in a Carefully Crafted Life: Eliza R. Snow's 'Poem of Poems.'" *Journal of Mormon History* 26, no. 1 (Spring 2000): 1–39.

———. "The Lion and the Lioness: Brigham Young and Eliza R. Snow." *BYU Studies* 40, no. 2 (2001): 55–101.

———. "The Significance of 'O My Father' in the Personal Journey of Eliza R. Snow." *BYU Studies* 36, no. 1 (1996–97): 85–126.

Derr, Jill Mulvay, and Karen Lynn Davidson, eds. *Eliza R. Snow: The Complete Poetry*. Provo, Utah: Brigham Young University Studies, 2009.

Dickinson, Emily. *The Poems of Emily Dickinson*. Edited by Ralph W. Franklin. Cambridge, Mass.: Harvard University Press, 1998.

Dimock, Wai Chee. "Afterword: The Hurricane and the Nation." *ESQ* 50, no. 1–3 (2004): 223–29.

———. "Deep Time: American Literature and World History." *American Literary History* 13, no. 4 (2001): 755–75.

———. "Epic and Lyric: The Aegean, the Nile, and Whitman." In *Walt Whitman: Where the Future Becomes Present*, edited by David Haven Blake and Michael Robertson, 17–36. Iowa City: University of Iowa Press, 2008.

Dippie, Brian W. *The Vanishing American: White Attitudes and U.S. Indian Policy.* Lawrence: University Press of Kansas, 1991.

Dixon, Melvin. *Ride out the Wilderness: Geography and Identity in Afro-American Literature.* Urbana: University of Illinois Press, 1987.

Dixon, William Hepworth. *New America.* Philadelphia: Lippincott, 1867.

Douglass, Frederick, J. Theodore Holly, William Watkins, and James M. Whitfield. *Arguments, Pro and Con, on the Call for a National Convention, to be Held in Cleveland, Ohio, August 24, 1854.* Edited by M. T. Newsom. Detroit: George E. Pomery & Co., 1854.

Drinnon, Richard. *Facing West: The Metaphysics of Indian-Hating and Empire-Building.* New York: Schocken, 1990.

Du Bois, W. E. B. *The Souls of Black Folk.* Edited by Henry Louis Gates Jr. and Terri Hume Oliver. 1903. New York: Norton, 1999.

Duffy, John-Charles. "'A Religion by Revelation': Emerson as Radical Restorationist." *ATQ* 14, no. 3 (Sept. 2000): 227–50.

Dunlap, W. "Ode to Time." *American Poems, Selected and Original.* Vol. 1. Edited by Elihu Hubbard Smith. Litchfield, Conn.: Collier and Buel, 1793.

"Editor's Easy Chair." *Harper's New Monthly Magazine*, Aug. 1860, 411.

"Editor's Easy Chair." *Harper's New Monthly Magazine*, Sept. 1860, 555.

Eitner, Walter H. *Walt Whitman's Western Jaunt.* Lawrence: Regents' Press of Kansas, 1981.

Eliason, Eric A. "Curious Gentiles and Representational Authority in the City of the Saints." *Religion and American Culture* 11, no. 2 (Summer 2001): 155–90.

Ellis, Clyde. "'Our Ill Fated Relative': John Rollin Ridge and the Cherokee People." *Chronicles of Oklahoma* 68, no. 4 (Dec. 1990): 376–95.

Emerson, Ralph Waldo. *Essays and Lectures.* Edited by Joel Porte. New York: Library of America, 1983.

———. *The Political Emerson: Essential Writings on Politics and Social Reform.* Edited by David M. Robinson. Boston: Beacon, 2004.

———. *The Portable Emerson.* Edited by Carl Bode. New York: Penguin, 1981.

Erkkila, Betsy. "The Federal Mother: Whitman as Revolutionary Son." *Prospects: An Annual Journal of American Cultural Studies* 10 (1985): 423–41.

———. "Public Love: Whitman and Political Theory." In *Whitman East and West*, edited by Ed Folsom, 115–44. Iowa City: University of Iowa Press, 2002.

———. "Revolution in the Renaissance." *ESQ* 49, no. 1–3 (2003): 17–32.

———. "Whitman and American Empire." In *Walt Whitman of Mickle Street: A Centennial Collection*, edited by Geoffrey M. Sill, 54–69. Knoxville: University of Tennessee Press, 1993.

———. "Whitman and the Homosexual Republic." In *Walt Whitman: The Centennial Essays*, edited by Ed Folsom, 153–71. Iowa City: University of Iowa Press, 1994.

———. *Whitman the Political Poet.* New York: Oxford University Press, 1989.

———. "Whitman, Marx, and the American 1848." In *Leaves of Grass: The Sesquicentennial Essays*, edited by Susan Belasco, Ed Folsom, and Kenneth M. Price, 35–61. Lincoln: University of Nebraska Press, 2007.

Esteve, Mary. *The Aesthetics and Politics of the Crowd in American Literature*. New York: Cambridge University Press, 2003.

Evans, E. Raymond. "Following the Rainbow: The Cherokees in the California Gold Fields." *Journal of Cherokee Studies* 2, no. 1 (1977): 170–75.

Fabian, Johannes. *Time and the Other: How Anthropology Makes Its Object*. New York: Columbia University Press, 1983.

Farwell, Willard B. *Oration Delivered Before the Society of California Pioneers*. San Francisco: Alta Job Office, 1859.

Fifer, Valerie. *American Progress: The Growth of the Transport, Tourist, and Information Industries in the Nineteenth-Century West*. Chester, Conn.: Globe Pequot Press, 1988.

Flanders, Robert Bruce. *Nauvoo: Kingdom on the Mississippi*. Urbana: University of Illinois Press, 1965.

Fletcher, Angus. "Whitman and Longfellow: Two Types of the American Poet." *Raritan* 10, no. 4 (Spring 1991): 131–45.

Folsom, Ed. "Lucifer and Ethiopia: Whitman, Race, and Poetics before the Civil War and After." In *A Historical Guide to Walt Whitman*, edited by David S. Reynolds, 45–96. New York: Oxford University Press, 2000.

———. "Talking Back to Walt Whitman: An Introduction." In *Walt Whitman: The Measure of His Song*, edited by Jim Perlman, Ed Folsom, and Dan Campion, 21–78. Duluth, Minn.: Holy Cow! Press, 1998.

———. *Walt Whitman's Native Representations*. Cambridge: Cambridge University Press, 1994.

Foreman, Carolyn Thomas. "Edward W. Bushyhead and John Rollin Ridge: Cherokee Editors in California." *Chronicles of Oklahoma* 14, no. 3 (Sept. 1936): 295–311.

Foster, Lawrence. *Religion and Sexuality: Three American Communal Experiments of the Nineteenth Century*. New York: Oxford University Press, 1981.

Fraistat, Neil. *The Poem and the Book: Interpreting Collections of Romantic Poetry*. Chapel Hill: University of North Carolina Press, 1985.

———, ed. *Poems in Their Place: The Intertextuality and Order of Poetic Collections*. Chapel Hill: University of North Carolina Press, 1987.

Frederickson, George M. *The Black Image in the White Mind: The Debate on Afro-American Character and Destiny, 1817–1914*. New York: Harper and Row, 1971.

Friedl, Herwig. "Making It Cohere: Walt Whitman's Idea of History." *Amerikastudien* 28 (1983): 295–307.

Frye, Northrop. *Anatomy of Criticism*. Princeton, N.J.: Princeton University Press, 1957.

Furniss, Norman F. *The Mormon Conflict, 1850–1859*. New Haven, Conn.: Yale University Press, 1960.

"The Future Home of the Mormons." *New York Times*, 10 Feb. 1858. *Proquest*, Lehigh University Research Database, ⟨http://www.proquest.com⟩. 1 Apr. 2009.

Gailey, Amanda. "Walt Whitman and the King of Bohemia: The Poet in the *Saturday Press*." *Walt Whitman Quarterly Review* 25, no. 4 (Spring 2008): 143–66.

Gardner, Thomas. *Discovering Ourselves in Whitman: The Contemporary American Long Poem*. Urbana: University of Illinois Press, 1989.

Genoways, Ted. *Walt Whitman and the Civil War: America's Poet during the Lost Years of 1860–1862*. Berkeley: University of California Press, 2009.

Gere, Anne Ruggles. *Intimate Practices: Literacy and Cultural Work in U.S. Women's Clubs, 1880–1920.* Urbana: University of Illinois Press, 1997.

Giles, Paul. "Transnationalism and Classic American Literature." *PMLA* 118, no. 1 (2003): 62–77.

Gilje, Paul A. *The Road to Mobocracy: Popular Disorder in New York City, 1763–1834.* Chapel Hill: University of North Carolina Press, 1987.

Giroux, Henry A. "National Identity and the Politics of Multiculturalism." *College Literature* 22, no. 2 (Jan. 1995): 42–57.

Givens, Terryl L. *By the Hand of Mormon: The American Scripture That Launched a New World Religion.* New York: Oxford University Press, 2002.

———. "Caricature as Containment: Orientalism, Bondage, and the Construction of Mormon Ethnicity in Nineteenth-Century American Popular Fiction." *Nineteenth-Century Contexts* 18 (1995): 385–403.

———. *People of Paradox: A History of Mormon Culture.* New York: Oxford University Press, 2007.

———. *The Viper on the Hearth: Mormons, Myths, and the Construction of Heresy.* New York: Oxford University Press, 1997.

Gohdes, Clarence. "Nationalism and Cosmopolitanism in Whitman's *Leaves of Grass.*" *Walt Whitman Review* 5, no. 1 (1959): 3–7.

Golding, Alan. *From Outlaw to Classic: Canons in American Poetry.* Madison: University of Wisconsin Press, 1995.

Gordon, David E. "Early California Journalism: John Rollin Ridge." *Overland Monthly and Out West Magazine* 44, no. 2 (Aug. 1904): 128.

Gordon, Sarah Barringer. *The Mormon Question: Polygamy and Constitutional Conflict in Nineteenth-Century America.* Chapel Hill: University of North Carolina Press, 2002.

Gourgouris, Stathis. "*Poiein*—Political Infinitive." *PMLA* 123, no. 1 (2008): 223–28.

Gray, Thomas. "The Progress of Poesy: A Pindaric Ode." *The Thomas Gray Archive,* edited by Alexander Huber, University of Oxford, ⟨http://www.thomasgray.org/⟩. 12 May 2009.

Greenfeld, Liah. *Nationalism: Five Roads to Modernity.* Cambridge, Mass.: Harvard University Press, 1992.

Greenspan, Ezra. *Walt Whitman and the American Reader.* Cambridge: Cambridge University Press, 1990.

[Griswold, Rufus W.] "[Review of *Leaves of Grass* (1855)]." *The Criterion* 1 (10 Nov. 1855): 24. *The Walt Whitman Archive,* edited by Ed Folsom and Kenneth M. Price, ⟨http:// www.whitmanarchive.org/⟩. 1 Aug. 2007.

Griswold, Rufus Wilmot, ed. *The Female Poets of America.* 2nd ed. Philadelphia: Henry C. Baird, 1853.

———, ed. *Poets and Poetry of America.* 2nd ed. New York, 1842.

Grossman, Jay. "'The Evangel-Poem of Comrades and of Love': Revising Whitman's Republicanism." *ATQ* 4, no. 3 (1990): 201–18.

———. *Reconstituting the American Renaissance: Emerson, Whitman, and the Politics of Representation.* Durham: Duke University Press, 2003.

Gruesz, Kirsten Silva. *Ambassadors of Culture: The Transamerican Origins of Latino Writing.* Princeton, N.J.: Princeton University Press, 2001.

Grünzweig, Walter. "Noble Ethics and Loving Aggressiveness: The Imperialist Walt

Whitman." In *An American Empire: Expansionist Cultures and Policies, 1881–1917*, edited by Serge Ricard, 151–65. Aix-en-Provence: Université de Provence, 1990.

Guillory, John. "Canonical and Non-Canonical: A Critique of the Current Debate." *ELH* 54, no. 3 (Autumn 1987): 483–527.

Gutjahr, Paul C. *An American Bible: A History of the Good Book in the United States, 1777–1880*. Stanford: Stanford University Press, 1999.

———. "Sacred Texts in the United States." *Book History* 4 (2001): 335–70.

Hale, Sarah Josepha, ed. *The Ladies' Wreath: A Selection from the Female Poetic Writers of England and America*. Boston: Marsh, Capen and Lyon, 1837.

Handley, William R. *Marriage, Violence, and the Nation in the American Literary West*. New York: Cambridge University Press, 2002.

Hansen, Klaus J. *Mormonism and the American Experience*. Chicago: University of Chicago Press, 1981.

———. *Quest for Empire: The Political Kingdom of God and the Council of Fifty in Mormon History*. Lansing: Michigan State University Press, 1967.

Hardy, B. Carmon. *Solemn Covenant: The Mormon Polygamous Passage*. Urbana: University of Illinois Press, 1992.

Harris, W. C. "Whitman's *Leaves of Grass* and the Writing of a New American Bible." *Walt Whitman Quarterly Review* 16, no. 3/4 (Winter/Spring 1999): 172–90.

Haslam, Gerald, ed. *Many Californias: Literature from the Golden State*. 2nd ed. Reno: University of Nevada Press, 1999.

Hayden, Dolores. *Seven American Utopias: The Architecture of Communitarian Socialism*. Cambridge, Mass.: MIT Press, 1976.

Hayes, Will. *Walt Whitman: The Prophet of a New Era*. 1905. London: Daniel, 1921.

Heater, Derek. *World Citizenship and Government: Cosmopolitan Ideas in the History of Western Political Thought*. New York: St. Martin's, 1996.

Heller, Dana. "Housebreaking History: Feminism's Troubled Romance with the Domestic Sphere." In *Feminism beside Itself*, edited by Diane Elam and Robyn Wiegman, 217–33. New York: Routledge, 1995.

Hereen, John, Donald B. Lindsey, and Marylee Mason. "The Mormon Concept of a Mother in Heaven: A Sociological Account of Its Origins and Development." *Journal for the Scientific Study of Religion* 23 (Dec. 1984): 396–411.

Hicks, Jack, James D. Houston, Maxine Hong Kingston, and Al Young, eds. *The Literature of California: Writings from the Golden State*. Vol. 1. Berkeley: University of California Press, 2000.

Hicks, Michael. "'O My Father': The Musical Settings." *BYU Studies* 36, no. 1 (1996–97): 33–57.

Higgins, Andrew C. "Wage Slavery and the Composition of *Leaves of Grass*: The 'Talbot Wilson' Notebook." *Walt Whitman Quarterly Review* 20, no. 2 (Fall 2002): 53–77.

Hinds, Michael, and Stephen Matterson. "Introduction: A Speaking Whole." In *Rebound: The American Poetry Book*, edited by Michael Hinds and Stephen Matterson, 1–9. Amsterdam: Rodopi, 2004.

Holland, Frederic May. *Frederick Douglass: The Colored Orator*. New York: Funk and Wagnalls, 1891.

Holliday, J. S. *Rush for Riches: Gold Fever and the Making of California*. Berkeley: University of California Press, 1999.

———. *The World Rushed In: The California Gold Rush Experience*. New York: Simon and Schuster, 1981.

Holly, J. Theodore, William Lambert, and James M. Whitfield. "Report of the Establishment of a Periodical, to Be the Organ of the Black and Colored Race on the American Continent." In *Proceedings of the National Emigration Convention*, 28–31. Pittsburgh: A. A. Anderson, 1854.

Holy Scriptures of the Church of Jesus Christ of Latter-day Saints. Salt Lake City: Deseret Book, 1960.

"Horace Greely Interviews Brigham Young." In *Among the Mormons*, edited by William Mulder and A. Russell Mortensen, 321–27. Lincoln: University of Nebraska Press, 1973.

Horton, James Oliver, and Lois E. Horton. *In Hope of Liberty: Culture, Community, and Protest among Northern Free Blacks, 1700–1860*. New York: Oxford University Press, 1997.

[Howells, William Dean]. "A Hoosier's Opinion of Walt Whitman." *New York Saturday Press*, 11 Aug. 1860, 1.

Huang, Guiyou. "Whitman on Asian Immigration and Nation-Formation." In *Whitman East and West*, edited by Ed Folsom, 159–71. Iowa City: University of Iowa Press, 2002.

Hughes, Langston. *The Collected Poems of Langston Hughes*. Edited by Arnold Rampersad. New York: Vintage, 1995.

Huhndorf, Shari M. *Going Native: Indians in the American Cultural Imagination*. Ithaca: Cornell University Press, 2001.

Hutchinson, George B. *The Ecstatic Whitman: Literary Shamanism and the Crisis of the Union*. Columbus: Ohio State University Press, 1986.

Iversen, Joan. "Feminist Implications of Mormon Polygyny." *Feminist Studies* 10, no. 3 (Fall 1984): 505–22.

Jack, Ian. "A Choice of Orders: The Arrangement of 'The Poetical Works.'" In *Textual Criticism and Literary Interpretation*, edited by Jerome J. McGann, 127–43. Chicago: University of Chicago Press, 1985.

Jackson, Virginia. "Who Reads Poetry?" *PMLA* 123, no. 1 (2008): 181–87.

James, William. *The Varieties of Religious Experience*. New York: Longmans, 1902.

"The Japanese Ball." *New York Times*, 26 June 1860, 4–5.

"The Japanese Embassy." *New York Times*, 18 June 1860, 1.

"The Japanese Embassy and What Will Come of It." *New York Illustrated News*, 26 May 1860, 1.

"The Japanese in New-York." *New York Times*, 18 June 1860, 4.

Jehlen, Myra. *American Incarnation: The Individual, the Nation, and the Continent*. Cambridge, Mass.: Harvard University Press, 1989.

Jensen, Beth. *Leaving the M/other: Whitman, Kristeva, and* Leaves of Grass. Madison, N.J.: Farleigh Dickinson Press, 2002.

Johannsen, Robert W. *To the Halls of the Montezumas: The Mexican War in the American Imagination*. New York: Oxford University Press, 1988.

Johnson, Dr. Ezra R., and James M. Whitfield. *Emancipation Oration By Dr. Ezra R. Johnson, and Poem By James M. Whitfield, delivered at Platt's Hall, January 1, 1867, in honor of the Fourth Anniversary of President Lincoln's Proclamation of Emancipation.* San Francisco: San Francisco Elevator, 1867.

Johnson, Susan Lee. *Roaring Camp: The Social World of the California Gold Rush.* New York: Norton, 2000.

Kadir, Djelal. "Introduction: America and Its Studies." *PMLA* 118, no. 1 (2003): 9–24.

Kamholtz, Jonathan Z. "Ben Johnson's *Epigrammes* and Poetic Occasions." *Studies in English Literature, 1500–1900* 23, no. 1 (1983): 77–94.

Kaplan, Caren. *Questions of Travel: Postmodern Discourses of Displacement.* Durham: Duke University Press, 1996.

Kaup, Monica, and Debra J. Rosenthal. Introduction to *Mixing Race, Mixing Culture: Inter-American Literary Dialogues*, edited by Monica Kaup and Debra J. Rosenthal, xi–xxix. Austin: University of Texas Press, 2002.

Keese, John, ed. *The Poets of America.* 4th ed. New York: S. Coleman, 1841.

Kennedy, William Sloane. *The Fight of a Book for the World: A Companion Volume to Leaves of Grass.* West Yarmouth, Mass.: Stonecroft, 1926.

Kenny, Maurice. "Whitman's Indifference to Indians." In *The Continuing Presence of Walt Whitman*, edited by Robert K. Martin, 28–38. Iowa City: University of Iowa Press, 1992.

Kern, Louis J. *An Ordered Love: Sex Roles and Sexuality in Victorian Utopias—The Shakers, the Mormons, and the Oneida Community.* Chapel Hill: University of North Carolina Press, 1981.

Kete, Mary Louise. *Sentimental Collaborations: Mourning and Middle-Class Identity in Nineteenth-Century America.* Durham: Duke University Press, 2000.

Kettell, Samuel, ed. *Specimens of American Poetry.* Boston: S. G. Goodrich, 1829.

Killingsworth, M. Jimmie. "The Voluptuous Earth and the Fall of the Redwood Tree: Whitman's Personifications of Nature." In *Whitman East and West*, edited by Ed Folsom, 14–25. Iowa City: University of Iowa Press, 2002.

———. "Whitman and Motherhood: A Historical View." *American Literature* 54, no. 1 (1982): 28–43.

———. *Whitman's Poetry of the Body: Sexuality, Politics, and the Text.* Chapel Hill: University of North Carolina Press, 1989.

Kinshasa, Kwando M. *Emigration vs. Assimilation: The Debate in the African American Press, 1827–1861.* Jefferson, N.C.: McFarland, 1988.

Kirkland, Caroline. Preface to *Dahcotah; or, Life and Legends of the Sioux*, by Mary Eastman, viii. New York: J. Wiley, 1849.

Klammer, Martin. "Slavery and Race." In *A Companion to Walt Whitman*, edited by Donald D. Kummings, 101–21. New York: Blackwell, 2006.

———. *Whitman, Slavery, and the Emergence of* Leaves of Grass. University Park: Pennsylvania State University Press, 1995.

Kowaleski, Michael. "Romancing the Gold Rush: The Literature of the California Frontier." In *Rooted in Barbarous Soil: People, Culture, and Community in Gold Rush California*, edited by Kevin Starr and Richard J. Orsi, 204–25. Berkeley: University of California Press, 2000.

Kramer, Michael P. "Imagining Authorship in America: 'Whose American Renaissance?' Revisited." *American Literary History* 13, no. 1 (2001): 108–25.

Kuebrich, David. *Minor Prophecy: Walt Whitman's New American Religion*. Bloomington: Indiana University Press, 1989.

Larson, Kerry C. *Whitman's Drama of Consensus*. Chicago: University of Chicago Press, 1988.

Lawrence, D. H. *New Poems*. New York: B. W. Huebsch, 1920.

———. *Studies in Classic American Literature*. New York: Viking, 1923.

Lawson, Andrew. *Walt Whitman and the Class Struggle*. Iowa City: University of Iowa Press, 2006.

León, M. Consuelo. "Foundations of the American Image of the Pacific." *Boundary* 221, no. 1 (1994): 17–29.

Leonard, Keith D. *Fettered Genius: The African American Bardic Poet from Slavery to Civil Rights*. Charlottesville: Univeristy of Virginia Press, 2006.

Levine, Herbert J. "'Song of Myself' as Whitman's American Bible." *Modern Language Quarterly* 48, no. 2 (June 1987): 145–61.

Levine, Robert S. *Martin Delany, Frederick Douglass, and the Politics of Representative Identity*. Chapel Hill: University of North Carolina Press, 1997.

[Lewes, George Henry (?)]. "Transatlantic Latter-Day Poetry." *The Leader* 7 (7 June 1856): 547–48. *The Walt Whitman Archive*, edited by Ed Folsom and Kenneth M. Price, ⟨http://www.whitmanarchive.org⟩. 5 Nov. 2009.

Lewis, R. W. B. *The American Adam*. Chicago: University of Chicago Press, 1955.

The Life and Labors of Eliza R. Snow with a Full Account of Her Funeral Services. Salt Lake City: Juvenile Instructor Office, 1888.

Lippy, Charles H. *Faith in America: Changes, Challenges, New Directions*. Westport, Conn.: Praeger, 2006.

Loeffelholz, Mary. "Anthology Form and the Field of Nineteenth-Century American Poetry: The Civil War Sequences of Lowell, Longfellow, and Whittier." *ESQ* 54, no. 1–4 (2008): 217–39.

———. "The Religion of Art in the City at War: Boston's Public Poetry and the Great Organ, 1863." *American Literary History* 13, no. 2 (2001): 212–41.

Longfellow, Henry Wadsworth. *Poems and Other Writings*. Edited by J. D. McClatchy. New York: Library of America, 2000.

———. *The Song of Hiawatha*. Cambridge, Mass.: Houghton Mifflin, 1936.

Loving, Jerome. *Walt Whitman: The Song of Himself*. Berkeley: University of California Press, 1999.

Ludlow, Fitz-Hugh. *The Heart of the Continent: A Record of Travel across the Plains and in Oregon, with an Examination of the Mormon Principle*. New York: Hurd and Houghton, 1870.

Maddox, Lucy. *Removals: Nineteenth-Century American Literature and the Politics of Indian Affairs*. New York: Oxford University Press, 1991.

Martin, Robert K. *The Homosexual Tradition in American Poetry*. Austin: University of Texas Press, 1979.

———. "Walt Whitman." In *The Gay and Lesbian Literary Heritage: A Reader's Companion*, edited by Claude J. Summers, 736–42. New York: Henry Holt, 1995.

———. "Whitman and the Politics of Identity." In *Walt Whitman: The Centennial Essays*, edited by Ed Folsom, 172–81. Iowa City: University of Iowa Press, 1994.

Marx, Leo. *The Machine in the Garden: Technology and the Pastoral Ideal in America*. New York: Oxford University Press, 1964.

Maslan, Mark. *Whitman Possessed: Poetry, Sexuality, and Popular Authority*. Baltimore: Johns Hopkins University Press, 2001.

Matthews, Glenna. "Forging a Cosmopolitan Civic Culture: The Regional Identity of San Francisco and Northern California." In *Many Wests: Place, Culture, and Regional Identity*, edited by David M. Wrobel and Michael C. Steiner, 211–34. Lawrence: University Press of Kansas, 1997.

Matthiessen, F. O. *American Renaissance: Art and Expression in the Age of Emerson and Whitman*. New York: Oxford University Press, 1941.

May, Caroline. *The American Female Poets*. Philadelphia: Lindsay and Blakiston, 1848.

McCormick, John O. "Walt Whitman: Orientalist or Nationalist?" *Tamkang Review* 10 (1979): 79–96.

McLellan, I., Jr. "The Hymn of the Cherokee Indian." *The Ariel*, 30 Oct. 1830, 4. *American Periodical Series Online*, ⟨http://proquest.umi.com/⟩. 23 May 2009.

McLoughlin, William Gerald. *After the Trail of Tears: The Cherokees' Struggle for Sovereignty, 1839–1880*. Chapel Hill: University of North Carolina Press, 1994.

Michaels, Leonard, David Reid, and Raquel Scherr, eds. *West of the West: Imagining California*. Los Angeles: University of California Press, 1995.

Mill, John Stuart. *Essays on Poetry*. Edited by F. Parvin Sharpless. Columbia: University of South Carolina Press, 1976.

Miller, Floyd J. *The Search for a Black Nationality: Black Emigration and Colonization, 1787–1863*. Chicago: University of Illinois Press, 1975.

Miller, James E. *The American Quest for a Supreme Fiction: Whitman's Legacy in the Personal Epic*. Chicago: University of Chicago Press, 1979.

Miller, Perry. *Nature's Nation*. Cambridge, Mass.: Harvard University Press, 1967.

———. *The Raven and the Whale: The War of Words and Wits in the Era of Poe and Melville*. New York: Harcourt, 1956.

Mills, Nicolaus. *The Crowd in American Literature*. Baton Rouge: Louisiana State University Press, 1986.

Miyoshi, Masao. *As We Saw Them: The First Japanese Embassy to the United States (1860)*. Berkeley: University of California Press, 1979.

Moon, Michael. *Disseminating Whitman: Revision and Corporeality in* Leaves of Grass. Cambridge, Mass.: Harvard University Press, 1991.

Mooney, James. *Myths of the Cherokee*. Washington, D.C.: U.S. Government Printing Office, 1900.

Moore, Marianne. *Complete Poems*. New York: Penguin Classics, 1994.

Moore, R. Laurence. *Religious Outsiders and the Making of Americans*. New York: Oxford University Press, 1986.

Morris, Timothy. *Becoming Canonical in American Poetry*. Champaign: University of Illinois Press, 1995.

Morton, Sarah Wentworth. "Odes to Time." In *My Mind and Its Thoughts, in Sketches, Fragments, and Essays*, 105–9. Boston: Wells and Lilly, 1823.

Nathanson, Tenney. "Whitman's Addresses to His Audience." In *Walt Whitman of Mickle Street*, edited by Geoffrey M. Sill, 129–41. Knoxville: University of Tennessee Press, 1993.

Newfield, Christopher. "Democracy and Homoeroticism." *Yale Journal of Criticism* 6, no. 3 (1993): 29–62.

Nibley, Preston. *Brigham Young: The Man and His Work*. Salt Lake City: Deseret Book, 1970.

Noble, Louis Legrand, and Elliot S. Vesell. *The Life and Works of Thomas Cole*. Hensonville, N.Y.: Black Dome Press, 2000.

Nolan, James. *Poet-Chief: The Native American Poetics of Walt Whitman and Pablo Neruda*. Albuquerque: University of New Mexico Press, 1994.

[Norton, Charles Eliot]. "[Review of *Leaves of Grass* (1855)]." *Putnam's Monthly: A Magazine of Literature, Science, and Art* 6 (Sept. 1855): 321–23. *The Walt Whitman Archive*, edited by Ed Folsom and Kenneth M. Price, ⟨http://www.whitmanarchive .org/⟩. 5 Nov. 2009.

O'Connor, William Douglas. *The Good Gray Poet: A Vindication*. New York: Bunce & Huntington, 1866. *The Walt Whitman Archive*, edited by Ed Folsom and Kenneth M. Price, ⟨http://www.whitmanarchive.org⟩. 15 Nov. 2007.

O'Dea, Thomas F. "Mormonism and the Avoidance of Sectarian Stagnation: A Study of Church, Sect, and Incipient Nationality." *American Journal of Sociology* 60 (Nov. 1954): 285–93.

O'Sullivan, John L. "The Great Nation of Futurity." *United States Democratic Review* 6, no. 23 (Nov. 1839): 426–30.

Owens, Louis. *Other Destinies: Understanding the American Indian Novel*. Norman: University of Oklahoma Press, 1992.

Parins, James W. *John Rollin Ridge: His Life and Works*. Lincoln: University of Nebraska Press, 1991.

Parke, Walter. "St. Smith of Utah." In *Parodies of the Works of English and American Authors, 1888*, edited by Walter Hamilton, 261–62. New York: Johnson Reprint, 1967.

Pearce, Roy Harvey. *Savages of America: A Study of the Indian and the Idea of Civilization*. Baltimore: Johns Hopkins University Press, 1953.

Pease, Donald. "New Americanists: Revisionist Interventions into the Canon." In *Revisionist Interventions into the Americanist Canon*, edited by Donald E. Pease, 1–37. Durham: Duke University Press, 1992.

———. *Visionary Compacts: American Renaissance Writers in Cultural Contexts*. Madison: University of Wisconsin Press, 1987.

Peeples, Ken, Jr. "The Paradox of the 'Good Gray Poet': Walt Whitman on Slavery and the Black Man." *Phylon* 35, no. 1 (1974): 22–32.

Perdue, Theda. *Mixed Blood Indians: Racial Construction in the Early South*. Athens: University of Georgia Press, 2003.

Perlman, Jim, Ed Folsom, and Dan Campion, eds. *Walt Whitman: The Measure of His Song*. 2nd ed. Duluth, Minn.: Holy Cow! Press, 1998.

Petrino, Elizabeth A. *Emily Dickinson and Her Contemporaries: Women's Verse in America, 1820–1885*. Hanover, N.H.: University Press of New England, 1998.

Phelps, C. Deirdre. "The Edition as Art Form: Social and Authorial Readings of William Cullen Bryant's Poems." *Text* 6 (1994): 249–85.

[Philips, George S.]. "Literature: *Leaves of Grass*—By Walt Whitman." *New York Illustrated News*, 26 May 1860, 2.

"Poems by Eliza R. Snow." *Latter-day Saints' Millennial Star*, 16 Feb. 1856, 105–6.

Polk, Dora Beale. *The Island of California: A History of the Myth*. Spokane, Wash.: Arthur H. Clark, 1991.

Porter, Noah, ed. *Webster's Revised Unabridged Dictionary*. Springfield, Mass.: G & C. Merriam Co., 1913.

Powell, Timothy B. "Historical Multiculturalism: Cultural Complexity in the First Native American Novel." In *Beyond the Binary: Reconstructing Cultural Identity in a Multicultural Context*, edited by Timothy B. Powell, 185–204. New Brunswick, N.J.: Rutgers University Press, 1999.

Price, Kenneth M. Introduction to *Walt Whitman: The Contemporary Reviews*, edited by Kenneth M. Price, xi–xxi. Cambridge: Cambridge University Press, 1996.

———. *Whitman and Tradition: The Poet in His Century*. New Haven, Conn.: Yale University Press, 1990.

The Principle of Life: A New Concept of Reality Based on Walt Whitman's Leaves of Grass. Advertisement. *Walt Whitman Quarterly Review* 10, no. 2 (Fall 1992).

Prins, Yopie. "Historical Poetics, Dysprosody, and the Science of English Verse." *PMLA* 123, no. 1 (2008): 229–34.

Proceedings of the National Emigration Convention. Pittsburgh: A. A. Anderson, 1854.

Qi, Li Shi. "Whitman's Poetry of Internationalism." *West Hills Review* 7 (1987): 103–10.

Ranck, M. A. "John Rollin Ridge in California." *Chronicles of Oklahoma* 10, no. 4 (Dec. 1932): 560–69.

Rawson, A. L. "A Bygone Bohemia." *Frank Leslie's Popular Monthly*, Jan. 1896, 96–107.

Reynolds, David S. *Walt Whitman's America: A Cultural Biography*. New York: Knopf, 1995.

Reynolds, Larry J. *European Revolutions and the American Literary Renaissance*. New Haven, Conn.: Yale University Press, 1988.

Richardson, Kelly L. "Collaboration, Materialism, and Masochism: New Studies in Nineteenth-Century American Sentimental Literature and Culture." *College Literature* 29, no. 3 (Summer 2002): 170–78.

Ridge, John Rollin. "Far in a Lonely Wood." *The American Native Press Archives*, edited by James W. Parins, ⟨http://anpa.ualr.edu/⟩. 18 Sept. 2007.

———. "Letter from John Rollin Ridge to Dennis N. Cooley, May 26, 1866." In *Comments and Objections of Certain Cherokee Delegates to the Propositions of the Government to Separate the Hostile Parties of the Cherokee Nation*. District of Columbia: Intelligencer Printing House, 1866. *The American Civil War: Letters and Diaries*. Alexander St. Press, ⟨http:// www.alexanderstreet.com/⟩. 27 Aug. 2007.

———. *The Life and Adventures of Joaquin Murieta, the Celebrated California Bandit*. San Francisco: W. B. Cooke and Co., 1854.

———. *Poems*. San Francisco: H. Payot & Co., 1868.

———. *A Trumpet of Our Own: Yellow Bird's Essays on the North American Indian*. Edited by David Farmer and Rennard Strickland. San Francisco: Book Club of California, 1981.

Robbins, Alexander, Jr. "Fourth of July Oration." *Mormon*, 21 July 1855, 2.

Roberts, B. H., ed. *History of the Church of Jesus Christ of Latter-day Saints*. Salt Lake City: Deseret Book, 1908.

Robertson, Michael. *Worshipping Walt: The Whitman Disciples*. Princeton, N.J.: Princeton University Press, 2007.

Roe, Remsey, Jr. *The Great Japanese Embassy*. New York: H. De Marsan, 1860.

Rohrbach, Augusta. "'A Blast That Whirls the Dust': Nineteenth-Century American Poetry and Critical Discontents." *ESQ* 54, no. 1–4 (2008): 1–8.

Rossetti, William Michael. "Prefatory Notice." In *Poems by Walt Whitman*, edited by William Michael Rossetti, 1–27. London: John Camden Hotten, 1868.

"Rough Poetry." *New York Saturday Press*, 21 July 1860, 3.

Rowe, John Carlos. "Nineteenth-Century United States Literary Culture and Transnationality." *PMLA* 118, no. 1 (2003): 78–89.

Rubin, Joseph Jay. *The Historic Whitman*. University Park: Pennsylvania State University Press, 1973.

Said, Edward W. "Invention, Memory, and Place." *Critical Inquiry* 26, no. 4 (2000): 175–92.

Salska, Agnieszka. "The Growth of the Past in *Leaves of Grass*." In *Utopia in the Present Tense: Walt Whitman and the Language of the New World*, edited by Marina Camboni, 35–51. Rome: Il Calamo, 1994.

Sánchez-Eppler, Karen. *Touching Liberty: Abolition, Feminism, and the Politics of the Body*. Berkeley: University of California Press, 1993.

Scheckel, Susan. *The Insistence of the Indian: Race and Nationalism in Nineteenth-Century American Culture*. Princeton, N.J.: Princeton University Press, 1998.

Scheick, William J. *The Half-Blood: A Cultural Symbol in Nineteenth-Century American Fiction*. Lexington: University Press of Kentucky, 1979.

Scott, David. "Diplomats and Poets: 'Power and Perceptions' in American Encounters with Japan, 1860." *Journal of World History* 17, no. 3 (2006): 297–337.

Scott, Sir Walter. *The Poetical Works of Sir Walter Scott*. Boston: Phillips, Sampson, & Co., 1852.

Sedgwick, Eve Kosofsky. "Whitman's Transatlantic Context: Class, Gender, and Male Homosexual Style." *Delta* 16 (May 1983): 111–24.

"The Sensation Yesterday: Magnificent Reception of the Japanese Embassy." *New York Herald*, 17 June 1860, 1–3.

Shaffer, Marguerite S. *America First: Tourism and National Identity, 1880–1940*. Washington, D.C.: Smithsonian Institution Press, 2001.

Shephard, Esther. *Walt Whitman's Pose*. New York: Harcourt, 1938.

Sherman, Joan R. *Invisible Poets: Afro-Americans of the Nineteenth Century*. 2nd ed. Urbana: University of Illinois Press, 1989.

Shibama, C., ed. *The First Japanese Embassy to the United States of America*. Tokyo: America-Japan Society, 1920.

Shipps, Jan. *Mormonism: The Story of a New Religious Tradition*. Urbana: University of Illinois Press, 1985.

———. "The Reality of the Restoration and the Restoration Ideal in the Mormon Tradition." In *The American Quest for the Primitive Church*, edited by Richard T. Hughes, 181–95. Urbana: University of Illinois Press, 1988.

Shuck, Oscar T., ed. *California Scrapbook*. San Francisco: H. H. Bancroft, 1869.

Smith, Elihu Hubbard, ed. *American Poems, Selected and Original*. Vol. 1. Litchfield, Conn.: Collier and Buel, 1793.

Smith, Fred Manning. "Whitman's Poet-Prophet and Carlyle's Hero." *PMLA* 55, no. 4 (1940): 1146–64.

Smith, Joseph. *The Personal Writings of Joseph Smith*. Salt Lake City: Deseret Book, 1984.

———. *Teachings of the Prophet Joseph Smith*. Edited by Joseph Fielding Smith. Salt Lake City: Deseret Book, 1976.

Snow, Eliza R. *The Personal Writings of Eliza Roxcy Snow*. Edited by Maureen Ursenbach Beecher. Logan: Utah State University Press, 2000.

———. *Poems: Religious, Historical, and Political*. Vol. 1. Liverpool: F. D. Richards, 1856.

———. *Poems: Religious, Historical, and Political*. Vol. 2. Salt Lake City: Latter-day Saints Publishing and Printing House, 1877.

———. "Woman, Jan. 30, 1855." *The Mormon*, 27 Dec. 1856, 2.

Soja, Edward. *Postmodern Geographies: The Reassertion of Space in Critical Social Theory*. London: Verso, 1989.

Soodik, Nicholas. "A Tribe Called Text: Whitman and Representing the American Indian Body." *Walt Whitman Quarterly Review* 22, no. 2/3 (Fall 2004/Winter 2005): 67–86.

Sowder, Michael D. "Walt Whitman, the Apostle." *Walt Whitman Quarterly Review* 16, no. 3/4 (Winter/Spring 1999): 202–10.

Stalin, Joseph. "The Nation." In *Nationalism*, edited by John Hutchinson and Anthony D. Smith, 18–21. New York: Oxford University Press, 1994.

Starr, Kevin. "Rooted in Barbarous Soil: An Introduction to Gold Rush Society and Culture." In *Rooted in Barbarous Soil: People, Culture, and Community in Gold Rush California*, edited by Kevin Starr and Richard J. Orsi, 1–24. Berkeley: University of California Press, 2000.

Stefanelli, Maria Anita. "'Chants' as 'Psalms for a New Bible.'" In *Utopia in the Present Tense: Walt Whitman and the Language of the New World*, edited by Marina Camboni, 171–88. Rome: Il Calamo, 1994.

Steinbrink, Jeffrey. "'To Span Vast Realms of Space and Time': Whitman's Vision of History." *Walt Whitman Review* 24 (June 1978): 45–62.

Steinman, Lisa. "Public Cultural Expression: Poetry." In *The Encyclopedia of American Cultural and Intellectual History*, vol. 3, edited by Mary Kupiec Cayton and Peter Williams, 601–10. New York: Scribner's, 2001.

Stenhouse, Fanny Ward. *"Tell It All": The Story of a Life's Experience in Mormonism*. Hartford, Conn.: Worthington, 1874.

Stevenson, Robert Louis. "The Gospel According to Walt Whitman." *New Quarterly Magazine* 10, no. 21 (Oct. 1878): 461–81.

Sturm, Circe. *Blood Politics: Race, Culture, and Identity in the Cherokee Nation of Oklahoma*. Berkeley: University of California Press, 2002.

Sweet, Timothy. *American Georgics: Economy and Environment in Early American Literature*. Philadelphia: University of Pennsylvania Press, 2002.

Symonds, John Addington. *Walt Whitman*. London: John C. Nimmo, 1893.

Taylor, P. A. M. *Expectations Westward: The Mormons and the Emigration of Their British Converts in the Nineteenth Century*. Ithaca: Cornell University Press, 1966.

Thobrun, Joseph B. "The Cherokee Question." *Chronicles of Oklahoma* 2, no. 2 (June 1924): 141–242.

Thomas, M. Wynn. *The Lunar Light of Whitman's Poetry*. Cambridge, Mass.: Harvard University Press, 1987.

———. *Transatlantic Connections: Whitman U.S., Whitman U.K.* Iowa City: University of Iowa Press, 2005.

———. "Whitman's Tale of Two Cities." *American Literary History* 6, no. 4 (1994): 633–57.

Thompson, Sith. *Tales of the North American Indians.* Bloomington: Indiana University Press, 1929.

Thornton, Russell. *The Cherokees: A Population History.* Lincoln: University of Nebraska Press, 1990.

Tichi, Cecelia. *Embodiment of a Nation: Human Form in American Places.* Cambridge, Mass.: Harvard University Press, 2001.

Tompkins, Jane P. "Sentimental Power: *Uncle Tom's Cabin* and the Politics of Literary History." In *Uncle Tom's Cabin*, by Harriet Beecher Stowe, edited by Elizabeth Ammons, 501–22. New York: Norton, 1994.

"The Torch-Bearers: A Paean for the Fourth of July, After Walt Whitman." *New York Saturday Press*, 7 July 1860, 4.

Trachtenberg, Alan. "The Politics of Labor and the Poet's Work: A Reading of 'A Song for Occupations.'" In *Walt Whitman: The Centennial Essays*, edited by Ed Folsom, 120–32. Iowa City: University of Iowa Press, 1994.

Traubel, Horace. *With Walt Whitman in Camden.* Vol. 1. Boston: Small, Maynard, 1906.

———. *With Walt Whitman in Camden.* Vols. 2–3. New York: Rowman and Littlefield, 1961.

———. *With Walt Whitman in Camden.* Vol. 4. Philadelphia: University of Pennsylvania Press, 1953.

———. *With Walt Whitman in Camden.* Vols. 5–7. Carbondale: Southern Illinois University Press, 1964–92.

———. *With Walt Whitman in Camden.* Vols. 8–9. Oregon House, Calif.: W. L. Bentley, 1996.

Travers, Len. *Celebrating the Fourth: Independence Day and the Rites of Nationalism in the Early Republic.* Amherst: University of Massachusetts Press, 1997.

Tullidge, Edward. *The Women of Mormondom.* Salt Lake City, 1877.

Twain, Mark. *Roughing It.* New York: Oxford University Press, 1996.

Ullman, Victor. *Martin R. Delany: The Beginnings of Black Nationalism.* Boston: Beacon, 1971.

"The Unity of Nations—Japan." *Frank Leslie's Illustrated Newspaper*, 28 Apr. 1860, 336.

Vendler, Helen. "*Tintern Abbey*: Two Assaults." In *Bucknell Review: Wordsworth in Context*, edited by Pauline Fletcher and John Murphy, 173–90. Lewisburg, Pa.: Bucknell University Press, 1992.

Virgil, Patricia M. Letter to the author from the Director of Library and Archives at the Buffalo and Erie County Historical Society. 2 Aug. 2003.

Wahnenauhi [Lucy L. Keys]. "The Wahnenauhi Manuscript: Historical Sketches of the Cherokees, Together with Some of their Customs, Traditions, and Superstitions." In *Anthropological Papers nos. 75–80*, edited by Jack F. Kilpatrick, 175–214. *Smithsonian Institution Bureau of American Ethnology Bulletin 196.* Washington, D.C.: U.S. Government Printing Office, 1966.

Waite, Catharine Van Valkenburg. *The Mormon Prophet and His Harem; or, an Authentic*

History of Brigham Young, His Numerous Wives and Children. Chicago: J. S. Goodman, 1867.

Wald, Priscilla. *Constituting Americans: Cultural Anxiety and Narrative Form.* Durham: Duke University Press, 1995.

Waldstreicher, David. *In the Midst of Perpetual Fetes: The Making of American Nationalism, 1776–1820.* Chapel Hill: University of North Carolina Press, 1997.

Walker, Cheryl. "Nineteenth-Century American Women Poets Revisited." In *Nineteenth-Century American Women Writers: A Critical Reader,* edited by Karen L. Kilcup, 231–44. Oxford: Blackwell, 1998.

Walker, Jeffrey. *Bardic Ethos and the American Long Poem: Whitman, Pound, Crane, Williams, Olson.* Baton Rouge: Louisiana State University Press, 1989.

———. *Rhetoric and Poetics in Antiquity.* New York: Oxford University Press, 2000.

"Walt Whitman." *New Orleans Sunday Delta,* 17 June 1860, 1.

Wardell, Morris L. *A Political History of the Cherokee Nation, 1838–1907.* Norman: University of Oklahoma Press, 1931.

Warner, Michael. "Civil War Religion and Whitman's Drum-Taps." In *Walt Whitman, Where the Future Becomes Present,* edited by David Haven Blake and Michael Robertson, 81–90. Iowa City: University of Iowa Press, 2008.

Warren, James Perrin. *Culture of Eloquence: Oratory and Reform in Antebellum America.* University Park: Pennsylvania State University Press, 1999.

Watts, Emily Stipes. *The Poetry of American Women from 1632 to 1945.* Austin: University of Texas Press, 1977.

Wells, Emmeline B. *Musings and Memories.* 2nd ed. Salt Lake City: Deseret News, 1915.

Wertheimer, Eric. *Imagined Empires: Incas, Aztecs, and the New World of American Literature, 1771–1876.* New York: Cambridge University Press, 1999.

Whitfield, James M. *America and Other Poems.* Buffalo, N.Y.: James S. Leavitt, 1853.

I, Too, Sing America: James M. Whifield's America and Other Poems, edited by Robert S. Levine, ⟨http://www.classroomelectric.org/volume1/levine/⟩. 5 Nov. 2009.

———. "Letter from J. M. Whitfield, Editor of the African-American Repository, (A Colored Man). Buffalo, New York, Feb. 1, 1858." In *The Mind of the Negro as Reflected in Letters Written During the Crisis, 1800–1860,* edited by Carter G. Woodson, 500–502. Washington, D.C.: Association for the Study of Negro Life and History, 1926.

———. "Poem by J. M. Whitfield." *San Francisco Elevator,* 6 May 1870, 3.

Whitley, Edward. "Presenting Walt Whitman: 'Leaves-Droppings' as Paratext." *Walt Whitman Quarterly Review* 19, no. 1 (Summer 2001): 1–17.

Whitman, Walt. "American Workingmen, Versus Slavery." *Brooklyn Daily Eagle,* 1 Sept. 1847, 2. *Brooklyn Daily Eagle Online,* ⟨http://www.brooklynpubliclibrary.org/eagle⟩. 25 Feb. 2010.

———. *The Collected Writings of Walt Whitman: The Early Poems and the Fiction.* Vol. 6. Edited by Thomas L. Brasher. New York: New York University Press, 1963.

———. *Complete Poetry and Collected Prose.* Edited by Justin Kaplan. New York: Library of America, 1982.

———. *The Complete Writings of Walt Whitman.* 10 vols. Edited by Richard Maurice Bucke. New York: G. P. Putnam's Sons, 1902.

———. *The Correspondence*. 7 vols. Edited by Edwin Haviland Miller. New York: New York University Press, 1961–77.

———. *Daybooks and Notebooks*. 3 vols. Edited by William White. New York: New York University Press, 1978.

———. "The Errand-Bearers: 16th 6th month, Year 64 of The States." *New York Times*, 27 June 1860, 2.

———. *The Gathering of the Forces*. 2 vols. Edited by Cleveland Rodgers and John Black. New York, G. P. Putnam's Sons, 1920.

———. *The Half-Breed and Other Stories*. Edited by Thomas Olive Mabbott. New York: Columbia University Press, 1927.

———. *I Sit and Look Out: Editorials from the Brooklyn Daily Times*. Edited by Emory Holloway. New York: Columbia University Press, 1932.

———. *Leaves of Grass*. Brooklyn: n.p, 1855. *The Walt Whitman Archive*, edited by Ed Folsom and Kenneth M. Price, ⟨http://www.whitmanarchive.org⟩. 15 Nov. 2007.

———. *Leaves of Grass*. Brooklyn: Fowler and Wells, 1856. *The Walt Whitman Archive*, edited by Ed Folsom and Kenneth M. Price, ⟨http://www.whitmanarchive.org⟩. 15 Nov. 2007.

———. *Leaves of Grass*. New York: William E. Chapin, 1867. *The Walt Whitman Archive*, edited by Ed Folsom and Kenneth M. Price, ⟨http://www.whitmanarchive.org⟩. 15 Nov. 2007.

———. *Leaves of Grass*. New York: J. S. Redfield, 1872. *The Walt Whitman Archive*, edited by Ed Folsom and Kenneth M. Price, ⟨http://www.whitmanarchive.org⟩. 15 Nov. 2007.

———. *Leaves of Grass*. Boston: James R. Osgood, 1881. *The Walt Whitman Archive*, edited by Ed Folsom and Kenneth M. Price, ⟨http://www.whitmanarchive.org⟩. 15 Nov. 2007.

———. *Leaves of Grass*. Philadelphia: David McKay, 1891–92. *The Walt Whitman Archive*, edited by Ed Folsom and Kenneth M. Price, ⟨http://www.whitmanarchive.org⟩. 15 Nov. 2007.

———, ed. *Leaves of Grass Imprints*. Boston: Thayer & Eldridge, 1860.

———. *Notebooks and Unpublished Prose Manuscripts*. 6 vols. Edited by Edward F. Grier. New York: New York University Press, 1984.

———. *Notes and Fragments Left by Walt Whitman*. Edited by Richard Maurice Bucke. London: Talbot, 1899.

———. "A Promise to California." Poem manuscript. *The Walt Whitman Archive*, edited by Ed Folsom and Kenneth M. Price, ⟨http://www.whitmanarchive.org⟩. 17 Sept. 2007.

———. *Prose Works, 1892*. 2 vols. Edited by Floyd Stovall. New York: New York University Press, 1963–64.

———. *Specimen Days & Collect*. New York: Dover Publications, 1995.

———. *The Uncollected Poetry and Prose of Walt Whitman*. 2 vols. Edited by Emory Holloway. Garden City, N.J.: Doubleday, 1921.

[———]. "Walt Whitman, a Brooklyn Boy." *Brooklyn Daily Times*, 29 Sept. 1855, 2. *The Walt Whitman Archive*, edited by Ed Folsom and Kenneth M. Price, ⟨http://www.whitmanarchive.org/⟩. 5 Nov. 2009.

[———]. "Walt Whitman and His Poems." *United States Review* 5 (Sept. 1855): 205–12.

The Walt Whitman Archive, edited by Ed Folsom and Kenneth M. Price, ⟨http://www.whitmanarchive.org/⟩. 5 Nov. 2009.

Whitney, J[osiah] D[wight]. "An Address Delivered at the Celebration of the Sixth Anniversary of the College of California, Held in Oakland, June 6, 1861." In *Catalogue of the College of California and College School in Oakland, California*, 3–50. San Francisco: Towne and Bacon, 1860.

Whittaker, David J. "Missionary Journeys to Foreign Countries." In *Historical Atlas of Mormonism*, edited by S. Kent Brown, Donald Q. Cannon, and Richard H. Jackson, 32–33. New York: Simon and Schuster, 1994.

Wilcox, Linda P. "The Mormon Concept of a Mother in Heaven." In *Sisters in Spirit: Mormon Women in Historical and Cultural Perspective*, edited by Maureen Ursenbach Beecher and Lavinia Fielding Anderson, 64–77. Urbana: University of Illinois Press, 1987.

Wilentz, Sean. *Chants Democratic: New York City and the Rise of the American Working Class, 1788–1850*. New York: Oxford University Press, 1984.

Wilkins, Thurman. *Cherokee Tragedy: The Ridge Family and the Decimation of a People*. 2nd ed. Norman: University of Oklahoma Press, 1986.

Willard, Charles B. *Whitman's American Fame: The Growth of His Reputation in America after 1892*. Providence, R.I.: Brown University Press, 1950.

Wilson, Ivy. *Specters of Democracy: Blackness and the Aesthetics of Nationalism*. New York: Oxford University Press, 2010.

Wilson, Rob. "Exporting Christian Transcendentalism, Importing Hawaiian Sugar: The Trans-Americanization of Hawai'i." *American Literature* 72, no. 3 (2000): 521–52.

Winn, Kenneth H. *Exiles in a Land of Liberty: Mormons in America, 1830–1846*. Chapel Hill: University of North Carolina Press, 1989.

Wolosky, Shira. "The Claims of Rhetoric: Toward a Historical Poetics (1820–1900)." *American Literary History* 15, no. 1 (2003): 14–21.

———. "Poetry and Public Discourse, 1820–1910." In *Nineteenth-Century Poetry, 1800–1910*. Vol. 4 of *The Cambridge History of American Literature*, general editor Sacvan Bercovitch, 147–480. Cambridge: Cambridge University Press, 2004.

Wrobel, Arthur. "'Noble American Motherhood': Whitman, Women, and the Ideal Democracy." *American Studies* 21 (Fall 1980): 7–25.

Wu, Frank H. *Yellow: Race in America beyond Black and White*. New York: Basic Books, 2002.

"Yahoo, *n*." *The Oxford English Dictionary*. 2nd ed. 1989. *OED Online*, ⟨http://dictionary.oed.com⟩. 17 Nov. 2007.

Young, Ann Eliza Webb. *Wife No. 19, or the Story of a Life in Bondage. Being a Complete Exposé of Mormonism*. Hartford, Conn.: Dustin, Oilman & Co., 1876.

Zitter, Emmy Stark. "Songs of the Canon: Song of Solomon and 'Song of Myself.'" *Walt Whitman Quarterly Review* 5, no. 2 (Fall 1987): 8–15.